BEYOND AGENDA SETTING:
Information Subsidies and Public Policy

COMMUNICATION AND INFORMATION SCIENCE

A Series of Monographs, Treatises, and Texts

Edited by
MELVIN J. VOIGT

University of California, San Diego

William C. Adams • Television Coverage of International Affairs
William C. Adams • Television Coverage of the Middle East
Hewitt D. Crane • The New Social Marketplace: Notes on Effecting Social Change in America's
  Third Century
Rhonda J. Crane • The Politics of International Standards: France and the Color TV War
Herbert S. Dordick, Helen G. Bradley, and Burt Nanus • The Emerging Network Marketplace
Glen Fisher • American Communication in a Global Society
Edmund Glenn • Man and Mankind: Conflict and Communication Between Cultures
Bradley S. Greenberg • Life on Television: Content Analyses of U.S. TV Drama
Robert M. Landau, James H. Bair, and Jean Siegman • Emerging Office Systems
John S. Lawrence and Bernard M. Timberg • Fair Use and Free Inquiry: Copyright Law and the
  New Media
Robert G. Meadow • Politics as Communication
William H. Melody, Liora R. Salter, and Paul Heyer • Culture, Communication, and Dependency:
  The Tradition of H.A. Innis
Vincent Mosco • Broadcasting in the United States: Innovative Challenge and Organizational Con-
  trol
Vincent Mosco • Pushbutton Fantasies
Kaarle Nordenstreng and Herbert I. Schiller • National Sovereignty and International Communica-
  tion: A Reader,
Dan Schiller • Telematics and Government
Herbert I. Schiller • Who Knows: Information in the Age of the Fortune 500
Dallas W. Smythe • Dependency Road: Communications, Capitalism, Consciousness and Canada
Janet Wasko • Movies and Money: Financing the American Film Industry

In Preparation:

William C. Adams • Television Coverage of the 1980 Presidential Campaign
Mary B. Cassata and Thomas Skill • Life on Daytime Television
Ithiel de Sola Pool • Forecasting The Telephone: A Retrospective Technology Assessment
Bradley S. Greenberg • Mexican Americans and the Mass Media
Cees J. Hamelink • Finance and Information: A Study of Converging Interests
Kaarle Nordenstreng • The Mass Media Declaration of UNESCO
Jorge A. Schnitman • Dependency and Development in the Latin American Film Industries
Indu B. Singh • Telecommunications in the Year 2000: National and International Perspectives
Jennifer D. Slack • Communication Technologies and Society: Conceptions of Causality and the
  Politics of Technological Intervention
Osmo Wiio • Information and Communication Systems

BEYOND AGENDA SETTING:
Information Subsidies and Public Policy

Oscar H. Gandy, Jr.

ABLEX PUBLISHING COMPANY
Norwood, New Jersey 07648

Printed in the United States of America.

Library of Congress Cataloging in Publication Data
Gandy, Oscar H.
    Beyond agenda setting.

    (Communication andinformation science)
    Bibliography: p.
    Includes index.
    1. Mass media—Political aspects—United States.
2. Communication in politics—United States. 3. Policy Sciences.   I. Title.   II. Series.
P95.82.U6G36   1982   302.2'34'0973   82-13823
ISBN 0-89391-096-1

ABLEX Publishing Corporation
355 Chestnut Street
Norwood, New Jersey 07648

Table of Contents

4. INFORMATION SUBSIDIES 61

5. THE INFORMATION SUBSIDY IN HEALTH 95

6. THE INFORMATION SUBSIDY IN EDUCATION 125

Preface

It has become almost trite to say that knowledge is power. And whereas its power may not be comparable to that which emerges from the barrel of a gun, knowledge, or the lack of it, largely determines when and how well that deadly power is used. Had it been possible for the generals to convince the rest of us that it was likely that we could win, or that we could at least survive a war fought with conventional nuclear weapons, this book would have no purpose, as it would have no readers.

Although relatively few matters of public policy have such global and dramatic consequences, all policies, whether in the area of health, education, social welfare, or industrial development, are dependent upon the success of interested parties in generating beliefs about an uncertain world. It is my intention in this book to focus scholarly attention upon the methods and techniques utilized by interested participants in the public-policy process to influence the decisions of others through systematic reduction of the costs of access to self-serving information.

Throughout their training, students of mass communication are exposed to a literature which is dominated by studies of the impact of media content on public attitudes, cognitions, or behaviors. Occasionally, programs may offer consideration of some peculiarities of the media production process; but even here, the focus is on the decisions made by individual journalists, editors, and producers, with only an occasional nod in the direction of professional or organizational constraints. Rarely will a student be exposed to a study of the activities of the primary sources of media content. This book aims to fill that gap in the mass communication literature by focusing primarily on the activities of sources who seek personal or collective advantage through their skillful manipulation of the mass media or other information channels.

Distributional questions, such as those concerned with the differential impact of media, have been explored to a certain extent in the process of examining the "knowledge gap" hypothesis. Very little has been done to examine the differential ability of sources to influence the content of information flows. This book dramatizes the extent of the disparity between corporate, government, and public sources to subsidize, and thereby influence the informational intake of others.

Studies of political communication have been limited almost entirely to electoral politics and formal campaign activities. Such a narrow focus ignores the day-to-day decisions of government and industry which form the basis of the issues debated in any electoral campaign. By concentrating on the public-policy process, this book is intended to broaden the field of enquiry in a way that will ultimately clarify some theoretical ambiguity about the role of media in the political sphere.

The study of mass communication and society has traditionally been approached from an interdisciplinary perspective. This tendency reflects in part the history of a discipline which has been dominated from time to time by sociologists, political scientists, and behavioral psychologists. Economics, or more correctly, political economy has been introduced only recently by the efforts of critical theorists like Herbert Schiller, Thomas Guback, and Dallas Smythe. This book attempts to integrate political economy more fully into this interdisciplinary mix, and I believe it reveals a marked degree of compatibility with psychological or intrapersonal explanations of information seeking, media use, and attitude formation or change.

As an integrative effort, the material in this book is neither technical, nor is it formally presented. It neither assumes, nor requires any background in economics. Instead, it seeks to utilize readily accessible notions of costs, benefits, and productivity to further our understanding of the essentially rational economic process of public decision making, through an examination of the incentives, resources, and techniques utilized by a variety of sources to influence that process.

The book begins with a discussion of agenda setting as traditionally explored by students of mass communication. After consideration of arguments for expanding the limited scope of the problem, the next three chapters develop a perspective on the role of subsidized information in the policy process in general. The next five chapters explore the use of information subsidies in a variety of specific policy areas: health, education, science and technology, and national economic planning. These five chapters may be read in any order as one's interest dictates. The final chapter identifies a number of theoretical issues, and suggests some potential approaches to structured research into the role of information subsidies in the public-policy process.

The book may be used most effectively as a source of material for classroom discussion and individual student projects. The introductory chapters provide a challenging alternative to traditional presentations of mass media "process and effects." One or more of the specialized chapters could serve to identify an area of interest that a student might pursue through content analysis, or through interviews with a variety of sources and media decision makers. More advanced students may elect to pursue some of the problems identified in the final chapter as a problem for a thesis or dissertation.

This book is the final product of some ideas that have been swirling around me, and within my head since my days at Stanford. Working with Bill Rivers and Susan Miller on a review of the literature on media and government relations revealed just how little we know about how the media agenda is set. Seminars with Hank Levin, Martin Carnoy, and Vick Fuchs on the economics of education and health provided an early introduction to these specific policy issues. Work with June Fisher, and later Noreene Janus on an analysis of health-related content in popular magazines provided some of the data utilized in Chapter Five. My dissertation, completed with the guidance and support of Bill Rivers, Emile McAnany, Bill Paisley, and Hank Levin served as the basis for Chapter Six. But it was the six months I spent as a postdoctoral fellow at the University of Pennsylvania that really brought these varied influences into focus. It was there that I delved more deeply into the literature on decision theory, the economics of information, and the nature of public choice. George Gerbner's foresight and generosity in making that fellowship possible is a debt that I can never repay.

I owe a debt as well to the faculty, staff, students, and administration at Howard University. Support for my research on media and public policy on health was provided through the Faculty Research Program administered through the office of the Vice President for Academic Affairs. Those grants made it possible for me to enjoy the services of Lenda Powell and Henry Forde, two graduate research assistants who spent countless hours tracking down obscure references. Generous support from my Dean, Lee Barrow, made it possible to present this research at international conferences where the critical comments of scholars like Jan Ekecrantz helped to clarify some of the relationships between purposive and structural influences on media content.

Like most authors, I owe my greatest debt to my family. There is no way to make up for the time you didn't spend together; there is no way to erase the hurts imposed by fatigue and short tempers. At one point, everybody in the family was involved in the project. My daughter and her grandmother shared the proofreading, while my wife Judy transformed my etchings into quite respectable figures. That we survived, I am no longer surprised; I am simply eternally grateful.

Oscar H. Gandy, Jr.

1

Introduction

In his contribution to Lerner and Nelson's ode to Wilbur Schramm, Steven Chaffee provides a useful organizing model for classifying the volumes of research reports on the effects of mass media.[1] An 18-cell matrix is described which serves to collect those studies into a data cube described by the intersection of three vectors within this tradition of empirical research.

One side of the cube distinguishes between studies which focus on the impact of media attributable to its form and the conditions of its use, and studies which examine the impact of mass media associated with exposure to its content. On another side, distinctions are drawn between three classes of studies which differ in the characteristics of the effects measured. Here we find studies that focus on either attitudes, cognitions, or behaviors that are in some way determined by exposure to mass media. On the third side, we distinguish between published studies on the basis of the units of analysis chosen for investigation. That is, studies differ in the extent to which they consider media effects at the individual, interpersonal, or higher levels of social organization.

The biases in the research system are immediately revealed. It is as though the data cube, filled with small beads of knowledge, had been tilted on its axis, so that all the beads move toward one corner. Thus, what we know from the "effects" tradition of research is limited almost entirely to the impact of mass media content on the attitudes of individuals. We know next to nothing about the impact of media structures on the behavior of major institutions in our society.

I have argued that this bias in the research system enters in the process very early, when research problems are first identified, and hypotheses are generated for empirical testing.[2] Bias in this formative stage is seen to be associated with the interests of the funds' source used in the research, with the class perspective of the researchers, or as is almost always the case, it is inherent in the dominant paradigms guiding mainstream communication research.

More recently, communication journals have begun to reflect aspects of a heated debate about the nature of the biases inherent in administrative or critical perspectives on media research. Jay Blumler has taken something of a conciliatory, integrative position between combatants like Elihu Katz, James Halloran, and Nicholas Garnham,[3] although Blumler still concludes that the eclecticism of American media research is attributable to the "professional-expert" orientation of its practitioners. Rather than pursuing research questions of demonstrable social or theoretical value, these researchers pursue "interesting questions" with innovative and challenging methodological tools, following the computer output wherever it leads. While Blumler does not explicitly condemn this use of resources, he does suggest that this orientation may "bias research output towards that which is most doable, most able to attract financial support, most likely to yield publishable findings, and most likely to advance investigators' careers."[4]

Within what is loosely characterized as a critical perspective, it is generally agreed that the goal of media research is the improvement of our understanding of the role of mass media in society. There is less agreement on whether that knowledge should be used to change that role, or merely to raise questions about traditional assumptions.

Critical scholarship tends to see the primary role of mass media as one of control, and differences between theorists emerge as they attempt to specify the nature and locus of that control.

Philip Tichenor, George Donohue, and Clarice Olien hold as a basic theoretical assumption that "all communication is under some form of human control in the interest of the achievement of objectives and goals."[5] Although they offer a systems-theoretic model to help clarify the relationship between media content and the attempts to bring it under functional control, their approach is based upon pluralistic notions about the nature and distribution of power within these systems.

They identify a variety of mechanisms employed at different levels of the social system that serve to maintain the entire system in a state of adaptive equilibrium. *Feedback Control* provides information about the performance of the system's parts, in order to maintain the overall functioning of the system. A thermostatically controlled furnace operates in much the same way, in that a thermostat relies on information about the temperature in the room in order to maintain it at some predetermined level. When the temperature drops below some criterion level, the furnace is turned on until information in the feedback loop indicates that the desired temperature has been achieved. The press is seen to serve as this feedback loop when it calls public attention to misbehavior, or deviance from cultural norms on the part of some member or unit in the system. Watergate and other exposés would be examples of media efforts to bring the system back into line.

Distribution Control operates in support of system maintenance without the requirement of feedback. The system may be maintained by the selective provision or withholding of information. News media coverage of complex issues may be presented in such a way as to oversimplify or to ignore the links between seemingly disparate events. The consumers of news are merely observers of stories that journalists unfold for them. This kind of news produces "knowledge of" events. For the public to participate in or influence events, "knowledge about" them is necessary. Distribution control ensures that this specialized knowledge is available only to the elite, highly motivated segments of the society.

They suggest that the timing of an information release may also play an important role in the use of the distribution control mechanism. It is often in the interest of some elements in the system to avoid releasing information about impending actions until it is too late for affected parties to take evasive or protective action.

Although this approach is based upon a conflict rather than a consensus orientation, and although the authors suggest that actions taken at one level of the system, which may be functional for those units, may be dysfunctional for units at other levels or for the system as a whole, they fail to identify actors or a class of actors as having the power to dominate the entire system.

Marxist and actors scholars within the critical tradition provide more explicit identification of the locus of power or dominance within social systems. In contrast with the pluralist view, radical theorists argue that the social order always involves a fundamental conflict between classes. While there are struggles or contradictions within these major class divisions, radical scholars argue that the primary conflict is that between the ruling classes, who own the means of material and cultural production, and the working classes, who own little more than themselves. The state, or institutions of government, are seen to operate primarily in the interest of the ruling classes—to offer protections for their property and privileges and to preserve order among the lower classes.

The mass media are seen as instruments of the ruling class—used to maintain a social order that is most supportive of the well-being of that class. Manipulation of consciousness is the principal means of social control, which is facilitated through the "control of the informational and ideational apparatus at all levels." Herbert Schiller's study of the mass media system is thus intended to

identify some of these conditioning forces and to reveal the means by which they conceal their presence, deny their influence, or exercise directional control under auspices that superficially appear benign and/or natural.[6]

Vincent Mosco and Andrew Herman divide the radical scholars into two camps on the basis of their instrumental or structuralist assumptions about the nature of the capitalist state.[7] The instrumentalists are concerned with documenting ruling class control by revealing the means through which this control is exercised. G. William Domhoff's *The Powers That Be* is identified as a classic example of that approach. The ruling class is seen to dominate the social order through the operation and control of four interrelated processes.

The *special interest process* is the most narrowly defined, where individual corporations, wealthy owners, or specialized industrial groups exercise control over government decision making to "satisfy their narrow, short-run needs." More general class interests are served through the *policy formation process*, which is facilitated through the *candidate selection process*. The management of social consciousness is seen to proceed through

> the *ideology process,* which involves the formation, dissemination and enforcement of the assumptions, beliefs and attitudes that permit the continued existence of policies and politicians favorable to the wealth, income, status and privileges of members of the ruling class.[8]

The structuralists are less accepting of the existence of a cohesive ruling class maintained through common education and social and corporate activities. Instead, according to Mosco and Herman, structuralists focus on the capitalist state itself, and on the dialectical processes that resolve conflicts within and between classes. Thus, Murdock and Golding argue that "an adequate analysis of cultural production needs to examine not only the class base of control, but also the general economic context in which this control is exercised."[9] They criticize more orthodox Marxists for their focus on content, which they see as providing only a weak base from which to infer the characteristics of the system that produced it.

It is impossible, they argue, to understand the role of the media in the production of the dominant ideology "without an analysis of the economic context within which it takes place and of the pressures and determinations which this context exerts."[10] They further suggest that this work might begin with a detailed analysis of economic relations within a particular sector of the information industry (such as the analyses of the motion picture industry offered by Thomas Guback).[11] They warn, however, that analysts who limit their analysis to relations within a particular sector fail to take note of increasingly more important conflicts between sectors in advanced capitalist states.

Thus, the structuralists would underscore the complexity of the capitalist system, and would reject the more mechanistic approach of the instrumentalists that tends to ignore or gloss over the reality of contradictions and the potential for change inherent in organized resistance to class domination. This potential for change is seen to increase when changes in technology or productive forces generate instability in the social order.

Mosco and Herman argue that the structuralists' focus on complexity and class struggle need not be seen as a variant of a pluralist model

> for it is not the direct pressures of a plurality of interests that is in the forefront of the state's concerns, but the need to set policies that advance capitalism . . . even without unified direct pressure from capital, the state in the United States pursues policies on information resources that are decidedly capitalist, simply because it is in the interest of state practitioners to maintain the capitalist system.[12]

The view taken in this book is somewhere between the instrumental and structuralist positions. By focusing on the processes whereby control over the flow of information is used in the pursuit of short- and long-term policy goals, complexity will most certainly be revealed. At the same time, it will also be demonstrated that there are vast inequities in the ability of groups and interests within and between classes to control the flow of information.

BEYOND AGENDA SETTING

Some 10 years before its explicit formulation by McCombs and Shaw, Kurt and Gladys Lang had begun to specify an agenda-setting function for the mass media. They argued that the mass media structured a reality which was so pervasive and so obtrusive that it was difficult, if not impossible, to escape its influence. On the basis of their analysis of the presidential campaigns of 1948 and 1952, they concluded that there was an important role for the media in defining the limits of political debate, and specifying the issues upon which voters would decide how to vote.[13]

Although based in part on the earlier work of Berelson, Lazarsfeld, and McPhee,[14] the work of the Langs offered some important insights that either had eluded researchers or had presented them with insurmountable methodological problems. They rejected Joseph Klapper's "limited effects"[15] view of media power, describing such findings as artifacts of the dominant research paradigm. Research then, as now, focused primarily on the period of the electoral campaign. And, as they suggest,

> the very emphasis on change *within* the span of a campaign makes it almost inevitable that whatever realignments occur are limited by the more permanent identifications and loyalties existing at the time the study is started. . . . All these habits and orientations have their roots outside the campaign . . . examination of change within this short span fails altogether to account for the cumulative impact of media exposure.[16]

In their view, *all* news is relevant to the vote, not merely the speeches made during the campaign. Media coverage of important events, the state of the economy, and relations with foreign governments all contribute to the public's impression of the kind of leadership they will accept at that particular moment in history.

In arguing for the extension of the boundaries of research on mass media, public opinion, and political behavior, they provided the theoretical basis upon which contemporary agenda-setting research is built.

Building on the work of the Langs, and incorporating similar theoretical departures in the area of political socialization (cognitive development and attitude formation), McCombs and Shaw provided the first empirical verification of what they called the agenda-setting function of the mass media.[17] By selecting a sample of undecided voters, they hoped to avoid the tendency toward selective exposure attributed to political partisans. Subjects were asked to identify the key issues in the campaign as they saw them, without regard to the positions on those issues taken by candidates. A content analysis of selected media provided a list of 15 categories of issues of major and minor importance to the press, as reflected in the number of appearances of those issues. The high correlation between what the media treated as important, and what the undecided voters considered to be important, was taken as evidence of the media's power to influence the salience of issues, thereby setting the public agenda.

This publication stimulated a great number of attempts to replicate the main effect, to see if it varied across media and across classes of issues.[18] As with other studies of mass media effects,[19] agenda-setting research efforts revealed the complexity of the phenomenon as different variables were used as the basis for comparisons. There were differences in the strength of the relationship between content and public agendas as researchers examined different contingent conditions. Media users were seen to differ in the extent to which they were interested in public affairs, were knowledgeable of issues and candidates' positions on them, engaged in discussion of political issues with family and friends, or expressed a "need for orientation" within a swirl of media content. These differences were reflected in varying degrees of agreement between media and personal agendas.

Methodological concerns about the measurement of media and public agendas have also been expressed.[20] It matters greatly how one asks respondents about the nature of their priorities. Black people, who have tended to set themselves apart from and in opposition to the policies and concerns of the Reagan administration, would give one response to the question: "What are the most important problems facing the government today?," and quite another to the question: "What are the most important problems facing black people today?"

It matters greatly whether one limits the assessment of the media agenda to the news items covered by the networks, or includes the agenda of problems faced by the principal characters in prime-time fiction. The strength of the correlations between public and media agendas varies with the number of categories or items arranged in any list of priorities—the longer the list, the lower the correlation.

There are even problems associated with determining just what the temporal relationship ought to be between media attention to an issue and its elevation to a place of importance in the public agenda.[21] Some kinds of issues or events move easily to the public agenda, others take more time, and the theoretical base of agenda-setting research is incapable of predicting just what that optimal lag should be. This problem of time is addressed by the Langs in their examination of Watergate as an issue that moved quite late onto the public agenda, despite its early coverage in the media.[22]

They describe certain issues as being "low threshold" issues, and because of the link between these issues and an individual's personal well-being, items covered in the press are of immediate importance. Those issues that do not touch the lives of most members of the audience are seen to have a high threshold, and require considerable media attention to achieve the same level of salience in the public consciousness. This notion may be seen to be somewhat akin to Gerbner et al.'s notion of *resonance,* where objective conditions and experiences serve to heighten the impact of media portrayals of violence or other social realities.[23] In the specific case of Watergate, the Langs also suggest that in addition to the fact that the break-in did not impinge on anyone's lives, the story "appeared outlandish to most people," and the "phenomenon of incredulity" served to keep the scandal off the public agenda for a long period of time.[24]

The list of conditions and cautions associated with gathering scholarly evidence in support of the existence of an agenda-setting effect is lengthy, and bound to grow longer. Researchers, anxious to earn additional publications through the presentation of significant differences, or strong, positive correlations, will continue to offer their own idiosyncratically defined formulations of the basic relationship between media and public consciousness. In the end, the conclusions will be the same as those always offered by the armies of equivocation: some media coverage will affect the agendas of some people, regarding some issues, some of the time.

By pursuing the infinite regress of individual differences, there is no question that research will find variations in the impact of media agendas. But does that really matter? Is it a difference that makes a difference in the final analysis of power?

As the Langs suggest,[25] the agenda-setting formulation is both too little and too much at the same time. All consciousness is not based on exposure to media. Although the amount is smaller all the time, *some* awareness is based on direct experience with our environment. At the same time, public issues and political action are not determined solely by the knowledge and perceived importance of issues and events. However, because McCombs and his colleagues[26] want to limit the agenda-setting construct to matters of issue salience, I suggest that we have to go beyond agenda-setting to determine who sets the media agenda, how and for what purposes it is set, and with what impact on the distribution of power and values in society.

In developing answers to these questions, I have turned toward political economy, and away from the traditional social-psychological base upon which much of the empirical work in mass communications is built. Knowledge and information are seen to have economic and political value through their relation to power, or to control over the actions of others. In capitalist societies in general, and in the United States in particular, the power of knowledge and information has been amplified by the tendency of such societies to transform essentially public goods into private property.

In addition, as with other commodities that are produced for sale in capitalist markets, the market for information is characterized by both shortage and surplus. Some information, like advertising and other promotional messages, is over-produced, and is provided free to its consumers. Indeed, in many cases, people are paid indirectly to consume advertising messages when the sources of the information sponsor entertainment or news in the mass media. Other information, such as that necessary to evaluate the risks associated with genetic research and development, is not available to the general population at any price.

Because information is at the heart of individual and collective decision making, control of information implies control over decision making. And, since the exchange of information is determined largely on an economic basis, mal-distribution in economic resources will be reflected in maldistribution of infor-mation. Such an economic perspective makes it possible to see control over the decisions and actions of others as flowing from the power to control their access to information.

Within a capitalist society, manipulation of prices is one way to control the consumption of information. With information, as with most commodities, when the price is lowered, the amount consumed increases; when the price is raised, the amount consumed generally decreases. Those with the power to control the price of information not only control its consumption, they also influence the decisions that are based on that information. Thus, if information opposed to the development of nuclear energy were made available at a lower price than that set for information in support of its use, more of the critical information would be consumed, and by extension, decision makers would be inclined to restrict its development. Persons who favor the development of nuclear energy would, therefore, have an incentive to lower the price of favorable information.

Indeed, all who have an interest in such decisions have an incentive to influence the prices faced by others for information related to those decisions. Efforts to reduce the prices faced by others for certain information, in order to increase its consumption, are described as *information subsidies*.[27] It is through the provision of information subsidies to and through the mass media that those with economic power are able to maintain their control over a capitalist society.

In turning away from social psychology in order to understand the role of information and media in the maintenance of the status quo, I have also turned away from the traditional focus on the audience or consumer as the target of mass communications. While the impact of information subsidies on individual and collective decision making is important to our understanding of power, much is already known. What we do not know, and what this book seeks to explore, are the relatively unknown dimensions of source behavior and the structural conditions that facilitate the use of information as an instrument of social control.

FOCUS ON THE SOURCE

There are a great many ways in which one can begin to characterize the sources of mass media content. The media may be viewed collectively, as is often the case in those agenda-setting studies that seek to demonstrate how ''the media'' set the public agenda with regard to the most important issues of the day. Other studies may divide the media into subgroups, print and electronic, in an effort to determine which wings of the monolith are more important and influential in setting the agenda of audience groups. In either approach, the media content is taken as given, and only peripheral interest is shown in determining how the agenda is set from day to day, from edition to edition.

A much smaller group of researchers begins with media content, but attempts to draw inferences about the nature of media organization on the basis of consistencies or patterns of attention and emphasis that characterize some sources and not others. Just as psychiatrists are able to draw inferences about the psychological ''states'' of their patients, content analysts draw inferences about the ''managerial assumptions'' that determine the content of mass media.[28]

A more direct approach, characterized by Gerbner as institutional process analysis,[29] uses the techniques of participant and nonparticipant observation to describe the procedures, pressures, and constraints that result in the production of a characteristic symbolic structure. This regularity in content is seen to be the result of the interplay of various institutional pressures imposed on the media by various sources of power, including

> the authorities who issue licenses and administer the laws; the patrons who invest in or subsidize the operation; organizations, institutions and loose aggregations of publics that require attention and cultivation; (and) the managements that set policies and supervise operation.[30]

Although Gerbner identified nine major sources of power or influence over message production, the bulk of mainstream research has been focused on the group he calls the Experts—the creative talent, technicians, or professionals who create, organize, and transmit media content. Within this group, the focus is even narrower, where researchers have tended to concentrate on the work of journalists, reporters, and editors as they operate the gates of the capitalist press. These ''gatekeeper'' studies traditionally view news content as the result of individual action, and seek to understand that action by understanding the background and personality of journalists.

The first, and perhaps the most important, of these studies was David Manning White's 1950 study of news selection by the opinionated "Mr. Gates."[31] White sought to discover the reasons behind the wire editor's selection of only 10% of the stories available to him during a given week. He classified the reasons given most frequently by the editor, and noted with particular interest the ideological character of many of the editor's comments. Stories were rejected because they were "propaganda" or "too red," and occasionally, because they were probably false, as indicated by the "B.S." label applied by Mr. Gates. Most important of all, however, was the limitation of space. Stories that made their way past other more personal filters were rejected because there was not enough space for their publication. In spite of this, White concluded that the editor had considerable independent power over media content and that "the community shall hear as a fact only those events which the newsman, as the representative of his culture, believes to be true."[32]

Walter Gieber, writing in 1963, had a somewhat more realistic view of the constraints or limits on the power of individual journalists or editors:

> the fate of the local news story is not determined by the needs of the audience or even by the values of the symbols it contains. The news story is controlled by the frame of reference created by the bureaucratic structure of which the communicator is a member.[33]

Paul Hirsch, in pursuing this structuralist view somewhat further, suggests that the requirements of the organization far outweigh any individual preferences that may guide any single gatekeeper.[34] His reanalysis of White's original study calls our attention to the surprising degree of consistency in the percentage of stories of a given type supplied by the wire services, and the percentages finally selected by the editor. While Mr. Gates may have had any number of *reasons* or personal justifications for the selections he made, he was "exercising discretion only within the latitude permitted for selecting particular stories to fit standard, widely agreed-upon categories, in the usual (expected) proportions that characterize a medium-sized, midwestern daily with a predominately conservative readership."[35]

GATEKEEPERS AND THEIR SOURCES

Within the context of organizational or structural requirements, recent studies of the nature of newswork have taken notice of the relationship between journalists and their sources. For some, this relationship is seen as social; for others, it is essentially economic. Herbert Gans, for example, uses a primarily social metaphor:

> The relationship between sources and journalists resembles a dance, for sources seek access to journalists, and journalists seek access to sources. Although it takes two to tango, either sources or journalists can lead, but more often than not, sources do the leading.[36]

Stephen Hess suggests that a kind of personal affinity brings journalists and their sources into contact. "Some news sources are automatic—people who must be approached because of the positions they hold. But otherwise, reporters seek news sources they prefer to be with . . . they like each other—and hate each other—because they are so much alike."[37] Hess suggests that certain sources, because of their styles, their use of bureaucratic language, and their reliance on documents and "boring statistics," are almost repellent to journalists.

Others suggest that regular contact between journalists and their sources may lead to some degree of personal identification, which may result in a hesitancy on the part of those journalists to reveal information that might harm or otherwise erect a barrier between them and their friends. This is seen to be particularly true for science writers, who because they are highly trained in their specialization, and are frequently in contact with scientists on a collegial basis, are "less likely to report science in a way that deviates from the norms of the scientific community, particularly in areas of controversy involving scientists."[38] Edie Goldenberg suggests that this interaction between journalists and their sources will, over time, tend to separate the reporters from their readership as the primary targets of their writing. Rather than writing for the mass audience, journalists who are in regular contact with government officials, and other reporters on the city hall beat, come to write instead for the friends they see each day.[39]

As important as these social explanations may seem to be, it is possible to reduce them to their basic economic considerations. Even social interaction can be seen in terms of costs and benefits, investments and rewards. Journalists have to meet deadlines, editors have to fill space, producers must fill the time between the commercials. In order to reduce their uncertainty about meeting these fairly standard organizational requirements, journalists enter into relationships of exchange with their sources that have many of the qualities of traditional economic markets. Although there is no exchange of cash, except in those few cases of "checkbook journalism," where reporters pay their sources for information, there is still an exchange of value. Journalists decide whether to invest time in the pursuit of one source rather than another, based on their estimation of the probable returns such an investment will produce. Those sources who have proved their value in the past are selected over those who are either unknown or have reduced their value by providing false information, or information in a form that was not easily converted into a publishable story.

Certain classes of sources have been identified as being more reliable than others. Official bureaucracies, or bureaucratically organized institutions, tend to be the most reliable, and as a result, bureaucratically supplied information comes to dominate mass media channels. Mark Fishman sees bureaucratic sources as doing much of the work of journalists.[40] Even when a journalist is aware that there is substantial self-interest involved in a particular controversy, and with a little effort the reporter could construct a balanced examination of the issues, Fishman suggests that the rule of least effort usually guides journalistic behavior:

> If reporters see that an agency in the beat territory has already claimed a contro-versy . . . then reporters will not take it upon themselves to assemble a constellation of interests around the event or establish a common framework with which accounts are brought into correspondence. This work is already done for them by officials.[41]

Investigative reporting, or enterprise news, is time-consuming, and jour-nalists have only so much time to invest in the production of a story. Where the average journalist may generate one ''think piece'' a week, the use of bureaucratic sources facilitates the production of two or more routine stories each day. In Goldenberg's terms, ''reporters had to have great energy and dedication to ferreting out stories to emerge from the overwhelming number of stories handed to them and do investigative journalism.''[42]

Reliance on bureaucratic sources is facilitated by the tendency of journalists to accept information from these routine sources as factual. When the factual nature of information is not questioned, journalists need not invest valuable time in an effort to obtain verification. While journalists resist the implication that they are the victims of bureaucratic propaganda efforts, and vehemently deny the possibility that they hold any sources as being above suspicion, Dan Nimmo would respond that the proof is in the pages.[43] Far too many news releases are successful in achieving publication for each to have been subjected to more than a cursory review.

Leon Sigal's analysis[44] of the stories appearing on page one of *The New York Times* and *The Washington Post* supports Nimmo's conclusion. Of nearly 1,200 stories, 58.2% were identified as coming through routine bureaucratic channels—official proceedings, press releases and conferences, and nonspon-taneous or planned events. Only 25.8% of the most important stories in these elite newspapers could be identified as the product of investigative or enterprise journalism. And, to the extent that interviews, the largest category of enterprise channels, could also be seen as the result of routine access to bureaucratic spokespersons, very little of the news has its origin in an investigatory mode.

Even when journalists are sure that the information bears checking, there are other economic considerations that lead them to go with the flow, to follow the pack. In Fishman's discussion of the case of a police department-created ''crime wave,''[45] a newly created police unit sought publicity by leaking stories about an increase in attacks by black and Hispanic youths against poor elderly whites. Despite the fact that police statistics had shown an actual decrease in such crimes, journalists were unable to resist the pressure to follow this ''non-story.'' Because other journalists and other media channels were covering the story, and publishing each new report as it was issued by the police unit, it was less costly to go along with the trend than to risk criticism or to invest in producing a more attractive alternative.

It is clear that journalists and other gatekeepers benefit from the relationships they establish with sources best able to meet their needs. It is also easy to see how they come to favor those bureaucratic sources who can provide a regular, credible, and ultimately usable flow of information, insight, and imagery with which to construct the news. But what value does the source receive in return?

The value of controlled access to target audiences through mass media channels is found ultimately in its contribution to source control over decisions made by the targets. Information is an important input in the production of influence, and the news media are primary means for the delivery of information. Because of the credibility normally associated with news, in comparison with that associated with commercial speech, sources would prefer to have their message delivered in a 30-second news item, than in a 60-second commercial.

In choosing between reporters and techniques for attracting the reporter's attention, sources are concerned with questions of cost-effectiveness. Press releases, briefings, and press conferences are seen to be economically efficient because they provide sources with access to several reporters at the same time, saving the time that would be spent in individual interviews. Some of the newer forms of what Dom Bonafede refers to as ''socialized journalism'' are even more efficient.[46] Special breakfasts and luncheon meetings where key officials and politicians are invited to speak before a select group of reporters have become popular with sources as well as reporters. These events not only ''offer the guests an opportunity to get 15 or so interviews out of the way at once,'' but do it in a more highly controlled atmosphere where the ''invitations-only'' nature of the event serves to screen out the ''kooks,'' who tend to ask embarassing questions or fail to follow the rules of the game regarding the use of background or off-the-record information.

Because the targets of these information subsidies vary from source to source, they will differ in their use of techniques to meet a journalist's needs. Altheide and Johnson suggest that bureaucrats generally aim their information subsidies at specialized rather than mass audiences.[47] Thus, they will select those channels which are used more regularly by high-level government officials and policy makers. Although it might take less effort to gain access to the editorial pages of several small-town newspapers, the expected value from such exposure is almost nonexistent when compared to that derived from positive editorial treatment in *The Washington Post*.

It is the goal of all sources to influence decisions by changing the stock of information upon which those decisions are based. Since the public is generally only marginally involved in the determination of public policy, and because the costs of molding public opinion are often quite high, sources have greater incentives to use the press to *define* public opinion than to influence it directly. Still, there are times when an effort to mobilize grass-roots support is economically justified. Then sources select those techniques that ensure the widest coverage for the least effort. Very often this means concentrating on the wire services and papers like *The New York Times*. A press release that is successful in gaining access to the Associated Press (AP) or United Press International (UPI) wires is more efficient than individual releases sent to each newspaper in the nation. And just as the wire services set the front page agendas of the nation's urban papers, the elite papers like the *Times* set the agenda for the networks. Assignment editors spend their mornings reading the *Post* and the *Times*. Adams and Albin suggest that "there are many topics that get newspaper coverage while being scarcely covered by television. There are virtually no topics that receive television news attention that are non-issues in elite newspapers."[48] In Gitlin's words, "the *Times* is, in fact, one of the main channels through which network newsworkers form pictures of the world, what is happening there, and what, within that world, deserves coverage."[49]

Often the value of an information subsidy for any source is increased to the extent that the source can disguise the promotional, partisan, self-interested quality of the information. This is often accomplished when news stories convey the desired information without identifying its source. Information that would be accepted only with caution if its source were identified as a partisan in a debate is much more powerful if it is received as objective fact, reported by an uninterested journalist.

On occasion, government policy deliberations involve struggles within the administration, or between administration and bureaucracy. Sources that want to influence the debate without risking the wrath of superiors seek journalists who will allow them to "leak" the information into the news media. Leaks are also important as techniques for launching "trial balloons." A policy maker who wishes to test public sentiment, or the receptiveness of others in the policy arena, without associating herself with a losing policy option, can avoid that risk by leaking the information first and taking responsibility for it later, if the response to the idea is favorable.

Whereas the journalist selects from an array of sources and events on the basis of perceived utility in producing news that will meet organizational requirements, sources select from an even larger array of techniques on the basis of their perceived effectiveness in being covered, reported, and transmitted in the right form, at the right time, and in the right channel. Techniques, gatekeepers, and channels are selected ultimately on the basis of their relative efficiency in the production of influence over the knowledge, attitudes, and behavior of others.

OVERVIEW

This book is about sources and their use of journalists and other gatekeepers to deliver information subsidies to participants in the policy process. Sources enter into an exchange of value with journalists in which (1) they reduce the costs of news work to increase their control over news content; (2) they reduce the costs of scientific research to increase their control over scientific and technical information; and (3) they even reduce the costs of writing and producing television fiction to increase their control over the cultural background against which social policy questions are generally framed.

Although sources may influence the pool of information by withholding information as well as by providing it, I have chosen to focus primarily on the subsidy, or cost-reduction aspects of the production of influence through information. In Chapter Two, the role of information in decision making is explored. There, a discussion of the economics of information provides a basis for examining the role of information subsidies in individual and collective decisions.

Chapter Three focuses primarily on the nature of collective decisions at the federal government level. Whereas discussions in Chapter Two are based primarily on the literature in psychology, economics, and decision science, political science provides much of the background to describe the incentives of major policy actors identified in Chapter Three. The chapter concludes with a review of the assumptions underlying the information subsidy approach to the production of influence.

Chapter Four examines in some detail the variety of techniques used by corporate and government sources to influence policy through the provision of information subsidies through direct and indirect means. Whereas Chapter Four provides numerous examples of advertising, public relations, research, and entertainment content published in support of a variety of policy goals, each of the remaining chapters concentrates on a single community of issues.

Chapter Five examines the use of information subsidies to influence public policy in health, with particular emphasis on the role of subsidized information in the creation and maintenance of demand for high-cost medical technology. Chapter Six takes a similar approach to the examination of a somewhat less successful effort to establish a market for instructional technologies in America's schools. Science policy in general and nuclear energy in particular provide the focus for the analysis in Chapter Seven.

In Chapter Eight, the focus is turned toward economics and public welfare, and the use of information subsidies by the Reagan administration and the representatives of the New Right to build public acceptance of "supply-side economics," or welfare for the rich. This theme is extended in Chapter Nine, where I examine the nature of information inequality, and its reflection in an unequal ability to influence public policy. Here, I reject the promise of new information technologies to reduce the knowledge and information gaps, and suggest instead that the new information utilities will only serve to further consolidate the power of the haves over the have-nots.

Finally, in Chapter Ten, I issue a call for a research effort by critical scholars to document and describe the extent to which information subsidies determine public policy, the extent to which these subsidies convey disproportionate power to their sources, and the extent to which subsidized information dominates international communication channels.

CHAPTER ONE FOOTNOTES

1 Chaffee, Steven. (1977). Mass media effects: new research perspectives. *In* D. Lerner, and L. Nelson (Eds.), "Communication Research—A Half-Century Appraisal," pp. 210–241. Honolulu, Hawaii: East-West Center.

2 Gandy, Oscar H., Jr. (1974). "The economics and structure of bias in mass media research." (Paper presented at the biannual Congress of the International Association for Mass Communication Research (IAMCR), Leipzig, East Germany.)

3 Katz, Elihu, Halloran, James, and Garnham, Nicholas. (1978). Social research on broadcasting: a colloquy on the Katz report for the BBC and the issues it raises. *Journal of Communication 28* (No. 2) (Spring), 89–141.

4 Blumler, Jay G. (1978). Purposes of mass communications research: a transatlantic perspective. *Journalism Quarterly 55* (No. 3) (Summer), 228.

5 Tichenor, Philip, Donohue, George, and Olien, Clarice. (1973). Mass communication research: evolution of a structural model. *Journalism Quarterly 50* (No. 4) (Autumn), 419–423.

6 Schiller, Herbert I. (1973). "The Mind Managers." Boston, Massachusetts: Beacon Press.

7 Mosco, Vincent, and Herman, Andrew. (1981). Radical social theory and the communications revolution. *In* E. McAnany, J. Schnitman, and N. Janus (Eds.), "Communication and Social Structure," pp. 58–84. New York: Praeger Publishers.

8 Domhoff, G. William. (1978). "The Powers That Be," p. 9. New York: Vintage Books.

9 Murdock, Graham, and Golding, Peter. (1977). Capitalism, communication and class relations. *In* J. Curran, M. Gurevitch, and J. Woolacott (Eds.), "Mass Communication and Society," p. 16. Beverley Hills, California: Sage Publications.

10 *Ibid.,* p. 19.

11 Guback, Thomas. (1969). "The International Film Industry: Western Europe and America Since 1945." Bloomington, Indiana: Indiana University Press.

12 Mosco, Vincent, and Herman, Andrew. Page 71 in footnote 7, 1981.

13 Lang, Kurt, and Lang, Gladys. (1971). The mass media and voting. *In* W. Schramm, and D. Roberts (Eds.), "The Process and Effects of Mass Communication," revised ed., pp. 678–700. Urbana, Illinois: University of Illinois Press.

14 Berelson, Bernard, Lazarsfeld, Paul F., and McPhee, William M. (1971). Political power: the role of the mass media. *In* W. Schramm, and D. Roberts (Eds.), "The Process and Effects of Mass Communication," revised ed., pp. 655–667. Urbana, Illinois: University of Illinois Press.

15 Klapper, Joseph. (1960). "The Effects of Mass Communication." New York: The Free Press.

16 Lang, Kurt, and Lang, Gladys. Page 683 in footnote 13, 1971.

17 McCombs, Max, and Shaw, Donald. (1972). The agenda-setting function of mass media. *Public Opinion Quarterly 36* (Summer), 176–187.

18 A comprehensive review of agenda setting and related studies is published *in* D. Shaw, and M. McCombs (Eds.). (1977). "The Emergence of American Political Issues: The Agenda-Setting Function of the Press." St. Paul, Minnesota: West Publishing.

[19] McLeod, Jack, and Reeves, Byron. (1980). On the nature of mass media effects. *In* Stephen B. Whithey, and Ronald P. Abeles (Eds.), "Television and Social Behavior: Beyond Violence and Children." Hillsdale, New Jersey: Lawrence Erlbaum Associates.

[20] De George, William F. (1981). Conceptualization and measurement of audience agenda. *In* G. Wilhoit, and H. de Bock (Eds.), "Mass Communication Review Yearbook," Vol. 2, pp. 219-224. Beverly Hills, California: Sage Publications.

[21] Eyal, Chaim, Winter, James P., and De George, William F. (1981). The concept of time frame in agenda setting. *In* G. Wilhoit, and H. de Bock (Eds.), "Mass Communication Review Yearbook" Vol. 2, pp. 212-218. Beverly Hills, California: Sage Publications.

[22] Lang, Gladys, and Lang, Kurt. (1981). Watergate: an exploration of the agenda-building process. *In* G. Wilhoit, and H. de Bock (Eds.), "Mass Communication Review Yearbook," Vol. 2, pp. 447-468. Beverly Hills, California: Sage Publications.

[23] Gerbner, George, Gross, Larry, Morgan, Michael, and Signorielli, Nancy. (1980). The mainstreaming of America: violence profile no. 11. *Journal of Communication 30* (No. 3) (Summer), 10–25.

[24] Lang, Gladys, and Lang, Kurt. Pages 458-459 in footnote 22, 1981.

[25] *Ibid.*, pp. 465–466.

[26] McCombs, Maxwell. (1981). Setting the agenda for agenda-setting research; an assessment of the priority idea and problems. *In* G. Wilhoit, and H. de Bock (Eds.), "Mass Communication Review Yearbook," Vol. 2, pp. 209-211. Beverly Hills, California: Sage Publications.

[27] Bartlett, Randall. (1973). "Economic Foundations of Political Power." New York: The Free Press.

[28] Gerbner, George. (1964). On content analysis and critical research in mass communications. *In* L. Dexter, and D. White (Eds.), "People, Society, and Mass Communications," pp. 476–500. New York: The Free Press.

[29] Gerbner, George. (1972). Communication and social environment. *Scientific American 227* (No. 3), 153–160.

[30] *Ibid.*, pp. 156–157.

[31] White, David M. (1964). The gatekeeper: a case study in the selection of news. *In* L. Dexter, and D. White (Eds.), "People, Society, and Mass Communications," pp. 160–172. New York: The Free Press.

[32] *Ibid.*, p. 171.

[33] Gieber, Walter. (1964). News is what newspapermen make it. *In* L. Dexter, and D. White (Eds.), "People, Society, and Mass Communications," p. 178. New York: The Free Press.

[34] Hirsch, Paul. (1977). Occupational, organizational, and institutional models in mass media research: toward an integrated framework. *In* P. Hirsch, P. Miller, and F. Kline (Eds.), "Strategies for Communication Research," pp. 13–42. Beverly Hills, California: Sage Publications.

[35] *Ibid.*, p. 23.

[36] Gans, Herbert J. (1979). "Deciding What's News: A Study of CBS Evening News, NBC Nightly News, Newsweek and Time," p. 116. New York: Pantheon Books.

[37] Hess, Stephen. (1981). "The Washington Reporters," p. 126. Washington, D.C.: The Brookings Institution.

[38] Donohue, George A., Tichenor, Phillip J., and Olien, Clarice N. (1973). Mass media functions, knowledge, and social control. *Journalism Quarterly 50* (No. 4) (Winter), 656.

[39] Goldenberg, Edie N. (1975). "Making the Papers," p. 79. Lexington, Massachusetts: D.C. Heath.

[40] Fishman, Mark. (1980). "Manufacturing the News," pp. 45–46. Austin, Texas: University of Texas Press.

[41] *Ibid.*, p. 132.

[42] Goldenberg, Edie N. Page 80 in footnote 39, 1975.

[43] Nimmo, Dan. (1978). "Political Communication and Public Opinion in America," p. 207. Santa Monica, California: Goodyear Publishing.

[44] Sigal, Leon V. (1973). "Reporters and Officials," pp. 119–130. Lexington, Massachusetts: D.C. Heath.

[45] Fishman, Mark. Pages 5–10 in footnote 40, 1980.

[46] Bonafede, Dom. (1981). Reporters' breakfast and lunch groups—good reporting or "socialized journalism?" *National Journal* (March 21), 487–491.

[47] Altheide, David, and Johnson, John. (1980). "Bureaucratic Propaganda," pp. 18–21. Boston, Massachusetts: Allyn and Bacon.

[48] Adams, William, and Albin, Suzanne. (1980). Public information on social change: TV coverage of women in the work force. *Policy Studies Journal 8* (No. 5) (Spring), 729.

[49] Gitlin, Todd. (1980). "The Whole World is Watching," p. 299. Berkeley, California: University of California Press.

2

Decision Making

All human behavior, no matter how complex, can be treated as a series of binary decisions—choices between two options. While emotions, attitudes, and values may play a role in these decisions, the process is essentially rational, and is based on the amount and quality of information available to the decision maker (DM) at the time the decision is made. This assumption of rationality is basic to a model of decision making which seeks to predict or explain the behavior of policy actors (PAs) who seek to influence the policy process through the provision of information subsidies.

The assumption of rationality is as troublesome as it is basic to a model of individual and collective decision making. The essential assertion in rationalist theories is that within the limits of possibilities in the actual or conceivable environment, an individual engages in "deliberate and intentional choice for the purpose of maximizing some objective function."[1] However, there are a number of premises within that very brief definition that are denied by critics of rationality. The most problematic of all threats to the rationalistic assumption is the impossibility of making fully rational choices in the face of unyielding constraints in the environment.

Herbert Simon, who is credited with the explication of this notion of "bounded rationality,"[2] suggests that the term "rational" should only be applied to decisions in the company of an appropriate adverb. A decision may be considered to be "objectively rational" if it is seen to actually result in the maximization of values. Another decision may be considered to be "subjectively rational" as long as it serves to maximize value within the limits of the knowledge available to the decision maker at the time. Decisions may not always be "consciously rational" in that they may involve choice behaviors which have become habituated through frequent performance, like the flick of a wrist of a Ping-Pong player returning a serve with topspin.

There are also critics of the rationalist assumption whom John Elster calls structuralists.[3] They argue that because all choices are constrained by structural influences, individual rationality is impossible. Ideology is identified as a structural constraint that is developed and exists external to the individual, and limits the range of possibilities considered to be appropriate to a given choice. And, to the extent that ideology or cultural values are the servants of the dominant classes, the behavior of the subordinate classes cannot be objectively rational if they are consistent with such an ideology. The only rational choices would be those that result in a transformation of the dominant social relations. Homans would reply that "our problem is not why they hold these values, but given that they do hold them, what do they do about them."[4]

Limits to rationality are also found within the individual and the limits of a person's ability to consider multiple objectives in the context of a complex and ever changing environment. Suboptimization is said to occur under a number of conditions where the individual is not able to select an option that will maximize even subjective utility.[5] We recognize, for example, that decisions are rarely independent of each other. When we act to optimize or maximize the attainment of one objective, that action can result in the limitation of some other desired objective. We cannot relax, and get our work done at the same time.

We recognize as well that decisions taken today may be less than optimal at some time in the future. Because decisions involving multiple objectives are so complex and involve so many sources of information and relationships, Herbert Simon suggests that we may engage in "satisficing" behavior where we select options that meet some minimal criteria, or are "good enough" considering the difficulty of arriving at a more well-informed decision.

At the heart of all discussions of bounded rationality is the recognition that there are limits on the availability of information relevant to most choices. Most choices would not be labeled as objectively rational because they are made under conditions of uncertainty where the DM has less than perfect information upon which to base a choice.

THE ROLE OF INFORMATION IN DECISION MAKING

We may think of decisions as the rational choice between options, based on the expected value to be derived from the pursuit of one option rather than another. The expected value is estimated on the basis of information available to the DM. That information may be available instantly from the DM's memory, or it may be available through some process of search involving the expenditure of time or economic resources. The information relevant to that decision may be classified into three major categories: (1) information about the range and probability of occurrence of different states or conditions of the DM's relevant environment; (2) information about the outcomes or consequences for the DM in the event that one of those possible states comes to be; and (3) information about the subjective value or utility the DM could expect, should that consequence be realized.

What we expect to occur in the relevant future is perhaps the most important component in the calcualtion of expected value, and it is also the component most susceptible to modification by those interested in constraining the choices of others. Our knowledge of the future is always imperfect; thus we are always operating under conditions of relative uncertainty. Our estimation of probable futures may be based in part upon our knowledge of the past and readily available information about recent changes in the environment. It is unlikely, however, that our knowledge of the past can be derived entirely from our personal experience. Such knowledge is bound to be based in part on the experiences of others. The extent to which we have confidence in those sources is a reflection of the credibility we assign to them.

The confidence we have in external sources of information also plays a role in determining the influence of those sources in defining the consequences that are likely to result from a particular change in the environment. An example may help to illustrate the nature of these three types of information and their relevance to individual and collective decisions.

A farmer makes a decision about what crops to plant for the coming year on the basis of information about a number of relevant possibilities. The first set of unknowns deals with the weather, and the farmer must estimate the probability of good weather. While there are many possibilities, we might consider that the weather might be quite good, variable or mixed, or quite bad. On the basis of personal experience gained from years of farming, the farmer might assign probabilities on the basis of what she has observed in the behavior of squirrels and other creatures that the folklore has linked to weather projections. Or, a more modern farmer may invest in the projections offered by the U.S. Weather service in order to compare those projections with those in the *Farmer's Almanac*.

Since the choice is between two crops, corn or cucumbers, the farmer needs information that will allow her to estimate the probable return she could expect from each crop if the weather was good, bad, or variable. While one crop might be more sensitive to weather conditions, its return per acre under good weather conditions might be as much as twice that for the less risky crop. Information about the productivity of corn and cucumbers might be based solely on past experience, or it might include information from the Department of Agriculture, or from seed salespersons. The expected prices for corn and cucumbers are also somewhat uncertain since they are dependent in part on the number of farmers who decide to plant that crop, and how well their acres produce. The choice between corn and cucumbers would be made on the basis of the total expected value for each crop, based on subjective estimates of prices and probable weather conditions. The crop with the highest expected value is the one the rational farmer *should* plant.[6]

Where the outcomes associated with a given policy are not then traded in the marketplace, the problem of assigning values is substantially more complex. Indeed, the same activity may vary in its utility over time, or in relation to a DM's experience with it. Where the assignment of dollar values in the marketplace is considered to be objective, many other consequences of public and private policy are decidedly subjective. How for example do we individually and collectively value national security? What dollar value do we assign to the sense of well-being we are supposed to experience after the installation of an ultrasonic burglar alarm? The extent to which there are no objective, external sources for information upon which to determine individual or collective values for these outcomes is the degree to which those values may be influenced by external sources of information.

In all these cases, the credibility of information sources is an important factor in determining their influence on a given decision. Credibility is seen to be a function of several factors, including what is known about source intentions, expertise and trustworthiness.[7] Of course, estimates of expertness vary with the information being provided—an expert in animal husbandry is not necessarily a credible source of information about atomic waste disposal (except of course when the government is proposing to dispose of that waste a few miles upriver).

The information sources to which we turn are determined in part as a function of our experience with them in the past. McLeod and O'Keefe, in their somewhat novel application of the term "socialization" to such communication behaviors as information seeking and media exposure, suggest that in order to understand the differential use of these sources, we must understand the social origins of such behaviors and the processes through which they are learned and maintained.[8]

Whatever the processes are that result in men being seen as more credible than women, whites as more credible than blacks, social workers as more credible than their clients, and print as more credible than speech, they all add up to an inequitable distribution of the power to influence others. McLeod and O'Keefe suggest that we stand to learn the most about these processes if we direct our attention to those social interactions in which the exchange of information serves functional goals.

INFORMATION STRATEGIES

In that persuasive communication has as its goal the production of influence over the decisions of others, such communications may be characterized according to the strategies they employ, as well as by their relative success. Strategies may be classified in terms of their focus on various stages of the decision process, and the techniques used to influence the conclusions arrived at in each one of those stages. Wright and Barbour[9] identify four fairly distinct stages that precede some decision or action. The first, *the problem recognition stage,* is the one that is essential for the initiation of an information-search procedure. Perhaps because its necessity is so obvious, researchers in the field of decision making have paid little attention to the nature of the problem-recognition phase of the process.

In order for a DM to recognize the existence of a problem requiring a decision, the individual must perceive that there has been a change in the immediate or future state of a relevant environment that would require some change in present or future activity. The sudden appearance of dark clouds on an otherwise pleasant day introduces the necessity of decision making about behaviors appropriate in the event of rain.

Efforts to influence the behavior of others may therefore be concentrated at this initial phase, where one sounds the alarm and attracts attention to expected changes in the environment. Such messages are directed at influencing the target's belief that the environment has changed, or its subjective assessment of the probability that it will change in the relevant future. Such messages may vary in the extent to which they provide verifiable evidence to support such assertions. "Reliable sources in the Pentagon report a three-fold increase in Soviet troop strength along the Polish border" is the kind of assertion we might find in a message intended to increase the target's estimation of the probability of an invasion. No evidence is provided, though there is an attempt to waive the factual requirement through the identification of a credible source.

At the problem-recognition stage, we may find that attempts are frequently made to influence decisions by changing the relative importance of environmental conditions without making reference to their probability of occurrence. That is, messages may be constructed so as to increase the salience of those conditions or outcomes presumed likely to occur under such conditions.

I recall one large billboard that played on the largely racist fears of the commuters that streamed past it each evening on their way back to the suburbs surrounding Philadelphia. "You wouldn't want to have to walk home from here, so invest in a Brand X, long-life battery today." The fact that the billboard was planted in the most devastated part of the West Philadelphia urban renewal area served to reinforce the implied threat in the ad, which focused not only on the probability of battery failure, but also on the consequences of such failures.

The ad also sought to influence behavior by suggesting a specific alternative—the purchase of a particular battery. While the thinly veiled threat might have been avoided by taking another route out of the city, there was no incentive for the battery manufacturer to suggest that option. Thus, we see that the *definition of alternatives* is the second phase in the decision process, and like the first, represents an opportunity for interested parties to influence decisions by providing information about the range of available options.

Some strategists may attempt to influence decisions by limiting the number of options considered by DMs. Recognizing that the probability of the preferred option being selected will vary with the number of relevant options identified, the interested source would want to limit that number once they had ensured that the preferred option was among those to be considered. Assertions made in such persuasive attempts might suggest which options the preferred alternative should be compared with. By specifying the makeup of the comparison group, the strategist may ensure that the other options are easily recognizable as inferior. For most choices, whether between political candidates or bars of soap, the attractiveness of one alternative is sure to vary with the attractiveness of the options with which it is compared.

In the third phase of the decision-making process, DMs engage in *information sampling behavior* to review what is known about the options and their consequences. At this stage, strategists want to influence the pool of information available to the target so as to ensure that information favorable to the selection of the preferred option dominates any sample. Assertions may try to link the preferred option to a particular level of worth or value, such as that implied in the message which claims that "if you drink Brand X, you'll feel like a kid again." Or, a similar message might simply describe a property of outcome associated with the preferred option, which has a known, implicit value: "the synfuels program will guarantee us energy independence." Then again, assertions focused on this stage of the process might suggest that the associated outcome has some particular value: "a limited nuclear war is a much better prospect than anything we can hope for with today's conventional weapons systems." Or finally, an assertion might suggest that a primary property or outcome is related to some other property or outcome with a known valuation: "a delayed response is a sign of weakness."

The fourth stage of decision making involves the *application of a decision rule,* which the DM feels is appropriate to the decision at hand, or is more generally characteristic of the DM's behavior across decisons. Decision rules determine which information is given the greatest weight in the process of selecting between options. If DMs have preferred routines for arriving at decisions, they will be more receptive to information that is structured to flow easily through the process to its conclusion. Information that is difficult to assess, because of its seemingly irrelevant nature, is likely to slow down or otherwise interfere with the process. Strategists who know the preferred routines of their targets structure their messages so as to provide compatible information flows. When the preferred routine is unknown, the strategist may suggest which rules are appropriate for a given decision, and then supply information best suited to that approach. Wright and Barbour identify five decision models a strategist might encounter or propose.[10]

The *affect-referral strategy* is seen as the least involved of the five because the DMs rely on loosely defined "feelings" about options. What one feels about a political party might be captured in a single index or effective category: "the Democrats are for the poor folk, the Republicans are for the rich." A complex economic policy might be reduced to a single value, such as its impact on the poor, or its status as "welfare for the rich." Options might be compared with each other in terms of their overall utility or value, or they might be held up against some minimum standard of acceptability: "such a program would no longer provide the basic level of income a family would need to survive in the inner city," or, "a tax program like that wouldn't provide enough of an incentive to attract the average investor into the market."

Somewhat more complex is the *compensatory model,* where the DM computes a weighted average of expected values or benefits for each option. Here choices are made between options on the basis of the sum of the expected values of the outcomes likely to occur under a variety of environmental conditions, weighted according to the DM's subjective estimation of the probability of their occurrence. In order to influence the final choice, messages may be directed at determining the value of *any* of the items included in the calculation of expected value. That is, assertions may be made about the properties of some option, their respective values, or their relative probability of occurrence. The less information the DM has about any of these aspects of a given choice, the greater the potential for influence by a source willing and able to provide that information.

The third model, which Wright and Barbour call a *lexicographic* strategy, involves the pairwise comparison of options on a single dimension or attribute that is most important to a particular DM. If there were no clear winners on the first dimension, the pairwise compairsons would continue on to the next most important dimension. Attempts to influence DMs known to follow lexicographic rules might begin with assertions about which dimensions are the most important, and then provide information about the performance of the preferred option on that dimension. During the so-called gasoline shortage, when long lines were the order of the day, advertising strategists focused on the range, or the number of miles between fill-ups, rather than considering the mileage or even the cost per mile as being relevant to the selection of an automobile.

The *conjunctive model* has criterion levels for each of several relevant dimensions. Options are examined to determine if they fall within the personal minima and maxima that might be associated with considerations of price, convenience, flexibility, and the like. If, for example, options were all to fall within the traditional limits set by a given DM who also followed a satisficing rule and would select the first option that was "good enough," then a strategist would attempt to ensure that the preferred option was considered first. As with other decision strategies, influence might be produced by messages that attempt to set a minimum or a maximum for a particular dimension in such a way that it would cause the rejection of a competitor that might be superior on four out of five relevant dimensions, but failed to meet minimum requirements on the last. "Of course those foreign sports cars may be fast, good looking, handle well, and even provide pretty good gas mileage. But remember, if anything goes wrong, it could take months for you to get a spare part."

The final decision model is predicated on *considerations of risk*. While there is not much known about how individual DMs assess the risk involved in a decision, Wright and Barbour suggest that the consideration nearly always involves some estimation of the magnitude of the loss one might incur with a particular option. Strategies of influence involve efforts to convince the DM that the costs associated with selection of the non-preferred option are excessively high, and their probability of occurrence almost certain. It is important to distinguish between the costs of pursuing an option, such as the purchase price of a small foreign car, and the costs one might incur as a consequence of its use. Efforts to reduce the attractiveness of these options might involve messages that highlight the accident rate and severity of injuries likely to befall the driver of such a vehicle. The difficulty with influencing DMs who base their decisions on considerations of risk is that there is great variety in the extent to which a person is risk averse.[11] It is unlikely that a persuasive message will succeed in changing a person's preference for certainty; thus we find that strategists focus instead on perceptions of the magnitude of a loss.

If we consider the decision to take the series of shots being offered as insurance against the swine flu, we will recall that not everyone rushed down to their neighborhood health center. Persuasive messages from the health bureaucracy were focused on the probability that the flu would spread, the probability that any individual would get it, some estimates of the probability of death for groups in the population at the greatest risk, and, until the end of the campaign, very little about the risks associated with the inoculation itself. Messages favoring inoculation were focused on the magnitude of the costs one would face if one chose *not* to be inoculated. When word emerged about the possibility of paralysis and death accompanying inoculation, the balance, in terms of relative risk, shifted dramatically.

In an effort to determine which strategies were most characteristic of commercial advertisements on television and in popular magazines, Wright and Barbour analyzed a sample of television commercials aired during prime time, and a sample of ads from *Ladies Home Journal, Esquire,* and *Harper's* magazine. They reported that the most widely used strategy involved assertions about the attributes of the products and the outcomes likely to accompany their use. They also noted that the general tendency was toward modification of DMs' subjective estimates of probability, rather than subjective valuations. No doubt these findings reflect an awareness on the part of Madison Avenue strategists that it costs more to influence personal values than to modify perceptions of the unknown. If the final outcome is the same, the rational strategist pursues the less expensive option.

THE ECONOMICS OF INFORMATION

Anthony Downs in his 1957 explication of an "economic theory of democracy," draws a fine distinction between rational errors and irrationality by suggesting that one could make a rational error because one acted on the basis of imperfect information. In his view, it was "the cost of information (which) can lead rational men to make systematic errors in politics."[12] Downs describes citizens as DMs fraught with uncertainty—uncertainty about their own utility, about the impact of government activity on their personal welfare, and about how best to influence government to act on their behalf.[13] His recognition of the widespread nature of uncertainty served as the basis for some speculation about the nature of persuasion, and lay the groundwork for a theory of information subsidization.

> Persuaders are not interested *per se* in helping people who are uncertain become less so; they want certainly to produce a decision which aids their cause. Therefore, they provide only those facts which are favorable to whatever group they are supporting.[14]

Downs' notion of subsidization is based on his realization that some of the costs of rational political decision making are transferrable. That is, the costs of gathering, selecting, analyzing, and interpreting information can be borne by others. Rational citizens are expected however, to take steps to ensure that persons they entrust with the responsibility of reducing their uncertainty are likely to "provide them with versions of events that closely approximate the versions they would formulate themselves were they expert on the spot witnesses."[15]

After discussing the nature of costs associated with information gathering and use, Downs describes the use of *some* subsidized information as being entirely rational—or at the very least, impossible to avoid. Where Downs stops in his consideration of information subsidies, Randall Bartlett continues in great detail.[16] Not only is subsidized information problematic, in that "the selection principles embodied in the data may differ from those of the decision maker,"[17] but the source of the information is likely to have made it available specifically for its impact on policy. Indeed, in Bartlett's view, all participants who stand to gain more from their influence over the decisions of others than it cost them to produce that influence are required by the assumption of rationality to utilize *any* means at their disposal. Notions of disproportionate power to influence decision making are developed in a careful analysis that explores the nature of information, its cost, and its contribution to the production of influence. Only the skeleton of that analysis will be presented here.

Utility maximization is the goal or motivation underlying all rational economic behavior. Economists and others pursuing an economic logic in their attempts to explain human behavior have adopted the concept of subjective utility as a way of avoiding the frustrations of psychologists faced with a dizzying array of motivations, drives, and urges. McGuire notes that "any attempt to choose a list of human motives confronts us with an embarassment of riches."[18] He then proceeds to identify a variety of schemes, some with as many as 18,000 different trait names linked in some way to the concept of motivation, and concludes that "any attempt to compile still another list of basic motives risks simply adding other plausible but non-compelling classifications to those already available." There simply is no limit to the number of ways that one can divide and redivide the content of this theoretical domain.

Because utility is subjective, it is not directly observable, and not comparable. What we are left with are attempts to estimate utility functions on the basis of behaviors which reveal preferences. Assumptions about utility functions include a few basics: (1) people usually want more rather than less of a good that contributes to utility, although the value or utility of that good declines or is reduced as the amount possessed or consumed increases; (2) preferences for goods are transitive, such that if A is preferred to B, and B is preferred to C, then A is preferred to C; and (3) preferences are relatively stable, but subject to change through experience. The third basic assumption has been modified somewhat by modern economists concerned with information and the production of influence, who suggest that "the relation between satisfaction levels and utility are easily influenced by the promotional action of other economic agents."[19]

If we think of utility in terms of satisfaction—some subjective state of being that is produced or maintained by the consumption of goods or activities (like rest and contemplation)—the relationship between consumption and utility is clear. However, for many goods and activities, where there is no direct experience upon which to base our evaluation of their potential contribution to utility or satisfaction, we base that evaluation on whatever information we have available to us. Our decision to invest in information gathering is dependent upon a number of subjective estimations of value: how much we would risk by acting on only limited information, how much information is available to us in a form we can use, and how much it will cost. How much we invest in the search for information is determined in part by the resources we have available and the degree to which we are risk averse.

The *value of information,* like the value of different commodities, is largely subjective. Information that *you* cannot use is of little value, even though it may trade at a very high price in a market for specialists. Clearly, there is substantial economic value in a computer program that produces four-color pictures of the earth's surface, making it possible to identify potential oil fields or other mineral deposits. Because that information is transmitted to earth in the form of digital pulses, it is unintelligible to anyone without the appropriate program to transform those pulses into line and color.

The utility of information may also vary with time. Speculators will not pay for information about the price of gold last week, but would pay almost anything for reliable information about the price at the end of trading next week. Knowledge about the winner of the next race at the *Meadowlands* loses its value the instant the betting windows close. In a related consideration, we might note that the value of information varies indirectly with the number of people who possess it. If one person knows the *Meadowlands* winner, the value of that information is high; that same information is worthless if everyone knows the fix is in.

Depending upon the information one possesses, the value of additional information that does not measurably change your preference or intention is worth less than information that changes your perception of the world, or your estimation of its impact on you.

The value of information is also based upon an estimation of the reliability of the source. This reliability estimate might also be considered to be based on information—information gained from experience with the source in the past, or information provided by the source or the source's agent designed to influence those estimates. As we have discussed, credibility—a reflection of competence and trustworthiness—is at the root of our subjective estimation of the value of information from an identifiable source. Information from less credible sources is said to be "discounted," such that it takes more information from questionable sources to reach the same level of certainty produced by information from a reliable source.

The *market price of information* is much less likely to equal its subjective value to the average consumer because of the peculiar qualities of information as a commodity. Unlike other goods, information is not consumed when it is used. Two or more people can possess the same information. Indeed, information makes the best kind of gift in that you can give it away and still keep it for your own use. We may assume, however, that with all other things being equal, the market price for information from reliable sources will exceed that charged for information from unknown or questionable sources, and that information with a limited distribution will cost more than information more widely available.

Although this discussion will be concerned primarily with the value of information used to reduce uncertainty about decisions of personal and collective importance, price and utility considerations are not based solely on such utilitarian factors. Because of its value, information may be used as currency for exchange. People trade information, just as they trade other goods and services outside the boundaries of traditional markets. Gossip is a kind of informal exchange of information that follows economic rules. Ralph Rosnow[20] describes three kinds of trading patterns that characterize the use of this "small talk with social purpose": (1) *redistributive* trading of gossip is said to be guided by considerations of fairness and equity where people give what they can and take what they need; (2) rules of *exchange* are more explicitly economic in that they require that information be sold or exchanged to the highest bidder; and (3) *reciprocative* trading rules govern more equitable transactions where people give as much value as they receive.

The *demand for information* can be seen to be a function of its price and the resources available to a DM. The lower the price of information, the more it is likely to be acquired. By the same token, the more income a DM has, the more willing he is to spend it on information. However, there are different "elasticities" of demand for information goods, just as there are different elasticities for more traditional commodities. The amount of gasoline demanded by the American consumer did not drop at the same rate the prices rose, because of the rather inelastic nature of the demand for fuel. Necessities like gasoline are rather insensitive to variations in price and income. Part of that inelasticity may be attributed to a lack of realistic substitutes. Television films may be substituted for theatrical films when the price of movie tickets goes too high, or unemployment brings about a reduction of income. Television news may also be a substitute for much of the content of the daily newspaper, although it often appears that the elasticity of demand for *Doonesbury* is near zero.

The notion of substitutibility is useful in understanding how the demand for information can change independently of a change in its price or its availability. A change in the price of a substitute may result in a change in the amount of information demanded. If a DM is indifferent between television and print as a source of news, an increase in the price of the newspaper will result in an increase in the amount of television watching. Where the relationship is between information and uncertainty, or knowledge and ignorance, a change in the cost of ignorance will be reflected in a change in the demand for knowledge. Thus, information seeking generally increases when a change in the environment increases the level of uncertainty. The greater the risk of acting on the basis of limited information, the greater the incentive to substitute information for uncertainty. The *salience* or importance of an issue may be seen as an indication of the costs of ignorance: the higher the costs, the greater the demand for information.

The notion of *information subsidies* is based on a recognition that the price of information may be reduced selectively by interested parties in order to increase the consumption of preferred information. A consumer subsidy may reduce the subjective price for any commodity by lowering its market cost, or increasing the income available for the purchase of such commodities. Government policy is a patchwork of economic subsidies designed to either increase production or increase consumption. Food stamps reduce the cost of agricultural products, housing subsidies reduce the cost of rent, and a variety of tax subsidies reduce the cost of money used for special purchases, like insulation and child care. Information subsidies reduce the cost of gathering and processing information. Most information subsidies take the form of direct and indirect transfers of information. Very rarely do we find tied grants, refunds, or discounts associated with efforts to increase the use of preferred information, although we might consider "free samples" or "discount coupons" for commercial products as efforts to reduce the cost of gathering information through *experience* with the product.

Information providers follow rules quite similar to those of consumers. Where consumers seek to maximize utility, producers also seek to maximize some objective function—whether profits or power, or both. Four our purposes, we will limit our discussion of producer behavior to actors interested in the production of influence, where information is seen as an input, just as steel is an input in the production of automobiles. DMs purchase or otherwise acquire information on the basis of its expected contribution to the reduction of uncertainty about a decision. Influence producers utilize information on the basis of its expected contribution to control over the decisions of others. Both invest in information until the expected benefits just equal the cost of the information.

Information providers are sensitive to price and quality, but they are also concerned about the nature of demand for information. Too much information is wasteful, too little may be ineffective. Concern for efficiency is reflected in the choice of distribution channels and the effort to match style and quality with the tastes and preferences of the target population.

Advertisers are the best-known members of the community of information providers who do not sell their information, but provide it free, occasionally even paying others to use their informational output. The information provided by advertisers, while not necessarily false, is almost always incomplete. There is no incentive to provide more information than necessary to influence a consumer's decision, and there are clear disincentives for providing information that would lead the consumer to select a competitor's product.

Information providers concerned with the production of influence give careful consideration to the *economies of scale* associated with the use of information. With certain technologies, there may be a change in the relation of input to output at different scales of operation. We may note, for example, that one worker can produce one fully assembled and tested chair in eight hours; perhaps two workers can produce two chairs, and three workers three chairs. This would be characterized as constant returns to scale. It might be the case, however, that with five workers, it is possible to reallocate their responsibilities in such a way as to increase the efficiency of the operation—less walking back and forth for materials. These same five workers might be able to produce six chairs in eight hours, and 10 workers, similarly organized, might produce 15. This relationship is described as increasing returns to scale. We can find important parallels in the use of information to produce influence.

It might be the case that there is a certain inherent resistance to new ideas or new products, thus the rate in which changes in knowledge, attitudes, or behaviors move in the desired direction changes with the amount of information received. The ogive or S-shaped curve (Figure 2.1) may illustrate the relationship between the number of messages received, and the probability of the DM taking the preferred action. Up to a certain point, the returns to scale or negative; that is, the probability of action is less than the proportional increase in messages received. After a certain point, however, the relationship changes and the returns to scale are positive. We might consider curves A, B, and C as being either different issues, or different channels of communication.

The different rates associated with different issues may be a reflection of the amount of information the DM already has, which opposes the position taken in the various messages. Issue C might involve a basic cultural belief, where experience and ideology provide information that may be useful for a while in

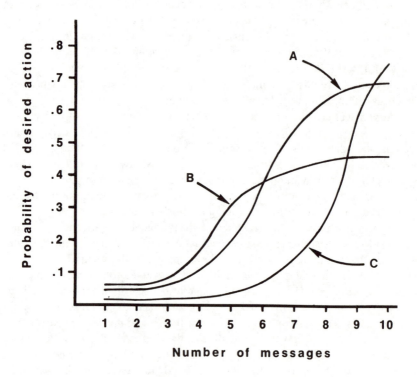

2.1 Informational Returns to Scale

resisting the influence of new information. The amount of competing information available about issues A or B is considerably less, and the transformation of belief takes place much earler.

If we think of A, B, or C as different channels of communication, we would interpret the different shapes of the curves as reflections of the accessibility of the information, or the credibility of the source. Difficult or unfamiliar material must first overcome that barrier, and repeated exposure is one way of achieving that goal. By the same token, the discount we apply to information from less than credible sources may be overcome by the legitimacy that flows from media exposure. It might also be that Channel A is *The New York Times,* and Channel C is *People Magazine;* a message would have to appear almost twice as frequently in one in order to achieve the same level of effectiveness as in the other.

The importance of these economies of scale is increased when we introduce the consideration of their cost. For information, as with many commodities, the nature of production is such that the *cost* per unit declines rapidly as the number of units increases. This is due in part to the nature of fixed and variable costs. If we consider that the most costly item in the production of a printed page is the cost of the information and the plate used for printing, then we see that after that plate is made, the additional costs are for paper and ink. If only one page is printed, the price for that page must be the same as the total cost of its production. By printing more pages, that cost is divided between more and more units. The same would apply to a video-taped commercial. It might cost as much as $500,000 to produce a 30-second message about the wonders of some new deodorant soap. The cost of showing it to one consumer would be $500,000 and change. With the technology of network distribution, the cost of delivering that information to *each* of 30 million viewers is a fraction of the total cost.

Advertisers and other rational communicators choose between channels of communication on the basis of their estimation of the marginal contribution of information in that channel to the achievement of their ultimate goal of influence. But, just as consumers must choose between commodities on the basis of their price and perceived utility, within the limits of their resources, communicators seeking to influence the behavior of others must also work within their resource constraints.

Budget constraints may be the most important determinants of the inequitable distribution of power to influence the decisions of others. DMs are constrained in their decision making by the cost of information relevant to their decisions. Those who would influence their decisions are limited by the costs of providing information through different channels, at different levels of scale. I would argue that it is no accident that those with the most limited resources are also those with messages requiring the highest level of output to influence the perceptions and intentions of others. By this I mean that persons and groups who take positions at variance with the dominant ideology would require a much larger budget to overcome the pool of existing information, and achieve any degree of conversion. These same persons would find that they would be forced to make use of less efficient technologies because their budgets would be exhausted by the purchase of only a single minute of prime-time television.

Although the economics of information are important in all aspects of human interaction, and we may characterize most communications as attempts to influence other by reducing the costs they face for preferred information, our focus in this book is at the level of collective, rather than individual, decision making. In the next chapter, we examine the nature of policy making at the federal level, focusing primarily on the incentives of key participants in the policy process, and the means at their disposal for the production of influence through the provision of information subsidies.

CHAPTER TWO FOOTNOTES

[1] Elster, John. (1979). Anamolies of rationality: some unresolved problems in the theory of rational behavior. *In* L. Levy-Garboua (Ed.), "Sociological Economics," p. 65. Beverly Hills, California: Sage Publications.

[2] Simon, Herbert A. (1965). "Administrative Behavior," 2nd ed. New York: The Free Press.

[3] Elster, John. Pages 66–68 in footnote 1, 1979.

[4] Homans, George C. (1961). "Social Behavior. Its Elementary Forms." New York: Harcourt, Brace and World.

[5] Miller, David W., and Starr, Martin K. (1967). "The Structure of Human Decisions," p. 48. Englewood Cliffs, New Jersey: Prentice-Hall.

[6] *Ibid.*, p. 114

[7] Brembeck, Winston L., and Howell, William S. (1976). "Persuasion: A Means of Social Influence," p. 256. Englewood Cliffs, New Jersey: Prentice-Hall.

[8] McLeod, Jack M., and O'Keefe, Garrett J. (1972). The socialization perspective and communication behavior. *In* F. Kline, and P. Tichenor (Eds.), "Current Perspectives in Mass Communication Research," pp. 127–128. Beverly Hills, California: Sage Publications.

[9] Wright, Peter, and Barbour, Frederick. (1976). The relevance of decision process models in structuring persuasive messages. *In* M. Ray, and S. Ward (Eds.), "Communicating with Consumers," pp. 57–69. Beverly Hills, California: Sage Publications.

[10] *Ibid.*, p. 62.

[11] Schneeweiss, Hans. (1974). Probability and utility—dual concepts in decision theory. *In* G. Menges (Ed.), "Information, Inference and Decision," pp. 115–116. Boston, Massachusetts: D. Reidel Publishing.

[12] Downs, Anthony. (1957). "An Economic Theory of Democracy," p. 10. New York: Harper and Row.

[13] *Ibid.*, p. 80.

[14] *Ibid.*, p. 83.

[15] *Ibid.*, p. 213.

[16] Bartlett, Randall. (1973). "Economic Foundations of Political Power." New York: The Free Press.

[17] Downs, Anthony. Page 230 in footnote 12, 1957.

[18] McGuire, William J. (1974). Psychological motives and communication gratification. *In* J. Blumler, and E. Katz (Eds.), "The Uses of Mass Communications," pp. 170–173. Beverly Hills, California: Sage Publications.

[19] Lesourne, Jacques. (1979). Economic dynamics and individual behavior. *In* L. Levy-Garboua (Ed.), "Sociological Economics," p. 36. Beverly Hills, California: Sage Publications.

[20] Rosnow, Ralph L. (1977). Gossip and marketplace psychology. *Journal of Communication, 27* (No. 1) (Winter), pp. 158–163.

3

Collective Decision Making

As has been noted by numerous contemporary observers of the U.S. political economy, the distinction between public and private policy is fast losing its meaning. There is, as Mark Nadel suggests: (1) extensive cooperation between public and private institutions, with the defense industry as the foremost example; (2) the delegation by government of many policy functions to the corporate sector; and (3) the dominance of public activity by private elites.[1] While many students of public policy have limited their investigations to the formal products of legislative, judicial, and administrative action, Nadel argues quite persuasively that public policy of no less importance is made each day by the corporate sector. Corporate public policy is characterized as action that is binding on a public, in that it produces consequences without reasonable alternatives. The extent to which corporate DMs are aware of the negative consequences of their action, and thereafter decide what levels of injury may be reasonably imposed on the public, is the extent to which they make public policy. Nadel concludes:

> It is an empty exercise in formality to say that the corporate decisions about automobile safety were not public policy while the government's decisions were public policy. In both cases, the decisions had binding consequences for most citizens.[2]

For Nadel, the only differences between corporate and government-determined public policies is the extent to which there is some degree of public accountability for the policies of government. This accountability, largely undefined, is limited to that exercised by the public, acting as individuals, participating in elections and referenda; or as conceived as a collectivity, whose intention to act is reflected in some measure of public opinion. To the extent that corporate DMs are sensitive to public opinion—and the amount of corporate image advertising we see would suggest that they are to some degree—then they may be seen to be similarly accountable for their actions. By some stretch of the analogy, we might also liken the "vote" of the consumer in the marketplace to the vote of the citizen at the polling place. The decision to boycott nonunion grapes, or the products of the Nestlé company are actions taken in response to corporate public policy. Votes at the polls and votes in the market may at times be intended to punish, and at other times to communicate displeasure. But nearly always, both classes of votes are based on shamefully incomplete or biased information.

Where the real differences between government and corporate policies emerge is in their public nature. While government may make policy by inaction, most of its policy making takes place in full public view. While I do not mean to imply that deals are not made in back rooms, and often behind closed doors with the lights out, public access to the deliberative process in government is so much greater than access to the corporate board rooms that more precise comparisons need not be drawn.

It is this accessibility that makes the study of government policy so popular with social scientists. And, while it is true that research undertaken because of the availability of data may be compared to the drunk searching for his keys under the lamppost because the light is better, it is expected that public actions are not unrelated to those taken in private. With the proper analytical frame, we should be able to draw some inferences about the nature of corporate processes as well. With that end in mind, this chapter will focus on policy making at the federal government level, identifying the key participants in the process, their incentives, and their use of information subsidies to influence the ultimate outcome—the distribution of economic values in society.

PUBLIC POLICY

Government policy may be determined at a variety of different levels, each theoretically independent of the other. All students of U.S. government learn of the ultimate wisdom of the founding fathers in drafting a Constitution that would guarantee the independence of the executive, legislative, and judicial functions of government. At the executive level, the president and his advisors are usually described as taking the initiative in the *policy formation* phase of the process. Here we find the chief executive exercising primary responsibility for identifying the major problems facing the nation, and developing the broad outlines of a response in a manner consistent with the ideological stance of his party.

The president is heavily dependent on advisors and consultants to reduce the complexity of domestic and international issues into a series of recommendations that can be passed on to the legislative branch for implementation. While the president is ultimately responsible for the policies of each administration, there is great variety in the ability of U.S. presidents to comprehend let alone develop policy recommendations in all the areas touched by the modern government. It is for this reason that ideological considerations are so important in the selection of presidential advisors and staff. Ideological consistency provides the chief executive with the confidence that the recommendations made by his Council of Economic Advisors are those he would have arrived at if he only had the time and the training to deal with the complexities of fiscal management.

At the legislative level, the Senate and the House, working independently at first, and then later forging a common policy instrument, have responsibility primarily at the *policy adoption* phase of the process. Policy making in Congress is a fairly complicated undertaking with thousands of occasions for influence. Unlike the executive branch, there is no final authority. In the view of one observer, "congressional policies are not 'announced' but are 'made' by shifting coalitions that vary from issue to issue."[3] While much of what we know about legislative policy making tends to focus on the decisions of individual representatives on an issue-by-issue basis,[4] we know very little about how legislative policy changes over time.[5]

Because of the responsibility that rests with the Congress for the allocation and appropriation of funds necessary for the *implementation* of policies, Congress may be seen to have a role at that level of the process as well. Administrative agencies, and regulatory commissions, structurally identified with the executive branch, find their responsibilities and powers constrained by legislative mandate.

Administrative agencies are involved in the policy process through their detailed specification of guidelines and procedures for the distribution of federal revenue, and through the procurement of goods and services by the government. Policy making at the bureaucratic level is not as well studied as that at the legislative level, but it is no less important in terms of the allocation of resources. The regulatory commissions engage in a curious brand of policy making, in that most combine administrative, legislative, and judicial functions within a single bureaucratic agency. The Federal Communications Commission (FCC) engages in rule making that results in a series of regulations with the rule of law. Entities whose activities fall under the jurisdiction of the Commission may be fined for activities in conflict with those regulations. Questions of fact and interpretation are decided by administrative law judges within the context of hearings, not unlike those before state and federal courts.

Just as the administrative agencies play a role in *interpreting* the laws passed by the Congress, the judiciary has the responsibility for ensuring that not only is the application of the law fairly and consistently applied, but also that its application does not threaten or deny any rights guaranteed by the Constitution or by statutory law. As little as we know about policy making in regulatory and administrative bureaucracies, we know even less about the development of judicial policy. But clearly, there are judicial standards that develop case by case in the system of common law. The Supreme Court can be said to develop policy in several key areas, often taking a position of leadership in opposition to the will of Congress.[6] Robert McClosky suggests that the greatest value in the U.S. Supreme Court is that it tends to take the long-term view and develops a policy perspective for an era, rather than responding to whatever issue is most hotly debated at the time:

> The Court's greatest successes have been achieved when it has operated near the margins rather than in the center of political controversy, when it has nudged and gently tugged the nation, instead of trying to rule it.[7]

In this chapter, we will be concerned primarily with policy making in the executive and legislative branches at the formation, adoption, and implementation stages of the process. The policy process will be revealed through the actions of its key participants.

Although the pluralist models of political reality dominate current thinking,[8] Nicholas Henry suggests that the economics of information make it impossible for a truly pluralistic system to work.[9] For interest-group politics to produce policies truly in the public interest, Henry suggests that three requirements must first be met: (1) that all groups or individuals that might be affected by a particular policy are aware that such an effect is likely; (2) that they all understand how their welfare would be affected by each of the options that might be considered; and (3) that even if some groups are not immediately aware of their self-interest in a particular policy, they find out about it in time to prepare themselves to act on their own behalf. The fact that a non-trivial part of public policy is determined in secret, and that much of what is public is either too costly, or is largely unintelligible to the vast majority of the electorate, is quite enough to falsify the pluralist assumptions.

Some of the difficulty in the development of pluralist or interest-group models of policy development rests in the seeming instability of these groups across issues, and across relatively short periods of time. While race, class, and sexual groups are fairly stable in U.S. society, and individuals' positions on broad issues should be predictable from their membership in those groups, such is clearly not the case. Witness the variety of positions taken by black folk on questions of integration, cultural nationalism, and black capitalism; or the different positions taken by women on ERA, abortion, and the draft. J. David Greenstone suggests that we must place interest group membership in the context of "political reality," and separate what we see as the groups' objective interests from what may be the subjective interpretations of those interests.[10] It is because those subjective interpretations of personal and collective interest are sensitive to the influence of information subsidies that we find group actions may be led to depart from those actions that better-*informed* interest would demand.

As an alternative to the impossible task of specifying a complete set of interest groups with a role in the policy process, Randall Bartlett[11] suggests that we can understand the policy process by focusing our attention on only four principal groups: politicians, bureaucrats, producers, and consumers.

POLICY ACTORS AND THEIR INCENTIVES

Within each of the four groups of PAs, there are differences in power and perspective that militate against full cooperation in pursuit of collective group interests. That is, there are class distinctions and class struggles within these groups, and class interests that run across group boundaries will always come to dominate the policy process. While the Assistant Secretary of Commerce is a bureaucrat, and the vice president for development at Exxon is a producer, both are either members or allies of the ruling class, and are therefore more likely than not to pursue policies that serve those interests. In this section, I identify the major actors within each policy group, focusing primarily on their incentives or motivations, and note some of the differences between them in terms of their allies and foes.

Politicians, like the rest of us, are utility maximizers. The benefits derived from political activity cannot be limited to present or potential economic gains, although former presidents have done "quite well, thank you." There is likely to be some kind of personal satisfaction or ego gratification that accompanies the exercise of and the association with *power*.

However the utility of politicians is defined, that utility is contingent upon their election to office. All other considerations are secondary. Because election is a dichotomous variable—you're either elected or you're not—it would not be the best choice for a model that argues that policy actors seek to *maximize* values. It might be suggested then, that a politican is a *vote* maximizer. The more votes one is able to generate, the greater the probability of election.

While it is possible to conceive of a politician who is not a vote maximizer, choosing instead to generate only enough votes to ensure reelection with some comfortable margin—to "satisfice"—this politician would be an exception. And, to the extent that there are secondary benefits associated with demonstrated "vote-getting ability," then maximization is still the best choice for the rational politician. Indeed, vote maximization would be rational for the politician who knows that she has *no* chance of being elected in a particular election, but knows as well that a good showing will demonstrate her worth to the party and other financial backers, and that this support may be available for the next election campaign.

Economic logic would argue then, that the rational politician would invest in a variety of activities, including communication, as long as their contribution to the production of votes is not exceeded by their costs. The rational politician chooses between activities and strategies on the basis of a subjective estimation of their relative efficiency in producing votes.

What must be kept in mind, however, is that there are many intermediate inputs in the production of votes. A politician may invest in activities that will result in an assignment to a particular committee. This committee may be one with high visibility. Visibility is an intermediate input that is highly valued in the production of votes. Indeed, much of the politician's investment in information subsidies is for the production of visibility—keeping his name and face in the view of his constituents. Visibility and other intermediate inputs, such as votes on policy issues favored by financial supporters, are combined in such a way as to maximize the votes received in the future.

The chain of intermediate inputs may become quite long and complex, involving votes on a number of seemingly unrelated legislative issues. A politician may vote on a bill independently of her conclusions about the bill's merit. Indeed, she may know very little about the bill, not having read even the committee report. Her vote will be cast at the request of a colleague in exchange for a vote on yet another bill—one that she supports because of its importance to her constituents.

Such vote trading is common, and is more likely to occur when the bills are non-controversial, have received little press coverage, and are not opposed by any significant constituent group.[12]

The president, as a politican, is a vote maximizer. Because he is dependent upon the votes of a national constituency, his chain of intermediate inputs may be the most complicated of all. The links between president and party are such that votes gained by other members of the party must be maximized in order to retain the strength and cohesiveness of the machinery needed for his own reelection. Thus, the president has an incentive to take actions which improve the image of other party members and supporters in the Congress with their constituents. Such actions would include instructions to executive agencies to distribute public works projects to the districts of House members in need of a boost.

While presidential efforts to facilitate the passage of a particular bit of legislation may be offered with genuine concern for the general public interest, that concern must ultimately be linked to vote maximization. Presidential policy, and its success in terms of stated goals, either in the party platform, or in presidential addresses, is the basis upon which the fate of many in Congress is decided in an off-year election.

Presidential advisors in the Cabinet or in the White House are included in the politician group, even though they are not elected directly. Vote maximization is still their goal since their fortunes rise and fall with the fortunes of their administration and party. If their activities are not seen as contributing to that ultimate success, they may be replaced between elections. Like politicians, Cabinet-level advisors may base decisions on their assessment of the demands of their constituents, but their constituency may differ from those of lower-level bureaucrats in the departments they administer.

Nathan Glazer suggests that Joseph Califano was unique in that he didn't seek his cabinet position as a stepping stone to elective office, but wanted the position for itself. Whether the visibility Califano gained from his service to the Johnson and Carter administrations will eventually be translated into votes, as it is presently being translated into legal fees, has yet to be determined. But his "insider's view" of the Cabinet provides numerous examples of conflict between personal preferences and political necessities, where politics won each time.[13]

Members of the Senate and the House differ in the degree to which electoral concerns are primary. Because senators are elected every six years, much of their strategy and planning may be directed toward the production of intermediate inputs that may either be stored up for later use, or consumed in the production of larger, more important, but still, intermediate goals.

Members of Congress take a variety of actions to ensure their reelection. They have an incentive to pass legislation that is favored by their constituents within their electoral district. The fact that they may personally agree with their constituents on many of the issues on which they vote should not be taken as evidence of constituent control. John Kingdon suggests that part of the reason may be that the electoral process tends to produce politicians that reflect (resonate with) the interests of the active electorate.[14] These politicians may seek assignments to committees whose activities most directly affect their constituents. Thus, their votes, and their other efforts to influence legislation within these committees and on the floor may be seen as motivated by a desire to produce constituent satisfaction, and through that, votes in the next election.

However, because the senatorial district is larger and more heterogeneous than the congressional district, the senator is required to be more of a generalist than her colleague in the House, in order to engage in activities of interest to such a broad constituency. Other committee assignments may be sought for their inherent power to produce intermediate inputs. Committees that are key to the overall legislative process, and therefore are more powerful, are important bases from which to build coalitions, or to negotiate agreement and compromise.

Bureaucrats have a different set of motivations guiding their policy actions. Although there is no direct link between the size of the budget and the size of a bureaucrat's personal income, budget maximization must be seen as the primary motivation of bureaucratic behavior. Bartlett describes bureaucrats as "security maximizers," whose goal is the increased security that can come only from the maintenance of the bureau as a legitimate area of government social policy, meeting a demonstrable public need, and managed in an efficient and altogether professional manner. The well-being of the individual career bureaucrat is linked to their success in contributing to the overall goal of bureaucratic expansion.

Distinctions might be made between executive departments, administrative bureaus, and regulatory agencies. Some bureaus have responsibility for the direct delivery of services, others provide the fiscal resources and guidelines for the delivery of services by others. Because employment in regulatory agencies provides important experiences and contacts, it may translate into higher salaries in the private sector after the bureaucrats retire, or move earlier through the "revolving door" that exists between regulatory agencies and the firms they regulate. For others, employment in the bureaucracy comes as the result of a political appointment—a reward for service delivered. Such a position provides the appointee with the opportunity to direct expenditures in such a way so as to ensure that political debts are repaid, and new friends are acquired for the future. A few others, committed to staying with the government until time for a comfortable retirement, have to develop a kind of ideological flexibility, and a reputation of irreplaceability in order to survive at fairly high levels of a highly politicized agency like the Office of Management and Budget.[15]

Like politicians, bureaucrats are attuned to the interests of their constituents. However, because of the complexities of the budgetary process, they often need to curry favor with sponsors in both the executive and legislative branches. Politicians in the executive branch may be more responsive to one constituent group, while the heads of key budget committees may be responsive to another group. The bureau chief must find a way to describe their current mission and past performance as meeting the needs of both groups.

That is, because the bureaucratic supply of goods and services is important to both clients and providers, and because politicians may be more sensitive to the interests of one rather than the other, representatives of bureaus have to convince these politicians that the expansion of the bureau's budget is the best way to serve those constituent interests.

Because there are important differences in the relative importance of client and provider groups in the political equation, bureaucrats in different agencies and departments may differ in their sensitivity to these interests. For the most part, however, providers of input factors are more important than consumers of government services. That is, while the general public might be seen as the ultimate beneficiary of government services, the bureaucracy is more responsive to a network of powerful, but geographically dispersed elites. Bureaucrats in the Department of Health and Human Services and the Department of Education are more responsive to the interests of big-city mayors, university presidents, hospital administrators, and professional association executives than they are to students, parents, patients, or clients not represented by organized groups.

This should not be taken to suggest that bureaucrats operate without regard for the demand for their services, or that the rational bureaucrat would not invest in efforts to increase that demand. Not only does the bureaucrat have an incentive to increase the genuine demand for his services, it is in his interest to make sure that the politicians are informed of that growth in demand. Where demand does not grow independently of government action, it is in the interest of bureaucrats to stimulate that growth in very much the same way that advertisers stimulate demand for goods and services sold in the marketplace. Research and development, demonstration and dissemination activities financed out of an agency's budget are, for the most part, investments in future demand.

The *producers* of goods and services are best described as profit maximizers. Their interest in government policy is derived from their recognition that their ability to grow and prosper in the economy is dependent upon government policy. They have an incentive to generate policies that increase demand, while reducing the costs of supply. Where they produce goods and services that are consumed by the government directly, or financed through restricted grants and transfers, they have an incentive to support the expansion of government activity.

—Despite protestations to the contrary, government regulations have most often been instituted at the behest of producers, rather than demanded by consumers, or enacted spontaneously by forward-looking bureaucrats, acting out of some independent commitment to the public interest.

—Tax policies that provide incentives for investment in plant and equipment, or reduce the costs of favored commodities, are defended as being necessary for the health of the economy. Without the tax deductions for interest expenses, the construction and housing industry would disappear overnight.

—Government-financed research and development projects often provide the facilities, equipment, and expertise that give these same firms a competitive advantage in doing business with government.

—Professionals willingly involve the state in the provision of licenses as government-imposed barriers to entry, which do more to inflate the cost of professional services than they do to ensure the quality of service delivered.

—Defense expenditures are more important for the preservation of foreign markets and the protection of overseas investments than for the protection of U. S. citizens.

—Even income transfers, criticized for their redistributive goals, provide a stable level of demand for goods and services that would disappear in the absence of government and would subject capitalist enterprise to a series of underconsumption crises of disastrous proportions.

Producer self-interest is not limited to the single firm or corporation. There is a recognition of a common interest among firms in the same industry where regulations, taxes, price supports, or tariffs may mean the difference between stagnation and growth in industry profits. This common interest is represented in the specialized trade associations. The American Petroleum Refiners Association, The American Gas Association, and other members of the "Oil Lobby" find their collective interests represented by an umbrella organization—the American Petroleum Institute. The connection between their common interest and the activities of government is reflected in the location of hundreds of association offices in the greater Washington area.

Fairfax Country, Virginia, in a full-page ad in *The Wall Street Journal* dominated by a picture of the Capitol Building, underscored this view:

ANY COMPANY INFLUENCED BY GOVERNMENT HAS TO BE IN A PO-
SITION TO INFLUENCE BACK . . . Fairfax County is across the Potomac River from Washington, D. C., and offers ready access to the legislative and regulatory bodies of government. And from here you can establish personal contact with key people on Capitol Hill, contacts that are next to impossible to maintain over long distances.[16]

Common interest is also recognized to exist by virtue of corporate size. The National Association of Manufacturers and the Business Roundtable have come to be concerned primarily with the interests of big business and multinational enterprise. The Business Roundtable differs from most business associations in that its membership is made up of the chief executive officers of the most important Fortune 500 firms. Small business interests are represented by the National Federation of Independent Businesses and the National Small Business Association.

Although it is somewhat more difficult for them to come to agreement on public policies that occasionally pit one business sector against the other, the U.S. Chamber of Commerce continues to serve as the collective voice of U.S. business, large and small. With its Washington office and staff of 400, the Chamber is well-equipped to pursue the policy interests defined by its board and standing committees.[17]

Professionals in the service sector are organized into protective associations so as to ensure that government policy provides them with opportunities for unrestricted growth. The health care industry is dominated by the American Medical Association as representative of the interests of numerous subspecializations. Research scientists in the universities and independent research centers are also dependent upon the expansion of government programs that support basic and applied research. Their collective interests are represented in Washington by well-financed associations like the Federation of American Societies for Experimental Biology with over 20,000 members. Other interest groups in the area of science and technology include the American Association for the Advancement of Science and the American Chemical Society. Leadership in American science is embodied in the National Academy of Sciences-National

Research Council-National Academy of Engineering nexus, which serves in advisory capacity on specific questions of science policy and practice.

Organized labor is included in the producer group because their interests have become increasingly aligned with those of business and the professions, and in conflict with the interests of the citizen/consumer. Mine workers, auto workers, machinists, and aerospace workers all have a direct interest in federal policy that parallels that of corporate managers. Those interests diverge primarily in the formulation of labor policy—minimum wages, employment security, safety standards, and labor relations. Like the corporations, workers' interests are represented by specialized trade and craft unions, many of which are represented in the American Federation of Labor-Congress of Industrial Organizations (AFL-CIO).

Like the business association, the AFL-CIO has an active interest in a broad range of policy issues. With business, they share a common concern for economic growth and relief from the pressures of inflation. They have a well-developed position on health insurance, tax reform, federal housing assistance, funding for education, and the repeal of the "right-to-work" provisions of Taft Hartley. Like the Chamber of Commerce, however, they occasionally experience some difficulty in formulating a position that meets the approval of their diverse membership.

Within the AFL-CIO, "there are 103 unions ranging ideologically from teachers and government employees on the left to traditional craft-based and building trades unions on the right."[18] These differences probably resulted in the Federation's defeat in the battle over common-site picketing legislation in 1977. Only the construction and building trades unions were actively in support of the legislation, and they were not able to match the organizational strength of a cohesive business lobby.

The educators represent another division of interest within labor. The National Education Association (NEA) is the largest association of teachers, with nearly two million members,[19] and an annual budget that exceeded $48 million in 1977. The NEA does not consider itself a union, instead preferring to serve its members as a professional association. Its closest rival, with under 500,000 members, is the AFL-CIO affiliate union, the American Federation of Teachers (AFT). These two groups lined up on opposite sides of the issue in the fight to establish a separate Department of Education. While both support the expansion of federal assistance to education, the AFT's opposition to the Department of Education was motivated by a desire to avoid giving the NEA any additional power over educational policy.

U.S. agriculture, although declining in importance in terms of its share of the Gross National Product (GNP), plays a role in the formation of domestic and foreign policy that can easily be underestimated. Farmers are concerned with price supports, import quotas, trade embargoes, the price of oil, environmental legislation regarding pesticides, foreign aid policy regarding the distribution of agricultural surplus, and the regulation of cigarette advertising.

Disagreements within the industry surface from time to time because of their differences in the use of agricultural products as intermediate inputs. High price supports for grain producers, liberal export agreements, even federal support for gasohol experimentation, may work to the disadvantage of dairy, poultry, and livestock producers. As with manufacturing, there are conflicts within agriculture that revolve around differences in scale and economic power. The small farmers find their interests no longer represented by traditional associations that have become dominated by agribusiness giants. Thus, the American Farm Bureau Federation often finds its efforts to influence the Department of Agriculture opposed by the National Farmers Union.

In recent years, farmers have had to engage in a subsidy effort to "correct" the public's impression of agricultural economics. The small farmers' profits were proportionately smaller and less secure than most people imagined, and they felt the public needed to understand the relationship between rising food prices and the add-on costs imposed by transporters, food processors, and other "middlemen" in the chain linking farmer to consumer.

Congressional Quarterly analysts[20] divide foreign interests into two camps. One group, described as "client states," is heavily dependent upon U.S. economic and military assistance to maintain shaky regimes in the face of internal resistance movements, or threats from hostile neighbors. It is in their interest, then, to influence U.S. foreign policy. As we have seen in the case of South Korea, the efforts of foreign governments may involve complex networks of influence touching all levels of government.

The other camp includes nations that fit more neatly into the producer category. The links between government and industry are considerably more explicit in many nations than they are in the U.S. As a result, some governments take a more active role in promoting the well-being of their export industries. The campaign to win landing rights for the joint French-British Concorde is a recent example. In excess of $4 million dollars flowed into some of the nation's leading law offices and public relations firms to win rights for the big bird to land in 13 U.S. cities.[21]

The Japanese are the most highly active participants in the policy arena, with twice as many registered agents as West Germany. In the face of a growing protectionist mood in Congress, Japan had more than 90 groups or individuals registered as agents by 1979—up dramatically from the 15 registered in 1977.[22] These representatives and consultants not only gather information about U.S. policy and practice, but engage in well-financed information subsidy campaigns to mold public opinion in support of favorable trade policy.

Congressional Quarterly estimated the number of foreign agents conservatively at 803 by late 1979.[23] This was considered an underestimate because many of the most active representatives, like lawyers, are not required to register under existing legislation.

Simply stated, *consumers* are utility maximizers. They seek to obtain the maximum benefits possible within the limits of their resources. They seek that utility in the market and they seek it through their government. As individuals, consumers have little possibility of capturing the benefits of changes in government policy equal to their costs of bringing about those changes. For most, voting in presidential elections is the closest they come to taking action to influence government policy.

William Niskanen's model of the public's demand for government services suggests that one group—those with the highest income, and by inference, the greatest demand for government services—has an incentive to influence the middle-demand group to join with them in seeking a still higher level of bureaucratic output.

> If the intellectual community, the press and Presidential commissions that are dominated by this group are successful in increasing the demand for public services by the middle-demand group, the high-demand group will be even better off, the middle-demand group will be no better off, and the low-demand group will be even worse off.[24]

On these occasions where individual consumers recognize that they have interests in common with others outside their immediate family, policy-related actions may be taken as members of national organizations. Citizen's groups are organized to influence public policy in a variety of narrowly specialized areas. Groups have developed with a concern for the well-being of particular racial and ethnic groups, others seek the improvement of the human condition through efforts to preserve the natural environment. On the whole, membership in these organizations is limited primarily to members of the educated elite, who are also more likely to take an active role in electoral politics, and who utilize the mass media for public affairs information.

Several national public interest organizations of liberal persuasion with a broad interest in government and corporate policy emerged in the 1970s, and have grown to occupy a highly visible position in the national policy arena. The most important of these organizations, Common Cause and Ralph Nader's Public Citizen, have in the neighborhood of 200,000 dues-paying contributors. Of the two groups, the Nader organization seems most willing to pursue consumer interests through Congress and selected regulatory commissions, while Common Cause appears to be more interested in reform of the electoral process.[25]

In recent years, several political action groups have been organized, and have come to play a very important role in the mobilization of support for conservative candidates, or for the defeat of liberal politicians. While the largest group, the National Conservative Political Action Committee (NCPAC)—or "nick-pack" to its detractors, spent nearly $7.5 million between 1979 and 1980 on broadly defined ideological targets, many of the new groups are organized around single issues.[26] In the next section we will examine the role that subsidized information—introduced into the policy process by politicians, bureaucrats, producers, and consumers—plays in the formation of government policy.

THE PRODUCTION OF INFLUENCE

It would be foolish to argue that information is the prime mover, the determining force in creation of public policy. Money and power drive this system and information merely guides the way. DMs in the policy system use information to develop policies that will ensure more votes, greater security, higher profits, and the maximum utility attainable within the limits of their resources.

The relationship between economic benefit and the day-to-day decisions of politicians and bureaucrats is not always as clear as in the more celebrated cases of political corruption and bribery. Politicians and bureaucrats alike are sensitive to the varying amounts of risk associated with the exchange of economic value for political favors. However, the courts have tended to see the legislature and politicians as somehow different from bureaucrats or civil servants; and what would be illegal bribery of a building inspector would be treated as a valid expression of constituent interest in the case of an elected official.

Representatives surveyed in a Brookings Institution study of congressional ethics were quite willing to err on the side of personal gain in their definition or what was or was not a conflict of interest.[27] Representatives felt it was a common and generally acceptable practice for legislators to favor bills that would result in personal gain through their private business activities. They felt no concern at all about the impropriety of such actions if their interests and the interests of their constituents could be seen to coincide.

When asked what they thought of the practice of inserting speeches or articles into the *Congressional Record* as a favor to contributors, the legislators differentiated between constributors who were inside or outside their constituency, but failed to see that giving such favors to either group was either clearly, or probably, unethical.[28] These same legislators saw very little wrong with the variety of ways that lobbyists provide favors: entertainment, transportation, campaign contributions, etc. Respondents did not even agree that it was clearly unethical for a legislator to play poker with lobbyists known to have interests in the business of his committee—even when he wins time after time.

The extent to which the exchange of gifts for legislative or bureaucratic action dominates the policy process is not the question at hand. Instead, we are concerned with describing the way that information is used to modify, resist, or reinforce these traditional pressures on the policy process. Although we have adopted Bartlett's scheme that identifies four classes of actors in the process, only politicians and bureaucrats *actually* make decisions that could be described

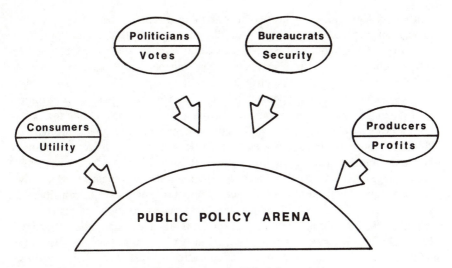

3.1 Policy Actors and Their Incentives

as government policy. Members of each of these four groups do, however, attempt to influence those decisions by subsidizing the information-gathering activities of other members of the policy process.

Policy actors (PAs) will invest in the production of influence as long as the benefits they expect to receive from government policy exceed the costs of influencing that policy. Because of the differences in their resources, and in the number of policy matters they consider to be relevant to their personal welfare, PAs will differ in the extent to which they utilize direct or indirect information subsidies.

Indirect routes may be more costly in terms of total expenditure required to induce another PA to take part in the production of influence on a particular policy issue. However, indirect channels may be preferred by certain PAs because they have other characteristics, like credibility, which may compensate for their cost, and seeming inefficiency. An example may help to clarify this point.

Representatives of the major companies in the trucking industry may want to convince members of Congress that they should not deregulate the industry. Their analysis of the legislation being considered suggests that deregulation would mean an increase in competition from independent truckers. A direct subsidy effort might involve sending a lobbyist or association representative calling on each member of the Interstate Commerce Committee or whatever subcommittee might be handling specific legislation. A more indirect method might include taking an ad in *The Washington Post,* with the expectation that all members of Congress will see the ad, and at the very least may be aware that such issues are on the congressional agenda. A more productive approach, still focused on legislators, might involve providing a reporter with a copy of an association-prepared "white paper" on the trucking industry, filled with references to public opinion polls, statistics about the number of accidents caused by independent truckers, and the estimations by "independent economists" of the total costs to society of such a change in policy.

An even more indirect approach would seek to mobilize grass-roots opinion against deregulation through a massive multi-media campaign including specially written news articles, complete with pictures of spectacular highway accidents, editorials, and a few made-for-television movies and serial episodes addressing the theme of irresponsible gypsy truckers. While some of the paid advertisements would suggest that concerned citizens write their legislators, others would merely paint a picture of impending doom. Since an outpouring of mail from constituents is recognized as more meaningful than a visit from an association lobbyist (unless of course, the lobbyist also left a check for $100,000 and the promise of more), the costs of the campaign may be justified in the long run. Thus, the trucking industry would have determined that its collective interests would be served by such expenditures, since the potential benefits to be derived from the defeat of the legislation far outweighed the costs associated with using an indirect approach. At the same time, the trucking industry association would not invest in a similar campaign to influence housing legislation. While some of their income is derived from the transportation of lumber and building supplies, they would see little chance of their capturing enough of the benefits of housing legislation to cover the costs of their information subsidy.

A citizen consumer of government services who wanted to influence the Senate's action on Social Security legislation might write to his senator. He might also take out an ad in the local paper suggesting that other members of the senator's constituency also write. Recognizing that a single senator can not pass a social security amendment, and wanting to increase the probability of success, this citizen would have to reach other senators as well. Perhaps a letter to the editor of the *Post* might be as effective as a full-page ad. While it would certainly be less costly, he could not be sure that his letter would be printed. Before he decides to spend the 20 dollars it would cost him to join the other senior citizens in a hastily called march on the capitol, he would give careful consideration to the likelihood that such a demonstration would change the minds of the new Republican majority in the Senate. Chances are he would stay home and do little more than hiss at the president when he appears on the evening news to lament the destruction of the "safety net."

The bureaucrat may also consider the utility of direct and indirect means of producing influence over legislative decisions. Direct testimony in congressional hearings is not only an opportunity, but an obligation for any bureaucrat who wishes to see her budgetary authority increase. She may also recognize the value of reaching other legislators as well, and may hold a press conference to issue a report on the great advances made in science as a result of one of her agency's research programs. Or, if she recognizes the importance of anonymity, she may release the report with less fanfare, or have it introduced through one of the beneficiaries of the program. Because it is important that members of the appropriations committees see the agency as having a mission that touches the lives of potential voters, the agency has an incentive to stimulate the grass roots to action every now and then. By informing the client groups about potential threats to their resources, bureaucrats hope that clients or client organizations will make more direct appeals to the politicians. Because the bureaucrat's budget for information subsidy efforts is subject to review, there is less freedom to pursue policy targets independently. When circumstances find the bureau chief in opposition to administrative policy, the leak and other undercover subsides will be used. The same official might make a public statement in support of administration efforts to contain waste and fraud in the administration of social welfare programs, and on the same day supply a sympathetic journalist with a confidential report estimating the impact of the administration's plan on senior citizens and the handicapped.

Aaron Wildavsky offers bureaucrats a guide to successful budgetary maneuvering. Success in the budgetary process is seen to be dependent upon three things: (1) the cultivation of an active clientele; (2) the creation of confidence in the agency and its officials; and (3) the development of skill in exploiting every opportunity to its maximum.[29] All three involve the use of information subsidies.

> Almost everyone claims that his projects are immensely popular and benefit lots of people. But how do elected officials know? They can only be made aware by hearing from constituents. The agency can do a lot to ensure that its clientele responds by informing them that contacting Congressmen is necessary and by telling them how to go about it if they do not already know. In fact, the agency may organize the clientele in the first place.[30]

Wildavsky suggests that such stage management is opposed only by those who are opposed to the mission of the agency. Those who support the agency are likely to suggest that the administrator mobilize client support.

The politician, as target of most direct and indirect subsides, is also quite frequently a source. After following six members of the House for 42 days, David Kovenock sought to determine the relative power of some 11,500 "factual and evaluative premises" that were directed at these DMs. Kovenock included messages within his relevant categories if they either: (1) alerted the DM of an occasion for a decision, such as a reminder that a vote was coming up on an important issue; (2) proposed an alternative position for the DM to consider; (3) explored the possible consequences that might follow a proposed alternative; (4) attempted to modify the DM's subjective estimation of the value of some outcome by offering an estimate of its probability; (5) attempted to modify the DM's subjective estimation of the value of some outcome by offering an evaluation of its utility; or (6) suggested, or in some cases ordered, the DM to take an action related to a policy decision.[31] Out of all the sources identified, non-governmental, or non-congressional informants accounted for only 28% of the qualifying messages. Kovenock concluded that members of Congress were the most effective sources of influence on the decisions of their colleagues, with representatives of organized interests coming in a distant second.

Because the elected official has such easy access to colleagues in Congress, direct means of producing influence are often chosen. We would include messages sent to the legislative staff as direct methods, in contrast to those methods that utilize the mass media or seek to mobilize support from the grass roots. This does not suggest that indirect means are not used at all. The mass media are very important to the maintenance of power in the Congress. While members of Congress are said to scan the *Congressional Record* each day, those who wish to ensure that their colleagues know what the key issues are on a particular piece of legislation, want to raise the importance of the legislation on the congressional agenda, or want to ensure that most of the senators have read the bill before it comes to a vote, will make every effort within their power to see that the bill and its importance is mentioned in the morning's edition of *The Washington Post*. Weaver and Wilhoit[32] report that senators who want to ensure that their activities on the floor and in committee win coverage in the media regularly issue supplementary press releases.

While indirect means are more frequently used to maintain the legislator's image at home than to mobilize support for a particular piece of legislation, Susan Miller suggests that indirect methods are also important in the agenda-setting stage of the process. When a representative's efforts were successful in attracting the attention of a reporter, those reporters

> sometimes increased the significance of the issue and made it easier for the chairman or the committee staff to get members to agree to the need for Congressional action. And coverage of hearings could increase the likelihood of reform or passage of legislation by feeding public demand for Congressional action . . . every eleven days, on the average, some person in Congress succeeded in moving a committee towards hearings by leaking material to the media.[33]

Finally, as party discipline continues to decline, and more and more legislators seek personal gain through national visibility, we see efforts to gain media coverage in order to appeal to a national constituency that might produce votes in an upcoming presidential primary.

THE FLOW OF INFORMATION AND INFLUENCE

The flow of information and the influence it produces can be seen as a continually changing pattern marked by shifts in the direction and strength of

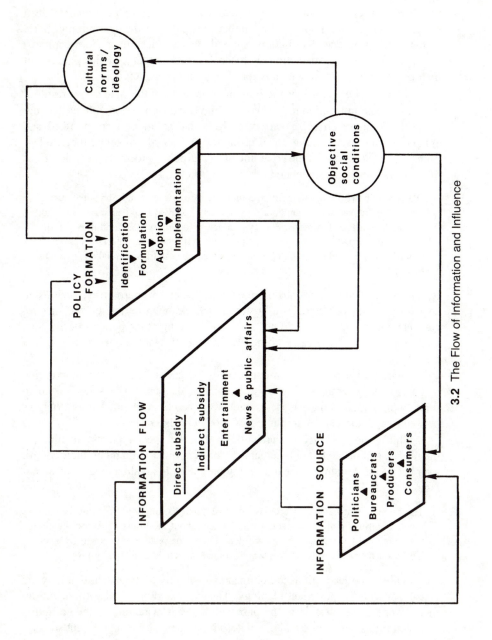

3.2 The Flow of Information and Influence

the flow. *Objective social conditions* may be seen as both cause and result of significant changes in public policy in that such policy is the determining factor in the production and distribution of goods and services in modern capitalist society, and that dissatisfaction with the level of output and the patterns of distribution gives rise to demands for change in that policy.

Sumner Rosen describes the present dominance of the state as the result of decisions taken in reaction to the shock of the Great Depression.[34] In an attempt to head off future crises, a variety of Keynsian solutions were adopted and applied to an ever-widening set of economic and social problems, thereby legitimating a central role for the government and its policy process. Rosen describes this role as somewhat anomalous:

> Directly or indirectly the state finances and maintains the arms industry, the housing stock, the transportation network—particularly highways and airways—and an increasing portion of domestic energy production; but it owns no aircraft or missile plants, no railroads, shipping, or airlines, and very little housing. This degree of subordination is without parallel in major industrial countries, capitalist as well as socialist.[35]

Rosen saw the movement into more explicitly social welfare areas, such as in education and health care, as a positive sign, although he recognized that recurring economic crises would not be avoided as long as the policies of the state were dominated by the same corporate interests that determined policy in the past.

Stuart Hall expresses a similar view of the necessity for state intervention to ensure the general welfare of the capitalist classes.[36] The state is said to function in pursuit of the long-term interests of capital while mediating struggles between capitalist classes in pursuit of short-term interests.

John Westergaard argues that while it is true that special interests manipulate the media, and through them the public agenda in order to maintain their control over economic resources, agenda setting only adds to an already present advantage:

> The point is that the dice were loaded by implicit assumptions, binding in hard practical terms on all contestants for influence, about the limits of policy: by the sheer inertia of the way "things are done," and the restraints imposed by such inertia on the policy alternatives which contestants could realistically propose.[37]

Realistic policy options are defined as such only to the extent that they are consistent with the dominant ideology. The expansion of social welfare entitlements were made possible in the past with a steady widening of the definition of which rights were basic and guaranteed to all members of an affluent society. The extension of social services to those without personal resources was justified on a moral basis, which some observers of the new conservatism suggest is being replaced by economics as the new public philosophy.

In the view of Sheldon Wolin, the replacement of moral and ethical considerations with estimations of economic efficiency serves to separate power from its traditional base in a political community. The dominance of the new economic ideology is seen even in the debate of issues:

> the change in public discourse implies that some of the things the old language was suited to express and emphasize are being lost or downgraded by a new public vocabulary, while some things which may have been devalued by the old vocabulary, or directly veiled, are being exalted.[38]

The debate now is not about what is morally right or wrong, but what is economically sound, and whether "supply side economics" will do a better job than the old Keynesian version.[39] It is important, however, not to see the adoption of an economic logic as somehow changing the fundamental hegemonic role of ideology. What Robert Zevin identifies as the Old Guard, and others would identify as the ruling class, has not veered from its constant path in 150 years.

> Often unconsciously or accidentally, they have gone about the truly conservative business of preserving the interests of those individuals and institutions that are already best served by our political economy. Their shifting doctrines make more sense if viewed as a succession of different techniques that are sequentially appropriate to achieving the same objective, like the series of tools employed by a dentist at work on a single cavity.[40]

Thus, whatever influence individual PAs may produce on the formation of public policy will be constrained by the influence of cultural norms, or ideological beliefs, which are themselves modified by changing objective realities.

Politicians, bureaucrats, producers, and consumers will each attempt to influence the identification of social problems, the formulation of policy options in response to those problems, the realization of those options in specific laws and budgetary appropriations, and the implementation of the legislative intent through a variety of bureaucratic systems. They will attempt to produce that influence through a great variety of means, but most frequently through the provision of information subsidies to other PAs by direct or indirect means. These information subsidies will define the problems and the available options, and will tend to do so in a manner consistent with the prevailing ideology. In so doing, those who seek to support the maintenance of the status quo will face lower costs than those who must swim against the tide of popular perceptions and cultural beliefs.

These same inertial forces must be overcome within the information channels used for the delivery of information subsidies. Figure 3.3 describes those factors contributing to the inclusion or exclusion of information from the public information environment.[41] Factors may be purposive, intentional, or deliberate, in that they represent conscious human action to facilitate, or restrict, the flow of specific information. Information subsidies are inclusive, in that they represent attempts to introduce information into media channels. Censorship, such as that imposed by the CIA on former employees trying to make a few bucks as authors,

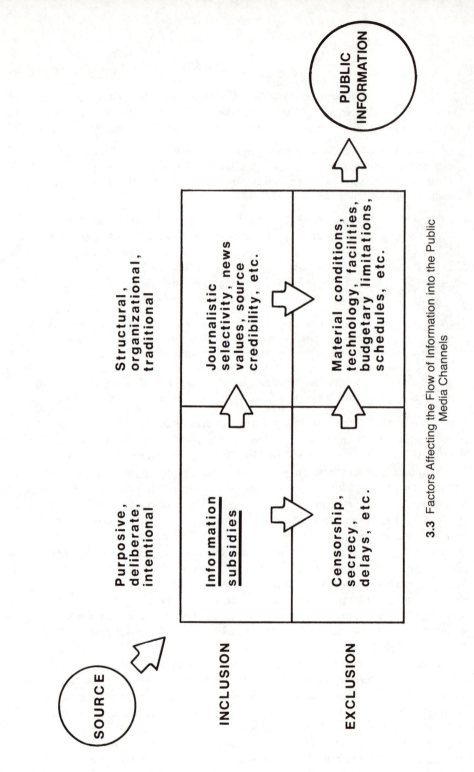

3.3 Factors Affecting the Flow of Information into the Public Media Channels

or court orders seeking to bar publication of plans for atomic weapons,[42] are examples of efforts to restrict the flow of information. These efforts may come from within media institutions, or they may be imposed from the outside by any agency with sufficient power to impose legal or economic sanctions on the media.

There are also structural, organizational, or traditional influences that meter the flow of information as a matter of day-to-day activity, rather than as a case-by-case, item-by-item attempt to construct a particular image of reality. Much of the hegemonic process is automatic, unconscious, and part of the "normal" practice of professional journalism. Journalistic practice has developed over the years in support of the expansionary needs of capitalism, and like an accomplished cyclist, the system is no longer conscious of the need to lean into a corner and accelerate coming out. Items are selected because of their news value, their aesthetic balance, their believability—their inherent or face validity. While other items or perspectives are not excluded in the same way that prior censorship keeps information out of the stream, content that is structured in such a way as to flow in sync with the media system's requirements has a greater probability of gaining entry into the public-information environment.

Just as objective conditions push and pull on the flow of information and influence in the policy process, material conditions may serve to exclude certain content from the media system. The absence of a satellite link in a foreign capital reduces the probability that news film from that nation will appear on the network news,[43] just as budgetary limitations determine that a full crew will not be assigned to cover a demonstration at the local school board, especially if that meeting is scheduled to begin at 4 P.M.

Contemporary gatekeeping or production research studies have attempted to describe the structural and intentional forces that interact to determine the attention, emphasis, evaluation, and analysis applied to issues in the policy arena. By and large these studies have failed to give serious consideration to the role of the information sources in controlling the flow of policy-relevant content. In the next chapter, we will explore the great variety of techniques utilized by PAs to influence decision making through the provision of direct and indirect information subsidies.

CHAPTER THREE FOOTNOTES

[1] Nadel, Mark. (1975). The hidden dimension of public policy: private governments and the policy making process. *Journal of Politics 37* (No. 1) (February), 2–34.

[2] *Ibid.*, p. 21.

[3] Oleszek, Walter J. (1978). "Congressional Procedures and the Policy Process," p. 9. Washington, D.C.: Congressional Quarterly Press.

[4] Kingdon, John W. (1973). "Congressmen's Voting Decisions." New York: Harper and Row.

[5] Burnstein, Paul, and Freudenburg, William. (1978). Changing public policy: the impact of public opinion, anti-war demonstrations, and war costs on senate voting on Vietnam war motions. *American Journal of Sociology 84* (No. 1), 99–121.

[6] Franklin, Marc. (1968). "The Dynamics of American Law." Mineola, New York: The Foundation Press.

[7] McClosky, Robert G. (1960). "The American Supreme Court." Chicago, Illinois: University of Chicago Press. Page 581 in footnote 6, 1968.

[8] Greenstone, J. David. (1975). Group theories. *In* F. Greenstein, and N. Polsby (Eds.), "Micropolitical Theory: Handbook of Political Science," Vol. 2, pp. 243–318. Reading, Massachusetts: Addison-Wesley.

[9] Henry, Nicholas. (1975). Bureaucracy, technology, and knowledge management. *Public Administration Review 35* (No. 6) (November/December), 572–578.

[10] Greenstone, David J. Page 307 in footnote 8, 1975.

[11] Bartlett, Randall. (1973). "Economic Foundations of Political Power." New York: The Free Press.

[12] Kingdon, John W. Footnote 4, 1973.

[13] Glazer, Nathan. (1981). Democratic difficulties. Book review of "Governing America" by Joseph Califano, Jr. *The New York Times Book Review* (June 14), 1 ff.

[14] Kingdon, John W. Footnote 4, 1973.

[15] Behr, Peter. (1981). If there's a new rule, Jim Tozzi has read it. *The Washington Post* (July 10), A21 ff.

[16] Fairfax County, Virginia. Any company influenced by government has to be in a position to influence back. Advertisement. (1981). *The Wall Street Journal* (January 29), 13.

[17] Ornstein, Norman J., and Elder, Shirley. (1978). "Interest Groups, Lobbying and Policymaking," pp. 36–37. Washington, D.C.: Congressional Quarterly Press.

[18] Moore, John (Ed.). (1979). "The Washington Lobby," 3rd ed., p. 110. Washington, D.C.: Congressional Quarterly Press.

[19] Ornstein, Norman J., and Elder, Shirley. Page 43 in footnote 17, 1978.

[20] *Ibid.*

[21] Jensen, Michael C. (1977). High lobbying and legal drive being pressed for the Concorde. *The New York Times* (May 10), 1.

[22] Farnsworth, Clyde H. (1980). Washington: the people who work for the Japanese. *The New York Times* (June 29), F3.

[23] Moore, John. Page 134, footnote 18, 1979.

[24] Niskanen, William A. (1971). "Bureaucracy and Representative Government," p. 179. Chicago, Illinois: Aldine-Atherton.

[25] Ornstein, Norman J., and Elder, Shirley. Pages 47–48 in footnote 17, 1978. Moore, John. Pages 169–176 in footnote 18, 1979.

[26] Clymer, Adam. (1981). Conservative political committee evokes both fear and admiration. *The New York Times* (May 31), 1 ff.

[27] Beard, Edmund, and Horn, Steven. (1975). "Congressional Ethics. The View from the House." Washington, D.C.: The Brookings Institution.

[28] *Ibid.,* p. 30.

[29] Wildavsky, Aaron. (1964). "The Politics of the Budgetary Process," pp. 64–65. Boston, Massachusetts: Little, Brown and Company.

[30] *Ibid.,* p. 30.

[31] Kovenock, David. (1973). Influence in the U.S. House of Representatives: a statistical analysis of communications. *American Politics Quarterly 1* (No. 4) (October), 407–464.

[32] Weaver, David H., and Wilhoit, G. Cleveland. (1980). News media coverage of U.S. senators in four congresses, 1953–1974. *Journalism Monographs* (No. 67) (April).

[33] Miller, Susan H. (1978). Reporters and congressmen: living in symbiosis. *Journalism Monographs,* (No. 53) (January), 3–4.

[34] Rosen, Sumner (Ed.). (1975). "Economic Power Failure: The Current American Crisis." New York: McGraw-Hill.

[35] *Ibid.,* p. 33.

[36] Hall, Stuart. (1977). Culture, media and the "ideological effect." *In* J. Curran, M. Gurevitch, and J. Woolacott (Eds.), "Mass Communication and Society," pp. 315–348. Beverly Hills, California: Sage Publications.

[37] Westergaard, John. (1977). "Power, class and the media." *In* J. Curran, M. Gurevitch, and J. Woolacott (Eds.), "Mass Communication and Society," p. 99. Beverly Hills, California: Sage Publications.

[38] Wolin, Sheldon. (1981). The new public philosophy. *Democracy 1* (No. 4) (October), 28.

[39] Greider, William. (1981). The education of David Stockman. *Atlantic Monthly* (December), 27–54; and Okun, Arthur M. (1975). "Equality and Efficiency. The Big Tradeoff." Washington, D.C.: The Brookings Institution.

[40] Zevin, Robert B. (1981). The new economic faith. *Atlantic Monthly* (April), 34.

[41] The relationship between inclusionary and exclusionary, purposive and structural influences was suggested by comments and sketches of Jan Ekecrantz at the Caracas conference of IAMCR, 1980.

[42] End of the H-Bomb Case. (1980). *The Progressive* (November 8), 8.

[43] Larsen, James F. (1979). International affairs coverage on U.S. network television. *Journal of Communication 29* (No. 2) (Spring), 136–147.

4

Information Subsidies

DIRECT AND INDIRECT SUBSIDIES

An information subsidy is an attempt to produce influence over the actions of others by controlling their access to and use of information relevant to those actions. This information is characterized as a subsidy because the source of that information causes it to be made available at something less than the cost a user would face in the absence of the subsidy.

As we have seen in Chapter Two, economic considerations enter into our use of information. Information is valued in terms of its expected utility in reducing uncertainty about some future action or decision. That utility estimation may be based on our perception of the credibility or reliability of the information source. Estimates of source credibility may be based in part on our knowledge of that source's personal interest in the information, such that information from interested sources is seen as less credible or less valuable than that from distinterested sources.

Because of the relationship between credibility and source interest, subsidy givers have an incentive to hide or disguise their relationship to the information they provide, in order to maximize its use by the relevant others. Scientific publications, legislative investigations, court testimony, and news reports are generally seen to be relatively objective, unbiased information channels. Subsidy givers have an incentive, therefore, to deliver information through these channels whenever the costs they face do not exceed the expected value, and less costly alternatives are not available.

While the ultimate target of an information subsidy effort may be an elected official or a government bureaucrat, a journalist may also be subsidized in order for that goal to be reached. That is, the delivery of an information subsidy through the news media may involve an effort that reduces the cost of producing news faced by a reporter, journalist, or editor. Faced with time constraints, and the need to produce stories that will win publication, journalists will attend to, and make use of, subsidized information that is of a type and form that will achieve that goal. By reducing the costs faced by journalists in satisfying organizational requirements, the subsidy giver increases the probability that the subsidized information will be used. The journalist receives a *direct* information subsidy, and the target in government receives an *indirect* subsidy when the information is read in the paper or heard on the news.

While most of the examples in this chapter involve efforts by PAs to influence policy decisions through such direct subsidies of news workers, other more direct means will also be discussed. And, while the concern for credibility is a primary consideration leading to the observed preference for news channels for the delivery of subsidized information, entertainment channels are also seen to be heavily subsidized. Because there is no tradition among writers and producers of fictional entertainment programs to identify the sources of their story ideas and themes, source credibility is rarely an issue or concern. Similarly, because self-interest or policy relevance is unexpected in entertainment fare, that aspect of credibility is rarely considered by consumers of entertainment media content.

Even though PAs may influence the use of information by others in the policy process by raising the cost of its use, as in government-imposed restrictions on access to classified material, or corporate classification of information as proprietary, our primary focus will be on subsidies, or efforts to increase the use of information by reducing its cost.

ADVERTISING

William Comanor and Thomas Wilson[1] have demonstrated that advertising messages distributed by firms in certain sectors of the economy generate considerable market power for those firms. Although their analysis is limited to advertising for consumer goods, their discussion of the economics of information bears directly upon our concerns with information and public policy.

Their analysis of the importance of advertising suggests that even though consumers may know that the source of such information has little incentive to provide objective, unbiased information about its product, consumers will accept much of that information because the cost of alternative, more objective information is perceived to exceed its expected value in making purchase decisions. In addition, because much advertising information arrives jointly with entertainment programming, consumers may even be seen to be "paid" for absorbing this biased information.

In commercial markets, advertising expenditures by some firms may serve as barriers to entry into that market by other firms without sufficient resources to mount similar promotional campaigns. The power of advertising to lift one firm's product above the field of virtually indistinguishable competitors through selective and largely spurious differentiation is a power that generally comes only at high cost. New firms, hoping to enter the market and distinguish their product from others already in the market, may be unable to do so if the products of competitors are heavily advertised. The cost of attaining brand recognition through advertising may exceed the resources of smaller firms, effectively barring them from the market.

The same conditions may obstruct a participant in the policy process that wants to offer a different perspective on an issue, or to offer an alternative policy. The cost of reaching the same level of awareness, or *salience* in agenda-setting terms, may be set artificially high by the expenditures of others in the debate.

Since the effectiveness of advertising messages may also vary with the number of such messages already received by the target audience, there may be economies of scale that further disadvantage some new entrants into the market. That is, the effectiveness of information subsidies may actually increase after some criterion level of salience has been achieved. Thus, new entrants into the market or debate would be forced to pay a higher price to achieve the same level of influence with each message produced.

Advertising messages produced by suppliers of goods and services to the government may be seen as attempts by those firms to influence government-procurement policy. With the government as consumer, ads placed by competitors in the defense industry have goals similar to the ads they design to promote the goods offered by their consumer products divisions. These ads are designed to convince government (1) that there is a need for a product of a particular type; (2) that there are differences between available products; (3) that the firm is a reliable and qualified supplier of products of that type; and (4) that the product can be delivered on time at a reasonable price.

The content of such ads may be seen to vary with changes in government and public attitudes toward the product class. In this period of growing militarism, striking in contrast with the immediate post-Vietnam period, the ads placed by defense industry firms are almost jingoistic.[2] These ads, aimed largely at procurement officers in the various branches of the armed forces, are placed in specialized publications, although several are placed in general interest newspapers and newsweeklies with a large elite readership. Those ads might be seen to serve as institutional self-promotion, helping to maintain the general image of the firm as a competitor, perhaps worthy of investment through the stock market.

However, because of the clear self-interest associated with paid advertising, corporate policy makers do not limit their information subsidies to this channel.

PUBLIC RELATIONS

It is the modern public relations firm that plays the central role in the design and implementation of information subsidy efforts by major PAs. Unlike the advertising agency, it is the responsibility and general practice of public relations (PR) specialists to generate *unpaid* publicity. It is, in fact, the PR specialist who is most often relied upon to deliver the undercover subsidy, where the source and the source's self-interest is skillfully hidden from view.

The PR specialist's resources for delivering an undercover subsidy include virtually every trick in the book; as evidenced by this Rafshoon proposal:

> favorable news stories in the thousands of smaller newspapers in the country are being published and will be reproduced for distribution to members of Congress; letters to editors replying to allegations made in antagonistic editorials are being prepared—and when published, those replies will be distributed to members of Congress; supporting journalists like Jack Anderson are considering further public reports favorable to the legislation; spokesmen for cargo preference will be making appearances in important television talk shows designed to increase public and, therefore political support.[3]

Popular textbooks in the field provide the hopeful practitioner with guidance in the use of these techniques to their client's best advantage. In discussing the value of PR approaches to the delivery of the client's perspective on complicated public issues, Harold Daubert's *Industrial Publicity* suggests the following:

> Technical and specialized papers are usually written for presentation before meetings, conferences and symposia sponsored by societies, associations and other special-interest organizations. They are sometimes written especially for publication in the official journal of an organization. Papers written for presentation are frequently published as proceedings or transactions.[4]

and, most importantly, in terms of the goal of hiding the source:

> a presented paper is another type of news opportunity. If the paper is on a subject related to a publicity objective, and if there is anything at all newsworthy about it, a press release should be prepared.[5]

And, where the issue is complex, or because the source's conclusions may be non-obvious, Daubert suggests that the press release "also serves to interpret the significance of the paper in case the editors and writers missed it."[6]

While increased sales and profits are the ultimate goals of corporate PR efforts, PR campaigns take many different forms as they are directed at varying intermediate targets. V.O. Key described the target of corporate PR as being largely ideological, aimed at influencing public opinion so as to create or maintain a climate supportive of unrestricted business activity:

> To gain public favor business associations and corporations employ in large numbers public-relations experts, those masters of the verbal magic that transmutes private advantage into the public good. While propaganda to win friends for specific legislative proposals or to make enemies for schemes opposed by business is important, of more fundamental significance is the continuing propaganda calculated to shape public attitudes favorably toward the business system as a whole or toward particular types of business.[7]

Public utilities were among the leaders of U.S. industry making use of PR to build public acceptance of their special brand of "private enterprise." But Key and others who have chronicled the growth of the profession suggest that PR did not come into its own until after World War II. And, in the postwar period, the focus of the information campaigns was not on the interests of a single company, or any short-term legislative objective, but on the transformation of public opinion toward big business in general.

> The great political triumph of large scale enterprise has been the manufacture of public opinion favorably disposed toward, or at least tolerant of giant corporations, in contrast to an earlier dominant sentiment savagely hostile to monopolies and trusts.[8]

Today we are witnessing the buildup of an ideological campaign that is sure to rival that of the postwar era. The public perception of big business is at an all-time low. In 1968, when interviewers for Yankelovich, Skelley, and White asked people whether they believed "business tries to strike a fair balance between profits and interests of the public," 70% of those surveyed agreed. By 1977, the percent in agreement had dropped to 15.[9]

Under the leadership of the Fortune 500 club members of the Business Roundtable, an effort to redirect public opinion in support of the "reindustrialization of America" was begun in all earnestness. The subsidy effort includes communications to customers, employees, and stockholders alike. The annual report, which has traditionally been used to provide information about the fiscal health of the corporation, and which is part of the effort to maintain investor confidence, has now been given a role to play in this larger campaign.

The most consistent message in these annual reports, and the one that reverberated throughout the Reagan presidential campaign, was "get the government off our backs."

Abbott Laboratories
The fundamentals of economic progress—initiative, incentive, innovation and investment—have been severely restricted over the past 20 years. The 1980 election provides encouragement that the primary objective of government will be to redirect

the course of this nation toward growth and prosperity . . . . The new administration has recognized the urgent need for a substantial reduction in the level of
government as a key ingredient to reduced inflation and economic recovery. The
elimination of unnecessary regulation would provide a good start toward this
target.[10]

Included in the Abbott annual report for 1980 was a quarterly magazine, *Commitment,* which has as its purpose "to report on Abbott's performance as a
corporate citizen and on issues affecting Abbott and the health care industry."
The Spring 1981 issue included an essay by Herbert Stein, senior fellow at the
American Enterprise Institute, entitled "Capitalism: Will we pay the price to
keep it," and a letter from Abbott's president to the ABC network, critical of
ABC's treatment of the infant formula debate. While Abbott, producer of several
infant formulations including *Similac,* was primarily concerned about its own
industry position, the letter was consistent with the larger collective campaign:

> You are well aware of the fact that the image of business, as perceived by the
> public has been eroded over the last decade. We are amazed that you, as an ethical
> businessman, condone unfounded anti-business tactics by certain parts of your
> organization—adding further fuel to the fire that all business is morally and
> ethically irresponsible.[11]

Commitment also included a plug for Abbott's program of "educational services
available to the public," including the broadly distributed film, the *Incredible
Bread Machine.* The promo describes the thrust of the message: "This film
explores government infringement in the free enterprise economic system, and
because they are dependent upon each other, on individual freedom."[12]

The Getty Oil Company, a leader among the energy firms engaging in a
broad-based subsidy effort, informed its stockholders of the need for their support
in the reindustrialization effort:

> *The 1979 Annual Report*
> The simple truth is that government regulators and their bureaucratic solutions to
> complex problems has been the cause of the nation's energy problems. The only
> sensible way to resolve these problems is by preserving the competitive market on
> which this country has thrived.
>
> You, the stockholders, can assist us. During this election year it is important that
> the free enterprise message be articulated not only to the electorate but to those
> people who propose to lead the electorate.[13]

Although the results of the 1980 election were interpreted by many to be a
victory for the "free enterprise" conservative view of government's role in the
economy, Getty Oil actually increased its subsidy effort. In the *1980 Annual
Report,* stockholders were informed about Getty's latest campaign, the "Something to Think About" series:

> Getty has launched a national effort to call attention to the costs we all bear when
> government overregulates our lives. Our corporate advocacy advertising program

this year on television and in publications is designed to remind Americans that it is only by bearing risk, by committing one's resources and by pursuing individual goals that one can hope for a brighter future.[14]

Although the "government off our backs" campaign represents a remarkable degree of cooperation between divergent corporate interests in pursuit of general goals, there are numerous examples where similar cooperative efforts were directed toward specific legislative targets.

George Schwartz describes the nine-year effort of business to defeat the creation of a consumer protection agency in the federal government. He suggests that "with relatively few exceptions, major U.S. enterprises and business associations vigorously opposed the CPA proposal."[15] The coordinated subsidy effort was directed by the Consumer Issues Working Group, an umbrella of more than 400 corporations and associations. As part of the group, the Grocery Manufacturer's Association hired the leading PR firm, Hill and Knowlton, to design their share of the effort.

The Business Roundtable hired the North American Precis Syndicate to distribute free of charge hundreds of editorials, cartoons, and feature stories for use by small papers, usually without attribution. The Roundtable also got Leon Jaworski to write a letter on their behalf to the Committee on Government Operations. Then, the U.S. Chamber of Commerce paid to have exerpts of that letter published in full-page advertisements, which conveniently "did not include that part of Jaworski's letter which stated that he was being compensated by the Business Roundtable."[16]

Although Ralph Nader's organization countered with an innovative mail-in campaign in 1977, where more than 43,000 separate nickels were mailed to legislators in opposition to the bill, it was finally defeated in February of 1978.

Other major campaigns have been more industry-specific. We may recall the effort by the American Medical Association to resist the introduction of national health insurance. V.O. Key argued that the AMA effort "exemplifies the capacity of an extremely small group—less than a quarter of a million persons—to exert a most impressive resistance to political change."[17] When President Harry Truman proposed compulsory health insurance in 1948, the AMA went to the ramparts, assessed its membership a $25 fee to build a war chest, hired a PR firm, and over the next 3½ years, "spent over $4.5 million in 'educating' the American people about the hazards of 'socialized medicine.' "[18] Key notes that the campaign was managed by the same PR firm that handled the successful Eisenhower-Nixon campaign. Their platform, not unexpectedly, included a declaration of opposition to compulsory health insurance.

The National Maritime Council hired Rafshoon Communications to provide support for its "Don't Give Up the Ships" campaign which had as its goals: (1) the establishment of the Maritime Council as "a major source of information on issues and problems confronting the U.S. flagshipping industry"; (2) dissemination of information on those issues; and (3) "to affect as widely as possible a greater awareness of the economic, technological, and security contributions of the U.S. flagshipping industry.''[19]

Similar campaigns have been organized to defeat the FDA's efforts to ban cyclamates, to retain oil depletion allowances, to defeat the windfall profits tax, or to respond to hundreds of other crises affecting specific industries or firms.

It is noted that a week after Three Mile Island (TMI) became a household word, the firm of Hill and Knowlton was retained by Metropolitan Edison, operator of TMI. Since the Nuclear Regulatory Commission had agreed to carry the ''public information'' responsibilities, the PR firm was left to improve the company's image with local communities, and to prepare them to provide coherent testimony when they were called before Congressional committees.[20]

When there are no specific crises, legislative targets, or mass ''educational'' targets to be addressed, the PR approach to information subsidies is focused on generating a sense of ''good will'' in the community about its corporate neighbors. Eric Barnouw calls this good will, an ''environment of confidence.'' What firms like ITT have done to create and maintain this environment is to invest some reasonable amount of money in good deeds, and then spend two or three times that amount telling everyone about it.

> The *Big Blue Marble* films cost $4 million to produce but were *given away* to television stations, with the result that they appeared mainly in the fringe periods. Not so the corporate commercials *about* the *Big Blue Marble* series and other intercultural good deeds. The commercials appeared in evening time at a cost of $4.2 million in 1974, and of $3.7 million in 1975.[21]

The oil companies have, for example, taken the lead in providing support for public broadcasting programs. A *TV Guide* survey of public broadcasting in 1981[22] found that 72% of the PBS prime-time schedule had been produced with funds from Exxon, Mobil, Arco, and Gulf. Mobil Oil estimated that it has spent more than $20 million on public television in the past 10 years, while Arco reported spending $15 million in the last five. The money spent on the programs is often only a fraction of the money spent promoting the program and the corporation's role in its presentation. John Wiseman reported that Gulf paid $350,000 for ''The Incredible Machine,'' an excellent program on the human body, and spent an additional $900,000 to promote it. It is the responsibility of the PR firms they hire to build the *right kind* of audience for the programs their clients underwrite . . . an audience dominated by the kind of people that vote and write to their congressional representatives.

Because Washington bureaucrats and legislators are such important targets of corporate PR campaigns, the metropolitan region surrounding the District of Columbia (D.C.) has become something of a satellite city for many of the nation's largest PR firms.[23] For a firm like Hill and Knowlton, work in the capitol is so important that its D.C. office requires a staff of 91, and an office larger than all but a few of the home offices of major firms in the industry.

Michael Gordon notes that the growth in the size of these firms' Washington offices is a fairly recent phenomenon. Five years ago, Burson-Marsteller's D.C. office had a staff of five; in 1980, that staff had grown to 25.

Although cautious about claiming too much success in influencing legislation and bureaucratic activity, representatives of these firms have claimed a few victories. Hill and Knowlton claims credit for the successful campaign against the Food and Drug Administration (FDA) and its efforts to ban cyclamates. Burson-Marsteller's successful assault on the embattled FDA was focused on its threat to ban television advertising directed at children. One firm, Fraser Associates, even claims responsibility for the successful effort to pass the Panama Canal treaty.

These Washington offices seem to have a "no-holds-barred" policy with regard to the techniques they might call into play. Although they avoid using the label PR, in favor of more management-oriented terms like "government relations," and "issue management," the tools used for delivering information subsidies on behalf of their clients are no less than classics in the art. In addition to providing training sessions for corporate executives to improve their ability to interact successfully with the press, firms like Hill and Knowlton also take direct responsibility for news management.

Employees of these firms have been known to pose as reporters in film and taped interviews, which are then sent to local markets for use on broadcast news programs. Special video tapes have been prepared, and sent to hundreds of stations along with prepared scripts in case the local broadcaster wanted to use their own reporters to ask the questions in cutaways or reversals. Burson-Marsteller reported a 50% success rate in getting stations to air its fake news event when a pharmaceutical firm wanted to spread the word about the FDA's positive evaluation of one of their products.

Editorials, considered to be products of socially conscious publishers, rather than the results of information subsidies, have also been claimed as evidence of success by D.C. firms. In 1978, Fraser Associates used the editorial route in its effort to defeat reforms in the labor laws. In many instances, papers in different cities simply printed the canned editorials verbatim. Others made use of Fraser's background materials to put together their own local versions. The North American Precis Syndicate, a firm that specializes in the distribution of such editorial copy, is said to guarantee a 10% success rate for each mailing.

The use of phony public opinion surveys completes the list of devices used by these firms to managing the flow of policy-related information. If the broad-based information campaigns are not successful in actually changing public opinion in an effort to bring it to bear on the policy process, PR firms will simply report the results of surveys by their own subsidiary.

Hill and Knowlton is described as using selected statistics from a poll by Group Associates that said that very few women were in favor of deregulation of the trucking industry. In a press release designed to have a human interest flavor, or to gain coverage in women's periodicals, Hill and Knowlton interpreted this poll in a headline claiming ''Women Fear Effects of Trucking Deregulation.'' Critics of the polling techniques used by the firm call attention to their failure to report the very high percentage of ''don't know'' responses to the trucking questions. Other critics question the ethics of Hill and Knowlton's failure to identify Group Associates as being owned by a PR firm under contract to the American Trucking Association.

ISSUE ADVERTISING

Corporate information subsidies delivered through paid advertisements can be seen as an approach to influence public opinion through more direct means than those described as PR. Such direct subsidy efforts have increased dramatically since Mobil Oil began its advocacy campaigns in 1970. S. Prakash Sethi estimated that 30 to 40% of all institutional advertising by American corporations in 1976 was devoted to discussion of controversial issues. This was a 40% increase over amounts spent in 1975.[24]

Advertisements of this sort may be directed at a number of different targets in the policy process, and as such, may take a variety of forms and be distributed through more or less specialized media buys. Robert Meadow[25] created a 10-category typography of issue, or nonproduct ads on the basis of his review of *The Wall Street Journal* and *The New York Times*. Ads placed in these two elite journals differed on a number of dimensions. The *Journal* was more likely to have what Meadow calls ''image'' ads, while the *Times* was seen as the more appropriate channel for the use of ''informative'' ads. The *Times*, because of the broader base of its elite readership, was also more likely to have more ''participation'' and ''patriotic'' ads, while the *Journal's* readers were thought to be more receptive to ''free enterprise'' copy. Thus, the choice of newspapers for the placement of political, or policy-oriented advertisements is guided by considerations of cost as well as by considerations of the characteristics of the readership.

Although a full-page, black and white ad in *The Washington Post* cost over $17,000 in 1981, the *Post*[26] was a favorite of corporate subsidy givers who wanted to reach key targets in the federal government. When the target is not limited to Washington DMs, but may include other businesses, or representatives of organized labor, ads may be placed in other newspapers and newsmagazines with broad readership among the power elite. When the issue is of importance to a particular subset of this group, the ads will be placed in trade publications.

For reasons of efficiency, as well as in recognition of the reluctance of broadcasters to trigger ''fairness'' complaints, issue ads directed to key PAs are less frequently designed for radio or television distribution. For campaigns aimed at the general public, designed to mobilize ''grass roots support,'' or merely to influence public opinion along some general ideological dimension, ads may be placed in local papers, general-interest periodicals, and wherever broadcast time can be obtained.

When Mobil began its movement along an increasingly visible path toward energy-policy leadership, it had little hope or intention of reaching the public at large. Instead, according to chairman Raleigh Warner, the campaign was aimed at:

> the movers and shakers who are often called opinion makers. These included, but were not limited to business leaders, people in important positions in government, reporters and editors in all communications media, members of the 'Establishment,' intellectuals.
>
> We felt that these people were best able to grasp complex issues, and were accustomed to dealing with ideas and with serious written material.[27]

Thus, Mobil felt that they were making a good investment by placing their messages on the editorial pages of *The New York Times*.

However, during the crisis of public confidence known as the "Arab Oil Embargo," Mobil was forced to take their appeal to the general public. They placed ads in more than 100 papers each week around the country during 1974–75. Warner reported that their "op-ed" campaign cost $1.4 million a year by 1978, but Common Cause researchers estimated Mobil's total expenditures for advocacy advertising in 1977 to exceed $4 million.[28]

Efforts to influence policy makers through paid advertisements are not limited to the oil companies, although by all accounts they are the most active. Utilities providing gas and electric service, subject to government regulation, and sharing a common interest in nuclear-energy policy, are frequent users of such ads. Most however have confined their media buys to local media, where they concentrated their energies on local legislators, utility commissioners, and local voters when public referenda were being considered. Financial, transportation, and telecommunications companies have also joined their colleagues in the Fortune 500 in an effort to mold grass roots opinion, and to stimulate them to political action.[29]

The ads produced for these corporations by advertising and PR firms reflect vast differences in corporate philosophy, and investment in creative talent. An *Advertising Age* review of the state of the art in advocacy advertising noted their overall tendency toward wordiness,[30] a trait attributable to the difficulty of discussing complex issues in the space of a full-page ad. Nevertheless, hundreds of ads followed tried and true advertising practice, and attempted to capture the essence of the issue in a single phrase:[31]

THE UNITED STATES DID NOT CONSERVE ITS WAY TO GREATNESS

Getty Refining and Marketing Company

YOU DON'T HAVE TO BE A NUCLEAR PHYSICIST TO UNDERSTAND AN ELECTRIC BILL

Allied Chemical

THE SOLUTION TO HIGH COSTS IN HEALTH CARE COULD BE SIMPLE. IF ONLY THE FACTS DIDN'T GET IN THE WAY

American Medicorp

WARNING: OPPONENTS OF NUCLEAR POWER MAY BE DANGEROUS TO YOUR FUTURE

Dresser Industries

Where some advocacy ads attempt to influence policy makers indirectly by asking voters to write their representatives, heads of congressional committees, or the President, and provide form letters or response cards to increase public compliance with their appeals, others bypass the public and offer policy makers their own interpretation of public sentiment. The National Association of Realtors used both methods in their "2% solution" campaign against government spending and high interest rates. The campaign began in 1979 with ads in papers in 25 major cities. More selective ads were placed in New York and Detroit papers in an attempt to influence the development of platform positions at the Democratic and Republican conventions. Finally, more than $130,000 was spent to place full-page ads around the country to coincide with the Presidential Inauguration in an effort to define what the election of Ronald Reagan, 18 new Senators and 74 new Representatives really meant:

THE AMERICAN PEOPLE DEMAND ACTION TO ATTACK INFLATION AND HIGH INTEREST RATES . . . AMERICANS WILL BE WATCHING FOR ACTIONS AND RESULTS. Americans expect new policies and new priorities. And their mandate is for action *now*. They will back tough decisions and actions that must be initiated in the days immediately ahead by the new administration and Congress. That is the message of November 4, 1980.[32]

The campaign of the National Maritime Council, acting on the behalf of its merchant marine constituents, covered a variety of media outlets in order to reach its target audiences in government and the business community. In the prospectus and strategy proposal by one of the advertising agencies contracted to handle the campaign, the importance of multi-channel subsidies was underscored:

we plan taking our story to two specific audiences—those influentials on the Washington scene who can affect legislation regarding our status and also to key business leaders who may have a voice in designating by what methods their goods are shipped.

It is extremely important that the campaign communicate with official Washington using media that is both reputable and influential among the selective audience and the Washington-based editorial staffs of the media itself . . . the three news-weeklies combined will virtually reach every member of Congress and the Executive branch. Because of the importance of these people to the magazines themselves, Congress, Cabinet members and high officials receive them on a complimentary basis. The publications provide these recipients with a convenient way of keeping informed . . . .

Face the Nation and *Issues and Answers* are recommended in the belief that these programs, even though they are low rating-wise, have great appeal among our target audiences . . . .

This is a long-range project. Attitudes change slowly, no matter how persuasive the arguments. But we see this as an exciting challenge. And we believe that this strategy—and the approaches that follow—can achieve the goals we set . . . to reach the people we want to reach and have them share our battle cry . . .

DON'T GIVE UP THE SHIPS![33]

As was the case in the efforts by the Maritime Council to muster support for specific legislation with the advice and counsel of government agencies, many of the ads by defense firms are placed at the instigation of their clients in the military service branches. Barred from producing such promotional material on their own behalf, procurement and legislative specialists in the Navy and Air Force have little hesitancy in asking their defense industry suppliers for help in selling their expansion programs in Congress and the White House through targeted advertising campaigns.[34] Thus we find ads from Lockheed calling for help to keep "The American Eagle's eyes sharp and talons strong" in magazines like *Time, Business Week,* and *Fortune,* and more specialized ads, highlighting Lockheed projects like its Viking planes, being run in magazines read primarily by Naval officers.

Although direct promotional ads of this sort are supposedly prohibited from use by government agencies, there are numerous channels for the delivery of information subsidies by government bureaucrats and elected officials.

GOVERNMENT INFORMATION AS SUBSIDIZED NEWS

Charles Steinberg describes the voluminous output of the federal government as being largely promotional, and the government's information workers as being primarily engaged in PR.[35] Such a focus on government information activity overlooks government's efforts to meet its responsibility to supply corporate America with information about markets and the resources for their continuous exploitation. Herbert Schiller notes the importance of this government information activity in his discussion of the government component of the "knowledge industry."[36] Government research, development, and dissemination activities are seen to have grown along with the state's increased responsibility for the reduction of uncertainty in domestic and international markets. Where government R&D efforts were initially limited to consideration of matters of national defense, the boundaries of government responsibility have been extended so far as to now include the use of geostationary satellites to gather information about weather and the availability of agricultural and mineral resources around the globe.

Still, the PR aspect of government information activity is worthy of special attention. Although estimates vary widely, there are at least 3,300 government workers whose principal goal is the generation of public information that produces or reinforces an impression of governmental competence and efficiency, or results in the adoption of a preferred perspective on some policy.[37] At every level of government, in every agency, there are information specialists whose responsibility it is to ensure that the nation's public media carry the desired message forward to the general public, other government officials, and key corporate leaders who have a role to play in the formulation and implemention of public policy.

The flood of information from government agencies has grown so much in recent years that a thriving cottage industry has developed in Washington to digest this material for corporations affected by regulatory policies. Described as the "fourth and a half estate," 400 newsletters report on the day-to-day actions of government agencies and the courts that affect business and industry planning and operations. While they ostensibly perform a news function, their audience is primarily interested in only one side of regulatory issues:

> Every time someone at the FCC farts, we write a story on it . . . . But if the industry gets together to kill some public interest legislation, my editors aren't too interested. I'm told to remember who I write for.[38]

Publishers of these newsletters range from the shoestring operations that fold after two or three speculative issues, to the giants in the field, like The Bureau of National Affairs, which employs a staff of 650 to publish 42 separate newsletters that generate revenues in excess of $50 million each year. Although there is some concern that the newsletters controlled directly or indirectly by the trade associations are dominated by self-interested reporting, it is not at all clear that the independent newsletters are anything more than conduits for the agencies they cover.

At the executive level, the President and the White House staff are constantly aware of the need to influence the public agenda, to define issues, to specify policy options, and to create an impression of active competence. The modern Chief Executive uses a variety of information channels and subsidy techniques to deliver messages to the general public, or to key DMs at home or in foreign capitals. Formal channels include the press release, and its pseudo-event, the presidential press conference, or the daily briefings by the presidential press secretary. The press corp is supplied with summaries of speeches by key administration officials before their scheduled delivery, background or position papers on issues under discussion at the cabinet level, and on a somewhat less frequent basis, access to high-level officials for on-the-record interviews.

More frequently, information subsidies from the executive branch are delivered to the press in the form of leaks, off-the-record interviews, or backgrounders, which provide reporters with enough information to construct a news story without identifying its source. Although the press appears to give more attention to the activities of Congress, in that the sources for a greater proportion of newspaper content are congressional rather than executive,[39] the executive branch is said to spend "more on publicity, news, views, publications, and special pleadings than is spent to operate the entirety of the Legislative and Judicial branches."[40]

The presidential press conference is a highly controlled, carefully planned event. Although there is the illusion of a fast-paced flow from question to answer, the President controls which questions will be asked, how much detail will be provided, and how far a point may be pursued. Although there are occasions, like the famous exchange between Dan Rather and Richard Nixon, where reporters fail to respect presidential control over the conference, they are so exceptional as to be newsworthy in and of themselves. Before the conference begins, the President is armed with a battery of carefully considered responses, often subjected to numerous drafts by full-time and special-assignment speechwriters.

Although the President is news whenever he acts, and is assured of instant access, on his own terms, whenever he wishes, the Washington Press Corps has only limited access to the Chief Executive. Instead, most information from the administration is delivered prepackaged through the White House Press Office. In order to ensure that presidential visibility is maintained in the hinterlands, and made more salient though the targeting of issues of regional importance, the White House Office of Media Liaison prepares a continual flow of special mailings, cooperatively arranged briefings and conferences for editors and editorial writers, and staffs an information desk, which is prepared to answer telephone queries from anywhere in the world.[41]

Much of the administration's subsidy effort is directed to the Congress, where White House and executive agency sources carry the administration's perspective throughout the halls and offices of Capitol Hill. The Carter White House is reported to have equipped its Congressional Liaison office with a computer to keep track of the votes and positions of each member of Congress on issues of importance to the administration. Carter's liaison team members were each assigned a roster of representatives, and they were equipped with beepers so they could be called into action by the White House on a moment's notice.[42]

Although considered part of the administration, the members of the Cabinet, and the cabinet-level agencies on occasion depart from the official script, and make use of a virtual army of information specialists to put forth their own perspective on issues and events. The Office of Management and Budget (OMB) in 1978 estimated that some 675 persons in 32 agencies were involved in direct efforts to influence congressional decision making. OMB estimated that expenditures for their salaries alone ranged between $12 and $15 million each year.[43]

Through their press secretaries and support staff of information officers, cabinet members and their assistant secretaries at the department level are almost in a daily competition to gain access to DMs through the public media channels. Some are more successful than others. Part of that success is due to the volume of information they release into the news stream, and part is due to the traditional news values associated with the activities of highly visible departments like State and Defense. Steinberg argues that even though the State Department is second only to the White House as a source of publishable news, news about the department emerges in somewhat more mysterious ways.[44] One of these anomalies is the apparent freedom given to the Assistant Secretary of State for Public Affairs to issue on-the-record statements. Steinberg suggests that the press officers in other departments are rarely empowered to issue statements on their own behalf.

Hess notes that diplomatic reporting differs from that on other Washington beats in that reporters were somewhat less dependent upon public-information officers, made more frequent use of career civil servants, and reported that fully 64% of the interviews used to generate stories were agreed to on the condition that the source would not be named.[45] Still, coverage of the State Department is preferred to coverage of Agriculture, and this preference on the part of Washington journalists is reflected in foreign policy stories topping the list for both newspapers and television coverage in a given week.[46]

Much of the news classified by Hess as foreign affairs had its origin in the Department of Defense (DOD). The Department is perhaps the most publicity conscious of all cabinet-level departments. Because of friction between the Pentagon and the administration over the growth of the defense budget, or competition between the various armed services for executive and legislative support for their pet projects, much of the information leaked on defense-related stories is directed at rather high-level policy targets. The public's steady diet of defense-related news during non-crisis periods is largely a by-produce of official use of public media channels to communicate with other officials through the most efficient means available.

Occasionally, as made famous in the CBS documentary, *The Selling of the Pentagon,* the DOD organizes the full reach of its resources to mount an assault upon public opinion. One such effort is described by William Rivers, who notes that in its attempt to garner public support for the ABM program, the Pentagon pulled out all the stops. Techniques used in that campaign included: (1) dependent or otherwise favorably disposed scientists were used to write articles for publication in general-interest magazines in support of the system; (2) briefings were arranged for selected supporters and influentials in Congress; (3) civilian contractors were encouraged to join in the promotional effort; and (4) press kits, containing pretaped commentaries, visual aids, and occasionally accompanied with portable displays for easy public viewing, were delivered to those areas that would be most heavily impacted by the ABM development program. At the height of the campaign, the logic of the DOD's argument running through these various channels was that "billions spent for the ABM might reduce casualties in a nuclear exchange from 100 million to 40 million."[47]

More recent examples of Pentagon information subisides may be seen in DOD's attempt to influence Justice Department policy with regard to its antitrust suit against AT&T. It was the position of the DOD that the nation's security depended on the preservation of AT&T's monopoly over domestic telecommunications. The DOD made use of AT&T-supplied statistics in making its case against the suit. It failed to reveal the source of its information, and it was later learned that AT&T used the same reports in its own defense before Justice.[48] DOD clients, like AT&T, have on occasion provided the Department with information to use in its pursuit of policy goals, and then, for reasons that are not immediately clear, provided contradictory information through other sources within the Department.

As part of its intervention in the AT&T case, the DOD introduced the findings of a poorly documented SRI study that concluded that divestiture of AT&T subsidiaries "will make it impossible to provide the essential system planning and engineering to adapt, enhance and modify the core network system for national security."[49] Two months later, the existence of another, more highly detailed SRI report that came to the opposite conclusion, was leaked to the press. In this later report, the AT&T system was shown to be highly vulnerable to attack, and would be effectively crippled by the loss of only 20 of its long-distance transfer facilities.

On occasion, State and Defense join forces in promoting a sense of crisis about the Soviet Union. These joint efforts are mounted when there is a need to focus the information subsidy on foreign as well as domestic policy makers. The U.S. International Communications Agency (USICA), the overseas information arm of the State Department, is called into play when defense and foreign policy concerns merge. In September 1981, Defense Secretary Caspar Weinberger held a press conference that was carried by USICA satellite links for rebroadcast to European capitals. The occasion of the conference was the release of a glossy, photo-filled, recently "declassified" report on "Soviet Military Power." The report, in the words of *Washington Post* reporter, Michael Getler, "paints an awesome portrait of the USSR as a military machine with an insatiable appetite for planes, tanks, submarines and missiles."[50] When questioned, Weinberger suggested that the timing of the report's release was merely "coincidential," and in no way related to the forthcoming announcements of Reagan administration plans for the MX missile or the B1 bomber.

The primary audience for the report was the leadership and population of Western European nations who had been less than receptive of Reagan's aggressive defense posture. Demonstrations in West Germany in recent months had sent a clear message of opposition to administration plans for the deployment of the neutron bomb, and in rejection of the possibilities of containing a "limited nuclear war" on European soil.

By November 1981, the role of USICA as the principal channel for the delivery of State/DOD information subsidies was made even more clear in the inauguration of "Project Truth."[51] As part of an "aggressive information campaign," federal agencies were being asked to declassify material that could be used by USICA to refute "misleading Soviet propaganda and disinformation."[52] A National Security Council memorandum describing the program reported that all USICA channels, the Voice of America (VOA), its specially commissioned films and videotapes, its speakers bureau, even the programs for international visitors and cultural exchange would be called into service in this effort. Specialized materials would include a monthly "Sovient Propaganda Alert," and a special news-feature service, "Dateline America," which would promote the best qualities of U.S. capitalism, while criticizing Marxist societies. Although there is no simple means for determining just how much of this particular subsidy effort will make its way back into domestic channels, past experience suggests that the amount may be considerable.

Steinberg's comprehensive and detailed description of the government information establishment provides examples of subsidy efforts by other cabinet-level Departments, as well as noting the promotional activities of key figures and spokespersons in the regulatory agencies, like the Federal Communications Commission (FCC) and the Securities and Exchange Commission (SEC). FCC chairman, Mark Fowler, has taken to the road on numerous occasions to put forward the administration's position on free enterprise, the First Amendment, and the deregulation of the telecommunications industry. In something of a unique, and creative twist on the usual economic relations governing information subsidies, Fowler has recommended that broadcasters and other associations wishing to have the thoughts of FCC officials expressed to their membership should pay for the privilege.[53] Whether they pay or not, participants at such conferences are treated to Fowler's appeals for their support of his initiatives in the Congress to eliminate the "Fairness Doctrine," and other policies that reflect a traditional view of broadcasters as "trustees" of a valuable public resource. Fowler's efforts on the road were not limited to expressing his views on policy matters but were an attempt to convince broadcasters that "they must carry their share of the burden in persuading Congress to adopt the proposals."[54]

There is every indication that the public information specialists, or "flacks," as they are called by less charitable observers, have gotten considerably more sophisticated in their use of public media channels to deliver an agency's message. The press release, the long-time standby of media sources, is said to be in a state of declining importance, replaced more and more by "more and more sophisticated tools—orchestrated advertising campaigns, television commercials, videotape cassettes, full-color brochures, and glossy magazines."[55] By taking policy matters to the "grass roots," agency information campaigns seek to influence all participants in the policy process. In one example, the Department of Transportation distributed 2.5 million copies of brochures promoting air bags and automatic seat belts through the nation's supermarkets. Many of these "consumer-oriented" publications have been withdrawn at the suggestion of OMB, to generate a savings of $1.2 million out of a fiscal 1982 publications budget of $302.2 million.[56]

On those occasions when government agencies decide that their own information resources are inadequate to meet the requirements of a particular campaign, there is little hesitation before calling in some professional assistance.[57] For public service announcements (PSAs)—that curious blend of public information, public education and self-promotion—many agencies let contracts with advertising agencies. Here, as in other aspects of government procurement, there is a tendency on the part of the government to favor monopolists. In the case of PSAs, the nod is frequently given to the not-for-profit Advertising Council. Described as the "godfather of public service advertising,"[58] the Ad Council dominates the allocation of "free" time on the nation's commercial broadcasting outlets.

CONGRESSIONAL INFORMATION SUBSIDIES

Susan Miller notes that Congress differs from the agencies in that there are no central information officers—no official spokesperson for Congress.[59] Instead, there are 535 officials free to issue statements on virtually anything. Blanchard's[60] classic compilation of what we know about Congress and the media suggests that the open hearing is perhaps the most important channel for congressional communications. In that volume, Douglas Cater suggests that the primary purpose of the hearing is publicity—the generation of headlines. "The most notable committee investigations are seldom in point of fact 'investigations.' They are planned deliberately to move from a preconceived idea to a preconceived conclusion . . . the hearing is the final act in the drama."[61] In Cater's view, such investigations have already arrived at a decision before witnesses are scheduled. William Small arrives at a similar conclusion that "all hearings develop a kind of legal brief intended to convince Congress and the American people of what it is the committee wants to announce."[62]

Michael Robinson and Kevin Appel's study of network coverage of Congress noted that congressional committee action was the most important source of broadcast information about Congress. When only non-campaign stories were considered, committee action was the source of 44% of the stories.[63] Part of this is due to the ease with which television reporters *can* cover hearings, and bring back the kind of images that television news items are made of.

Beyond hearings, the legislators may seek publicity and policy goals through a variety of activities which attract the attention of the press. These activities include the regular supply of press releases, reports, research summaries, and copies of items inserted into the *Congressional Record* for publication in the papers back home. Scripts, cassettes, slides, and video tapes are also prepared for use by local broadcasters. Steinberg notes that legislators, during lulls in congressional activity, make themselves available for interviews on as many stations as time will permit. National coverage tends to flow to those legislators with national visibility. And there is something of a self-reinforcing system that favors senators, because the Senate is seen as more newsworthy. However, the investigation of senatorial and congressional visibility in the press by Weaver and Wilhoit concludes that members of the House can overcome their structural disadvantages by energetic promotional activity.[64]

More often than may be generally realized, congressional staff members take the lead in leaking information to the press that either supports the position of their boss or attacks that of their opposition. Although congressional staff members are less frequently *cited* as the source for quotes or details published in the nation's press, Hess notes that staff members account for some 13% of journalist/source contacts, making them the second most important group of informants.[65] The congressional staff is also more likely to be familiar with, and able to digest, much of the technical reports and specialized documents provided by special interests, that many reporters find too boring to read through. These ''recent studies'' may be seen to play an increasingly important role in the formation of public policy.

RECENT STUDIES

S.M. Miller,[66] in heralding the arrival of the ''pseudo-technocratic society,'' warns of an impending push by big business to further consolidate its control over the U.S. economy by capturing its technocratic elite. He suggests that particular aspects of society, such as issues of economic efficiency and productivity, are likely targets for the development of this pseudo-technocracy under corporate control. Such a development is *required* by big business for five key reasons: (1) in the post-Watergate era, neither government nor business is held in high regard; (2) patriotism and morality seem incapable of supporting collective efforts by Americans; (3) the economic system seems likely to continue its decline; (4) the welfare state, at least that segment providing support for the poor, is likely to be abandoned; and (5) affirmative action for women, blacks, and other victims of discrimination will be increasingly ignored. In Miller's view, only the introduction of rational, objective, scientific opinion can make these five conditions tolerable by the majority of the population.

Thus, the pseudo-technocracy provides the image of ''experts rationally evolving decisions while the reality is big business groups and their political allies self-confidently making decisions in their own narrow interests with only limited concern for the broader population.''[67]

Social scientists are seen to be likely to go along with such a program for a number of reasons, not all of which are complimentary. First, the social scientist is part of a privileged class in society, and when pressed, is unlikely to do anything that threatens that position of privilege. Second, as Miller suggests, "social scientists are prone to the delusion that they have power or great influence."[68] Thus, while they think they are having an impact on policy consistent with what they perceive to be in the public interest, they find themselves trapped by the inherent conservatism of social science methods[69] or the very narrow definition of the problems set before them. In this way, they are subtly, but ultimately, manipulated by those they seek to advise.

Finally, social scientists may come to do the bidding of corporations because alternative sources of funding begin to dry up. Government funding for basic research in the social sciences has been hard to come by ever since the contract research system replaced the unrestricted grants from sources like the Office of Naval Research.[70] Increasingly, university-based researchers will have to turn to corporate sources for research support, and while much of that research will be related to product development, a considerable part of the work of social scientists will be directed toward the influence of public policy.

With the expected decline in the support for social sciences through government channels, we can also foresee an increased role for the independent research centers or "think tanks." Dan Morgan of *The Washington Post* described the already well-developed network of research and publication centers whose commitment to conservative ideas and policies had generated millions of dollars in research support from major corporations. Morgan identified some 74 organizations whose primary activity was research, publication, and the development of conservative policy initiatives.[71]

Organizations like Accuracy in Media, and the Media Institute concentrate their research efforts on the mass media, primarily radio and television. Their reports of impressionistic, and occasionally, well-constructed analyses of media content are introduced into the policy arena through books, newspaper columns, and radio commentaries delivered to stations "free as a public service." Accuracy in Media's commentary, "Media Monitor," is carried in *Broadcasting* each week as an advertisement, although it differs from most other ads in the trade publication in that it adopts the three-column format used for editorial copy.

The Media Institute, in addition to its publications, *Business in Media* and *The Television Business,* has published a number of content analyses for use in school media courses. *Crooks, Conmen and Clowns,*[72] a 1981 report on the treatment of businessmen in 200 prime-time episodes in the 1979–80 television season, brought empirical confirmation of the more impressionistic views of Ben Stein, whose *The View From Sunset Boulevard* described the Hollywood writers as liberals divorced from the mainstream of America. Both books were given favorable and prominent reviews in *Time* and *The Wall Street Journal.*

Television Evening News Covers Inflation: 1978–79 makes use of the Vanderbilt News Archives to classify news stories according to their origins. Here they find that government is the primary *source* of stories in the network news channel, and where nongovernment sources appear, they were usually presented as responding to government statements or actions. Because the new conservative economics requires the creation of a mistrust of government, to replace public mistrust of big business, the analysis was especially concerned with who or what was identified as the *cause* of inflation. While wages and prices were regularly identified, government monetary policy was rarely identified as the cause of inflation. They suggest that "the more one looks over the body of news stories dealing with inflation, the more one concludes that it represents a public relations triumph of sorts on the part of the White House, the Council on Wage and Price Stability, and Alfred Kahn."[73]

The Media Institute lists Herbert Schmertz, media whiz of Mobil Oil, on its Board of Trustees, and Murray L. Weidenbaum, Reagan's chief Economic Advisor, on its National Advisory Council. With an annual budget of $500,000, its activities represent little more than petty cash for contributors like the American Medical Association, Ashland Oil, Bristol-Meyers, Adolph Coors, The Dow Chemical Company, Gulf Oil, and several other prominent petroleum and pharmaceutical companies.

The most successful, in terms of both financial support and ideological impact, is the American Enterprise Institute (AEI). Peter Stone described the AEI as "probably the leading source of conservative intellectual firepower in the country today."[74] AEI serves as a home for conservative scholars both literally and figuratively. Some 45 researchers were in residence at the institute in 1981, working full time on various projects. Another 250 or so were reportedly teaching or in research positions at campuses around the country, but could be called upon from time to time to provide their expertise as consultants on the AEI projects.

The work of scholars associated with the Institute has come to hold considerable weight in the debates on Capitol Hill, within the White House and in the executive agencies. Murray Weidenbaum, one of 18 persons who left the staff to join the Reagan administration in its early days, is perhaps the most widely cited of the AEI authors. It is Weidenbaum's research into the economic impact of regulation that served as the basis for much of the deregulatory fever that began building momentum during the Carter administration. Stone suggests that "the special attraction of AEI is that it knows how to reach the right legislators and opinion-makers with studies that answer questions on issues at just the right time."[75] In contrast, it is noted by Carol Weiss and others, the general failure of social research to be utilized by DMs is due to the inability of most scientists to produce meaningful results quickly enough.[76]

The Institute is well endowed, just matching the annual budget of its liberal counterpart, the Brookings Institution. One important difference, however, is the extent of corporate support the AEI has attracted in recent years. A number of these supporters, including *Readers Digest,* have provided $1 million endowed chairs. In Stone's view:

> AEI has connected with a new consciousness and mood in the business community that emphasize the importance of funding research and writing that will help further the views of American corporations and shape public opinion accordingly.[77]

This comfortable economic base allows the Institute to publish a number of influential journals, including *Public Opinion* and *The Foreign Policy & Defense Review,* and to produce and distribute radio and television programs for broadcast by both public and commercial stations.

Other sources of research reports supportive of the conservative, pro-business view on most policy issues include the Hoover Institution at Stanford University, The Georgetown University Center for Strategic and International Studies, The National Bureau of Economic Research, and the Hudson Institute. The Heritage Foundation, which offered the Reagan administration a blueprint for reorganization in its 1,093-page report, *Mandate for Leadership: Policy Management in a Conservative Administration,* is also credited with having had a significant impact on the Department of Labor.[78]

Although we occasionally see an attempt on the part of some policy makers to influence the process through the use of nonexistent studies, such as the mythical Department of Agriculture study[79] referred to by representatives of the National Conservative Political Action Committee (NCPAC) in their effort to preserve commodity tax loopholes, most of the "recent studies" introduced into the process can be traced to some existing source of expertise. It is this dependence upon external sources of expertise that leaves elected officials and the bureaucracy so susceptible to the influence of information subsidies.

CONSULTANTS AND OTHER EXPERTS

Although the federal government has continued to increase the number of Ph.D.-qualified scientists and technicians within the executive-branch agencies,[80] the administrative bureaucracy still depends upon a reserve army of consultants in universities, independent R&D centers, and multidisciplinary consulting firms with offices within easy reach of the nation's capitol. The extent of government dependence on consultants is impossible to estimate with any degree of precision. Part of that difficulty is the great variety in the definitions used to classify information services procured outside government.

In 1976, a Senate subcommittee surveyed 178 executive-branch agencies asking them to identify all contracts for amounts exceeding $5,000, and to describe the parent firm and the nature of the services provided. The responses were considered to be "wholly inadequate." Some of what they discovered, however, has some important implications for our understanding of the role of information subsidies in the formation of public policy and administrative practice.

There were considerable difference between the agencies in their dependence on outside expertise. When expenditures for consultants' services were expressed as a percentage of the agency's total salary expenditure, the average for all respondents was 6%. Several agencies were considerably above that average:

Table 4.1
Consultant Fees Paid As a Percentage
Of Total Agency Salary, Fiscal Year 1976[81]

Agency	Expenditure	% of Total Salaries
Nuclear Regulatory Commission	$29.9 million	55.0
Federal Energy Administration	20.7 million	30.6
Energy Resource Development Administration (ERDA)	61.7 million	35.6

Agencies with greater-than-average dependence upon outside expertise are more vulnerable to the influence of subsidized information when the consultants to these government agencies are also consultants to firms in the regulated industry.

In a multi-part series on conflict of interest in government contracting, Johnathan Neumann and Ted Gup described four particularly glaring examples of "conflict of interest" involving Monsanto Research Corporation, Dow Chemical, Arthur D. Little, and the Exxon Research and Engineering Corporation.[82] Monsanto Research Corporation is a subsidiary of the Monsanto Company, a leader in the nation's chemical industry. Although technically a separate entity from its parent firm, Monsanto Research "borrowed" researchers from the parent company for the duration of the contract. The contract with the Environmental Protection Agency (EPA) was for an investigation of the amounts of pollution being emitted by chemical plants in general, and associated with the production of several compounds in particular.

Before the investigation began, the quality of the government's information was limited by an agreement that Monsanto would not be required to reveal which plants they investigated. To ensure that this information would not be disclosed, "EPA officials agreed to allow Monsanto to destroy certain original documents. The information contained in them was neither to appear in reports nor to be seen by anyone from the EPA."[83] Instead, the final report to the EPA made reference to data gathered from a "hypothetical acrylonitrile plant which was to represent the industry" in which Monsanto had just become the number one company. Of course, data presented in this form made it virtually impossible for the EPA to verify the accuracy of the representation.

Neuman and Gup note that when the report was complete, Monsanto Research sent the document to corporate headquarters for review *before* it was released to the EPA. The report concluded that acrylonitrile pollution represented no significant environmental problem. It was then published by the EPA with only perfunctory notice given of the role played by Monsanto in the development of the report. Two years after, they concluded that there was no need for emission controls or further EPA regulation; an investigation by EPA's regulatory branch reached the opposite conclusion: "that acrylonitrile is one of the biggest sources of hydrocarbons in the petrochemical industry."[84]

In the case of EPA and Arthur D. Little, the firm engaged in a subsidy effort where the report produced under contract for the EPA relied heavily on data gathered for a commercial customer. The A.D. Little study concluded that government regulation of its former client "would create a serious economic hardship that might force the firm to shut down." Although EPA officials at the time were critical of the Little study, and noted the absence of verifiable data, the report was eventually published under the EPA seal, and later introduced as evidence in the Asarco company's fight against EPA regulation. A second EPA-funded study of the copper industry produced by A.D. Little, reaching the same anti-regulatory conclusion, was introduced as evidence in the hearings on the Clean Air Act, and, in all probability, contributed to the 1977 grant by Congress of a 10-year exemption from EPA regulation to the nonferrous smelter industry.

Finally, Neumann and Gup reported on the EPA contract to the Exxon Research and Engineering Corporation for assistance in the creation of policies for off-shore oil rigs. Not unexpectedly, Exxon concluded that off-shore drilling did not represent a significant pollution hazard. Yet, the same day that Exxon had been awarded the contract, an Exxon project in Alaska began dumping polluted waste, which resulted in their being fined "the largest civil penalty assessed up until that date for a violation of the Federal Water Pollution Control Act of 1972."[85]

Examples of such obvious information subsidies abound in the pages of congressional hearings on government use of consultants. Where there is evidence that government agency heads are aware of the problems of dual loyalties on the part of their consultants, we find that these officials actually treat this duplicity as a plus. In the case of an award to Arthur Young and Company to develop energy allocation regulations, the contract review noted that the fact that Young had worked with Gulf Oil was a strength.[86] Similarly, SRI's (Stanford Research Institute) source of qualifying expertise for a synthetic fuels contract was based on their numerous contracts with Gulf and other energy companies in the development of their own synfuels programs.[87] Since Chase Manhattan Bank's Energy Information System was the primary source of statistics on the international flow of energy resources, why shouldn't Chase be allowed to nominate the consulting firm the government would hire to report those statistics to the International Energy Agency?[88] Indeed, since the Bechtel Corporation owned

40% of the coal transportation firm[89] targeted for government investigation, who would be better qualified to direct the study?

DOCUDRAMA AND OTHER FICTIONS

Most of the discussion in this chapter has focused on the attempt by PAs to produce influence through the provision of subsidized information to participants in the process. The bulk of the examples have dealt with efforts to manipulate the flow of news. News channels have been identified as productive sources of influence because of their high degree of credibility, maintained by the convenient fiction of journalistic objectivity. Fictional materials are rarely considered to have policy relevance because communication scholars have only recently begun to explore the links between social perception and social policies. Even fewer still have pursued the link between fictional content and the efforts by interested parties to influence public policy.

George Gerbner's Cultural Indicators[90] project is focused primarily upon the fictional portrayals of life that make up the bulk of prime-time television. These stories serve a symbolic or ideological function, in that they are seen to be the primary socializing agents in the modern world. The "lessons" of television have been shown to be well learned by those who spend more of their waking hours in the "world of television." Gerbner and his associates have suggested that these lessons have important social-policy implications, including the willingness of heavy users of television to accept a reduction in civil liberties in exchange for protection from crime and violence.

Althougl Cultural Indicators research is just beginning to extend its inquiry beyond the consideration of violence and the portrayal of criminality to the cultivation of "mainstream" views about science and health, there has been far less progress in documenting the process through which the dominant ideology is produced. Gerbner's original focus on content analysis as a tool for critical research[91] was expanded only briefly to include the production process. Early experience with "institutional process analysis" resulted in studies of decision making by network standards and practices executives with regard to representation of the mentally ill, and problems of mental health.[92] Following the publication of the Surgeon General's study of "Television and Social Behavior," Gerbner's attention turned less and less frequently to the analysis of power roles and the control of industrialized cultural production.

David Paletz and Robert Entman[93] suggest that entertainment production follows rules similar to those governing the production of news. Just as there are news values, there are entertainment production values. And, these values are based on shared perceptions of what will be sufficiently titillating and attractive to an audience, without exceeding the bounds of contemporary social values. They argue that television, as a cultural mechanism, does not struggle against change, but integrates new ideas and tendencies into the mainstream—by making "modifications and adjustments in the particular values and practices that at any one time comprise the accepted social order." Whatever changes take place occur incrementally to "take the oppositional bite out of social innovation."

Just as Gerbner and others suggest that the media's portrayal of social reality may support an acceptance of increased police action to defend us against threats in the "mean world," Paletz and Entman suggest that these portrayals support the acceptance of "autocratic and demagogic politicians." Because television presents only the most beautiful, talented, compassionate and understanding of persons as leading characters, viewers cannot hope to "measure up" to these ideals. As a result, a loss of self-esteem and a sense of personal efficacy and dependence on media-created authority are seen to grow.[94]

Joseph Turow has examined some of the factors influencing the range of human characteristics we see portrayed in popular television fiction.[95] Following the traditions of the gatekeeper studies of the press, Turow interviewed writers, producers, casting directors, and talent agents who are the principal determinants of the human background, or canvas, which ensures the realism of television fiction.

Two sets of guidelines, closely aligned with journalistic notions of news value, were identified—credibility and visual balance. Credibility requires that the person chosen for the part must be believable to the television audience. The person should fit within what the gatekeepers think is the public's conception of persons likely to have a given occupation, or position of authority. It does not matter that other people could or perhaps *should* be found in those positions; if the gatekeeper feels that a particular actor would draw viewer attention away from the main action because they are seen as unusual, that actor will not be recommended for the part.

The second criterion, visual balance, is a more personal, artistic notion of how well two characters appear together, how well they "fit next to each other from an aesthetic standpoint." On a few, rare occasions, these gatekeepers may stray from these guidelines and select actors who are only marginally credible, or weaken visual balance, out of a sense of social purpose, such as a desire to "help out minorities." Occasionally, as suggested by Kathryn Montgomery,[96] choices are made in response to political pressure from organized interest groups, such as that represented by gay activists, or by black artists. But by and large, Turow concludes that casting decisions are made on the basis of unverified estimations of public perceptions of normality.

The most comprehensive examination of the television production process in the U.S. is that offered by Muriel Cantor.[97] Building on the perspectives she developed in her sociological portrait of the Hollywood TV producer, Cantor seeks to provide some sense of how control is exercised over the production of prime-time television. As with most reviews of this sort, Cantor provides very few specific examples of control, and her conclusions about the nature of the process are stated in rather all-encompassing terms:

> The production and manufacture of television drama are rooted to the business interests in the United States. Consequently, the content must be produced by people who are either willing to suppress deep-seated dissident values, . . . or by people who are fundamentally in agreement with the system.[98]

Thus, Cantor, like Turow, sees the control of television content largely as an unguided, self-propelled process, where all who are involved, including the audience, have accepted the cultural and social values that the media portray. Whatever changes in content we might witness being introduced in response to pressures from the disaffected within the audience are changes at the margins of the ideological core. Such adaptive changes are never threatening to the larger system and the social relations upon which it is based.

In opposition to this pluralist view, Eric Barnouw specifies a more active role for the corporate and governmental "sponsor" for entertainment media. Whereas "objectivity" is the screen that increases the potential of information subsidies delivered through the news channel, Barnouw suggests that the label "entertainment" serves a similar function in fictional programs. The entertainment label lulls the viewer into a passive, uncritical state. "Diversion being the order of the day, we are not inclined to question or even identify unspoken premises of the game. This enables entertainment to play a leading role in shaping attitudes and ideas, including political ideas."[99] For many tasks, Barnouw's sponsors are seen to actually *prefer* entertainment for the delivery of information subsidies.

Although it is labeled as entertainment, Barnouw asks us to consider that many serial dramas, especially the action-adventure series, are given an "air of authenticity," which makes it difficult for some viewers to distinguish between fact and fiction. This authenticity is guaranteed in many such programs by the army of advisors from law enforcement and professional associations who review scripts, screen rough cuts, and suggest a variety of changes that blend the concern for authenticity with a desire to de-emphasize negative aspects of the professions.

Although not discussed by Barnouw, the current growth in long-form dramas, based on real-life experiences, can be seen to provide the maximum degree of authenticity possible within the context of entertainment television.

Too frequently to be mere coincidence, serial dramas, or the made-for-television movies we describe as docudrama, have been aired simultaneously with the discussion of related issues in the Congress. We have seen, for example, the airing of a program on the march of American Nazis in Skokie, Illinois,[100] coincidental with discussion of FCC chairman Fowler's[101] call for the elimination of fairness and equal-time requirements. The focus of the drama was not about racism, and its rise in the U.S., but on the moral and ethical issue of "Free Speech" and First Amendment rights. TV critic Tom Shales noted that these same issues were the focus of *Word of Honor,* a recent theatrical release starring

Karl Malden. The film did rather poorly in the theatres, and Shales suggests that "perhaps the addition of Nazis to the plot will entice viewers to Skokie the way a swastika on a book cover seems to guarantee a great literary success."[102]

Earlier, in March 1981, Jack Klugman, who plays a medical examiner on the television series *Quincy,* was featured as a key witness in congressional hearings on rare diseases like Tourette Syndrome. Klugman's only basis for expertise was the fact that the week prior to his appearance before the House subcommittee, Quincy had dealt with a young character afflicted with the disease . . . and, believe it or not, "testified before a 'Senate subcommittee' on the problem."[103] Of course, his appearance before Henry Waxman's committee did not take place because Klugman was an expert, but because his appearance would guarantee extensive press coverage of the hearings. What is not discussed in the newspaper accounts of the hearings is the process through which the writers and the producers of the series came to treat Tourette's and other "orphan diseases" in the first place. Very often, the suggestion for such stories come from the disease associations themselves, who seek to gain public support for their chosen malady through any activity that will increase the salience of the disease in the public consciousness.[104]

Other topical, policy-related docudramas include *Battered,* an NBC movie concerned with household violence. Karen Grassle, writer and lead actress in the film about housewives victimized by violent husbands, later testified during congressional hearings on a bill that would set up an Office of Domestic Violence in the Department of Health, Education, and Welfare. In her comments on the bill, Grassle said "I hope the legislation will pass. If I dreamed up a bill myself, it wouldn't be as good as this one."[105]

Occasionally, social relevance is merely the hook upon which more traditional audience builders are hung. One such example is *A Gun in the House,* a CBS thriller ostensibly aimed at addressing the social concerns at the basis of gun control legislation. Tom Shales suggests that gun control gets only "a cursory glance or two," while the rest of the film uses every standard theme of sexual violence in the catalog.[106] Similar criticism has been directed at the use of sex and violence to build the audience for ABC's dramatization of Alex Haley's *Roots,* and the less documentary and ever more controversial *Beulah Land.*

Less frequently than the reverse, popular fiction may emerge before the event it describes. *The China Syndrome,* in contrast with *Raid on Entebbe,* was released to the public before Three Mile Island (TMI) made its own spectacular debut. But, as Aaron Latham suggests, TMI was inevitable, and the producers of *The China Syndrome* had merely done their homework well, had studied nuclear reactors, the nuclear industry, and the regulatory establishment, and had concluded that it was just a matter of time.[107] Although the film gained financially from the TMI accident, the public may have gained in more important ways from the release of the film. Aaron reports that just before *The China Syndrome* was to open, the Nuclear Regulatory Commission (NRC) shut down five nuclear plants for failure to meet safety standards.

> It is not clear what role the movie played in the NRC's action, but the timing seems more than coincidental. Surely it occurred to the NRC that it would be better to close the plant before the premiere than after. That way it would seem less like cause and effect.[108]

Of course, these few examples do not provide evidence of regular, systematic use of entertainment programs to influence public opinion. As often as not, these programs are the result of DMs in the industry trying to capitalize on the salience or popularity of issues and events that have made their way onto the public agenda through the news media. Mitch Tuchman describes the frenzy within the Hollywood community when some news event becomes ripe for exploitation.[109] Yet, what evidence there is, suggests that direct and indirect information subsidies account for a substantial number of the themes treated in television series and movie specials.

INFORMATION SUBSIDIES

In this chapter, we have reviewed numerous examples of efforts by PAs in government and industry to influence the policy process through the provision of direct and indirect information subsidies to other participants in the process. Advertising, PR, expert advice, and even scientific research have all been used in the production of influence in matters of public policy. Although the links between popular fiction and public policy goals are not as clear as those between news reports and government action, such portrayals have been described as contributing to the overall climate of public opinion, within which the limits of public debate are set. In the next chapter, the role of fictional material takes on an even more critical role in stimulating demand for an ever-increasing array of costly medical techniques and services.

CHAPTER FOUR FOOTNOTES

[1] Comanor, William, and Wilson, Thomas A. (1974). "Advertising and Market Power." Cambridge, Massachusetts: Harvard University Press.

[2] Wilson, George. (1980). With Vietnam defused, weapon-makers ballyhoo their firepower. *The Washington Post* (November 25), A2.

[3] Rafshoon Communications. (1978). A proposed public education program and media relations campaign for the National Maritime Council. *In* U.S. Congress, House, Committee on Government Operations, Subcommittee on Commerce and Monetary Affairs. (1978). "IRS Administration of Tax Laws Related to Lobbying," Part II, p. 413, 95th Congress, 2nd Session, July. Washington, D.C.: U.S. Government Printing Office.

[4] Daubert, Harold. (1974). "Industrial Publicity," p. 145. New York: John Wiley & Sons.

[5] *Ibid.*, p. 146.

[6] *Ibid.*

[7] Key, Jr. Valdimer O. (1958). "Politics, Parties and Pressure Groups," 4th ed., p. 103. New York: Thomas Y. Crowell Company.

[8] *Ibid.*, p. 108.

[9] Paskowski, Marianne, and Donath, Bob. (1981). Telling the corporate story. *Industrial Marketing* (March), 44.

[10] Abbott Laboratories. *Annual Report,* 1980, pp. 4–5.

[11] Abbott Laboratories. (1981). *Commitment* (Spring), p. 8.

[12] *Ibid.*, back cover.

[13] Getty Oil Company. *Annual Report,* 1979, p. 3.

[14] Getty Oil Company. *Annual Report,* 1980, p. 5.

[15] Schwartz, George. (1979). The successful fight against a federal Consumer Protection Agency. *MSU Business Topics* (Summer), 51.

[16] *Ibid.*

[17] Key, Jr. Valdimer O. Page 138 in footnote 7, 1958.

[18] *Ibid.*

[19] Rafshoon Communications. Page 75 in footnote 3, 1978.

[20] Luxenberg, Stan. (1979). Image agencies thrive on crises. *The New York Times,* Sec. III (July 29), 9.

[21] Barnouw, Eric. (1978). "The Sponsor," p. 84. New York: Oxford University Press.

[22] Weisman, John. (1981). Why big oil loves public tv. *TV Guide* (June 20), 4 ff.

[23] Gordon, Michael. (1980). The image makers in Washington-PR firms have found a natural home. *National Journal* (May 31), 884–890.

[24] Sethi, S. P. (1978). Testimony in U.S. Congress, House, Committee on Government Operations, Subcommittee on Commerce and Monetary Affairs. "IRS Administration of Tax Laws Related to Lobbying," Part II, pp. 408–412, 95th Congress, 2nd Session, July. Washington, D.C.: U.S. Government Printing Office. See also Sethi, S. P. (1977). "Advocacy Advertising and Large Corporations." Lexington, Massachusetts: D.C. Heath.

[25] Meadow, Robert G. (1981). The political dimensions of nonproduct advertising. *Journal of Communication 31* (No. 3) (Summer), 69–82.

[26] Gordon, Richard. (1981). Tugging away at Uncle Sam's ear. *Industrial Marketing* (March), 74–78.

[27] Warner, Raleigh, and Silk, Leonard. (1979). "Ideals in Collision. The Relationship Between Business and the News Media," p. 15. New York: Carnegie Mellon University Press.

[28] Common Cause. (1978). The power persuaders. *In* U.S. Congress, House, Committee on Government Operations, Subcommittee on Commerce and Monetary Affairs. "IRS Administration of Tax Laws Related to Lobbying," Part II, p. 346, 95th Congress, 2nd Session, July. Washington D.C.: U.S. Government Printing Office.

[29] Garcia, Rogelio, and Laurencall, Suzanne. (1978). "An Analysis of Responses to a Questionnaire by the Commerce, Consumer and Monetary Affairs Subcommittee of the House Government Operations Committee Concerning Representational Activities of Large American Corporations and Companies." Washington, D.C.: Congressional Reference Service, Library of Congress, May.

[30] Edelson, Alfred. (1981). Advocacy advertising. *Advertising Age* (March 30), 47.

[31] Copies of newspaper advertisements included as appendices in footnote 29, 1978.

[32] Gordon, Richard. Page 74 in footnote 26, 1978.

[33] Vasant Dugdale & Company. (1978). *In* U.S. Congress, House, Committee on Government Operations, Subcommittee on Commerce and Monetary Affairs. "IRS Administration of Tax Laws Related to Lobbying," Part II, pp. 38–41, 95th Congress, 2nd Session, July. Washington, D.C.: U.S. Government Printing Office.

[34] Wilson, George. (1980). With Vietnam defused, weapon-makers ballyhoo their firepower. *The Washington Post* (November 25), A2.

[35] Steinberg, Charles. (1980). "The Information Establishment," pp. 38–39. New York: Hastings House.

[36] Schiller, Herbert I. (1973). "The Mind Managers," pp. 32–61. Boston, Massachusetts: Beacon Press.

[37] Steinberg, Charles. Page 39 in footnote 35, 1980.

[38] Selinger, Susan. (1977). Newsletters: the fourth and a half estate. *Washington Journalism Review* (October), 28.

[39] Hess, Stephen. (1981). "The Washington Reporters." Washington, D.C.: The Brookings Institution.

[40] Rivers, William L. (1970). "The Adversaries. Politics and the Press," pp. 49–50. Boston, Massachusetts: Beacon Press.

[41] Steinberg, Charles. Pages 96–97 in footnote 35, 1980.

[42] Hess, Stephen. Page 56 in footnote 39, 1981.

[43] Hagar, Barry. (1978). Executive lobbying. *Congressional Quarterly Weekly Report* (March 4), 579–586.

[44] Steinberg, Charles. Page 148 in footnote 35, 1980.

[45] Hess, Stephen. Page 56 in footnote 39, 1981.

[46] *Ibid.* p. 109.

[47] Rivers, William L. Page 42 in footnote 40, 1970.

[48] Brown, Merrill. (1981). DOD faulted for use of AT&T data. *The Washington Post* (August 21), D8 ff.

[49] Brown, Merrill. (1981). U.S. phone lines called vulnerable to attack. *The Washington Post* (May 6), B1 ff.

[50] Getler, Michael. (1981). Pentagon paints awesome portrait of Soviet arms. *The Washington Post* (September 30), A1 ff.

[51] Marder, Murray. (1981). U.S. sharpening information policy overseas. *The Washington Post* (November 10), A1 ff.

[52] Hughes, John. (1981). Published memorandum outlining "Project Truth" campaign. *The Washington Post* (November 10), A11. John Hughes was associate director, National Security Council.

[53] More to FCC proposals than meets the eye. (1981). *Broadcasting 101* (No. 13) (September 28), 41–44.

[54] Fowler out to slay big brother. (1981). *Broadcasting 101* (No. 13) (September 28), 19.

[55] Perry, James M. (1981). Washington PR staffs dream up ways to get agencies' stories out. *The Wall Street Journal* (May 23), 1.

[56] Struck, Myron. (1981). Publications come down to final word. *The Washington Post* (November 9), A12.

[57] Gordon, Michael. (1980). The image makers in Washington—PR firms have found a natural home. *National Journal* (May 31), 884–890.

[58] Baldwin, Deborah. (1977). Ad Council prescription: public service pablum. *Washington Journalism Review* (October), 36–39.

[59] Miller, Susan H. (1978). Reporters and Congressmen: living in symbiosis. *Journalism Monographs* (No. 53) (January).

[60] Blanchard, Robert. (Ed.). (1974). "Congress and the News Media." New York: Hastings House.

[61] Cater, Douglas. The fourth branch of government. Page 347 in footnote 60, 1974.

[62] Small, William. Congress, television and the war protests. Page 360 in footnote 60, 1974.

[63] Robinson, Michael J., and Appel, Kevin R. (1979). Network news coverage of Congress. *Political Science Quarterly 64* (No. 3) (Fall), 411.

[64] Weaver, David, and Wilhoit, G. Cleveland. (1980). News media coverage of U.S. Senators in four Congresses, 1953–1974. *Journalism Monographs* (No. 67) (April).

[65] Hess, Stephen. Page 99 in footnote 39, 1981.

[66] Miller, S. Michael. (1976). The coming of the pseudo-technocratic society. *Sociological Inquiry 46* (Nos. 3–4), 219–221.

[67] *Ibid.*, p. 219.

[68] *Ibid.* p. 220.

[69] Aaron, Henry. (1978). "Politics and the Professors: The Great Society in Perspective," pp. 30–31. Washington, D.C.: The Brookings Institution.

[70] Greenberg, Daniel S. (1967). "The Politics of Pure Science," pp. 133–134. New York: New American Library.

[71] Morgan, Dan. (1981). Conservatives: a well-financed network. *The Washington Post* (January 4), A1 ff.

[72] Theberge, Leonard J. (Ed.). (1981). "Crooks, Conmen and Clowns." Washington, D.C.: The Media Institute.

[73] Bethell, Tom. (1980). "Television Evening News Covers Inflation, 1978–79," p. 46. Washington, D.C.: The Media Institute.

[74] Stone, Peter H. (1981). Conservative brain trust. *The New York Times Magazine* (May 3), 18.

[75] *Ibid.*, p. 65.

[76] Weiss, Carol. (1980). Knowledge creep and decision accretion. *Knowledge 1* (No. 3) (March), 381–404.

[77] Stone, Peter H. Page 65 in footnote 74, 1981.

[78] Brown, Warren. (1981). Donovan to reorganize the Department of Labor. *The Washington Post* (July 10), A3.

[79] Knight, Jerry. (1981). Mythical study of market, NCPAC lobbying used in fight to keep tax straddle legal. *The Washington Post* (July 5), E1 ff.

[80] Nelkin, Dorothy. (1979). Scientific knowledge, public policy, and democracy: a review essay. *Knowledge 1* (No. 1) (September), 106–122.

[81] U.S. Congress, Senate, Subcommittee on Reports, Accounting and Management. (1977). "Consultants and Contractors," pp. 202–206. Washington, D.C.: U.S. Government Printing Office.

[82] Neumann, Jonathan, and Gup, Ted. (1980). Billion-dollar U.S. deals with industry unchecked. *The Washington Post* (June 22), A1 ff.

[83] *Ibid.*, p. A14.

[84] *Ibid.*

[85] *Ibid.* p. A15.

[86] Guttman, Daniel. (1979). Testimony in U.S. Congress, Senate, Subcommittee on Civil Services and General Services, Hearings. "Federal Government's Use of Consultant Services," p. 41. Washington, D.C.: U.S. Government Printing Office.

[87] *Ibid.*, p. 47.

[88] *Ibid.*, pp. 38–39.

[89] Hanrahan, John. (1979). Testimony in U.S. Congress, Senate, Subcommittee on Civil Services and General Services, Hearings. "Federal Government's Use of Consultant Services," p. 118. Washington, D.C.: U.S. Government Printing Office.

[90] Van Poecke, Luc. (1980). Gerbner's cultural indicators. The system is the message. *In* G.C. Wilhoit, and H. de Bock (Eds.), "Mass Communication Review Yearbook," Vol. 1, pp. 423–431. Beverly Hills, California: Sage Publications.

[91] Gerbner, George. (1964). On content analysis and critical research in mass communications. *In* L. Dexter, and D. White (Eds.), "People, Society and Mass Communications," pp. 476–500. New York: The Free Press.

[92] Gerbner, George. (1961). Regulation of mental illness content in motion pictures and television. *Gazette 6*, 365–385.

[93] Paletz, David L., and Entman, Robert M. (1981). "Media Power Politics," pp. 170–172. New York: The Free Press.

[94] *Ibid.*, pp. 180–182.

95 Turow, Joseph. (1978). Casting for TV parts: the anatomy of social typing. *Journal of Communication 28* (No. 4) (Autumn), 18–24.

96 Montgomery, Kathryn. (1981). Gay activists and the networks. *Journal of Communication 31* (No. 3) (Summer), 49–57.

97 Cantor, Muriel G. (1980). "Prime-Time Television." Beverly Hills, California: Sage Publications.

98 *Ibid.,* p. 83.

99 Barnouw, Eric. Page 101 in footnote 21, 1976.

100 MacPherson, Myra. (1981). Notes from the real life drama. *The Washington Post* (November 17), B1 ff.

101 Fowler out to slay big brother. (1981). *Broadcasting 101* (No. 13). (September 28), 19–20.

102 Shales, Tom. (1981). TV's look at the town's fight over "free speech." *The Washington Post* (November 17), B11.

103 Carmody, John. (1981). The TV column. *The Washington Post* (March 9), C10.

104 Beck, Mindy. (1975). Public interest groups tap into entertainment tv. *Access* (No. 18) (September 22), 8–11.

105 Shales, Tom. (1978). Violence at home. *The Washington Post* (September 26), C1 ff.

106 Shales, Tom. (1981). A gun in the house: taking cheap shots with a low caliber thriller. *The Washington Post* (February 11), C3.

107 Latham, Aaron. (1979). Hollywood vs. Harrisburg. *Esquire* (May 22), 77–86.

108 *Ibid.,* p. 86.

109 Tuchman, Mitch. (1977). Who's turning what into movies? *Esquire* (April), 72–74.

5

The Information Subsidy in Health

"I may be poor, but at least I've got my health," is a familiar refrain these days. Good health is a basic human desire or need. In the sense of economic rationality that we have discussed in Chapter Two, health is one of the goods or outputs that each individual or family unit seeks to produce using a variety of inputs, including food, shelter, rest, and recreation. Rational economic beings choose between potential inputs on the basis of their perceived costs and expected benefits. The great variety in approaches to the production of health can be seen to be a function of differences in economic resources, but much of the variation is associated with differential access to information about prevention and treatment of damage and disease. And, while much of our productive activity is directed toward acquisition and consumption, more important differences may exist in the kinds of inputs and activities we avoid. Thus, with an eye toward health, we either seek or avoid certain foods, activities, places, and people.

At the same time that individuals and families make decisions related to the production and maintenance of health, various levels of government may be seen to act to improve or maintain the collective health of the population. All of these decisions, to the extent that they take on regular patterns, can be considered health policy decisions.

Health policy, like defense policy, involves the expenditure of substantial human and economic resources. Also like defense policy, health policy at the national level involves the active participation of powerful interests that seek to influence that policy to their own benefit. The formulation, adoption, and implementation of health policy are controlled in large part by those participants in the process most able to define the problems, specify the alternatives, and differentiate between them in terms of their probable benefits and costs.

As we have seen, ideology plays an important role in determining the effectiveness of information-subsidy efforts directed toward public policy. Information consistent with the dominant ideology flows more easily, is accepted more readily, and is less likely to be discounted in the reduction of uncertainty. The dominant medical ideology in the U.S. is one that focuses on cure rather than prevention, and is driven by a view of the body as a machine, hospitals as repair shops, and physicians as master mechanics. It is a view that sees cost as no barrier, and to a certain extent, prefers to ignore the common or mundane, in pursuit of the technical or engineering challenge.

In this chapter we will examine the roots of this ideology, its reflection in medical practice, and its place in the larger arena of national economic and social policy.

THE HEALTH CARE INDUSTRY

Medicine is big business. By 1980, total expenditures for health care in the U.S. had exceeded $247 billion.[1] Hospitals serve as the primary channel for the delivery of these goods and services, but the primary beneficiaries of the seemingly boundless demand for medical inputs are the suppliers of professional services, drugs, and disposable supplies, and sophisticated diagnostic and monitoring instruments.

Unlike other industries, the health care industry is protected from the vagueries of consumer demand by a variety of exceptions to the rules of the competitive market. On the supply side, the industry is characterized by substantial barriers to entry. Physicians dominate the industry, and their entry into the profession is characterized by a lengthy education and apprenticeship program. Competition for these educational opportunities is fierce, and the number is determined somewhat arbitrarily. These barriers are reinforced by a system of licensure supported by a criminal sanction for unlicensed practice.

Monopoly-like behavior on the part of the physicians has included price discrimination and restricted sales to "target populations." Although government insurance programs have increased access to medical services by the poor, Karen Davis[2] reports that the benefits from such programs have been disproportunately low for blacks and other minorities.

As Victor Fuchs[3] notes, physicians themselves account for only a small portion of actual health care expenditures, but their decisions determine the amount and distribution of the lion's share of what remains. Once a patient decides that it is time to "adopt the sick role" and seek professional help, virtually all remaining decisions are made by the physician. This includes ordering a battery of expensive tests, which have come to protect the physician as much as they provide her with information about the patient's condition.

Whereas in other markets, the consumer is expected to have ready access to sufficient information to make a choice between alternatives, in the health care market, most consumers have little or no basis upon which to choose between diagnostic approaches or treatment plans. Therefore they tend to turn over that responsibility to the physician.

The exchange relationship in the health care market is similarly unique. In most markets, there is an expectation that payment is based upon satisfactory service, as evidenced by results. When one pays the bill for automobile repairs, one can reasonably expect that the vehicle will operate within reasonable limits. There is no such expectation in the health care market. Payment is made on the basis of service delivered, not upon effects produced. Indeed, some of the most costly medical care is provided to the terminally ill.

Perhaps the most important difference between health care and other markets is the role of third-party payers. Economic decision making involves the consideration of personal costs and benefits, but the introduction of insurance distorts the relation between payment and consumption. The portion of medical expenditures actually paid by the individual consumer had declined to 35.4% by 1974, from 52.5% in 1965.[4] As employee benefit packages expand the number of health-related services covered, and as the corporate share of the insurance premiums increases as well, that portion must continue to decline. Thus, while consumers as a group ultimately bear the costs of health care through increased taxes and lower real wages, the individual consumer sees less of a direct link between the consumption of services and their personal cost.

Because of this separation of cost from service received, there is less of an incentive for consumers to economize. On the supply side, because current policy and practice results in third-party payment of "all reasonable costs" for service, there is virtually no incentive for economy.

What appears as a technological imperative in the health care industry—a necessity to have the latest, or the state of the art, in medical technology—is not entirely explained by the drive for profits that characterizes most industries of comparable size. In the profit-maximizing firm, new technologies are chosen because they will either increase the output or reduce the costs of some input (usually labor). In health care, new technology nearly always creates a demand for additional labor inputs. Thus, the observed tendency within the medical profession to choose highly visible, innovative technologies or techniques must be based in part on their status and prestige value. Barbara and John Ehrenreich[5] note that this prestige factor is most important in the university-related hospitals and medical centers, where the latest technology is necessary to attract the high-level professors, who in turn attract the best residents and interns.

Next, we have to see the demand for new technology as being externally imposed to a large extent by federal research and development (R&D) programs. Rosemary Stevens suggests that by 1970, "the medical schools had become in large part arms or branches of NIH. Their facilities and their interests responded to the availability of an apparently never-ending stream of federal wealth channeled through a byzantine system of national peer review groups and advisory committees."[6] She supports this conclusion by noting that in 1968–69, nearly half of the faculty of U.S. medical schools received some portion of their salaries from the National Institutes of Health (NIH)-sponsored research, and one-third received nearly all their support in this manner.

Even though the nonprofit community hospitals are not in direct competition with the university centers for prestige awards, they are still in competition for physicians, and are thereby affected by the same technological fix. The publicity generated by "stars" at the nation's leading medical centers sets a standard for modern medical practice. Colleagues at nearby teaching facilities spread the gospel more directly through frequent professional and social contact. Hospitals are forced to continually update their facilities to meet the ever-changing demands of their privileged tenants. The availability of federal funds for expansion and improvement of community hospitals has resulted in what critics see as senseless duplication of resources.

Where physicians largely control the demand for new and costly technologies within the hospitals, their own demand is influenced in no small degree by the efforts of manufacturers and suppliers. Defense-electronics firms, household names because of their domination of the consumer-electronics field, have also come to dominate the highly competitive market for diagnostic and monitoring equipment. With the decline of federal support for the aerospace industry, the expanding medical field was a natural alternative for many of these firms. General Electric, Hewlett-Packard, and Motorola have all entered the health care industry, either through the development of their own devices, or through the purchase of smaller technical innovators. Their efforts to stimulate demand for these devices involves both direct and indirect information subsidies, and, as we will see, their ingenuity is matched only by the pharmaceutical firms who have developed the techniques of "undercover promotion"[7] into a high art.

Where government policy toward medical R&D serves to stimulate and support the influence of the technological or engineering approach to health care delivery, the government is also a direct consumer of the output of the medical supply industry. Silverman and Lee[8] report that direct purchases for the military, VA, and Public Health Service facilities have made the U.S. government the "largest single drug buyer in the U.S. and the world." They suggest that with the indirect payments through Medicaid and Medicare, the government must be responsible for 80% of the drug industry's output.

The parallels between the defense industry and the health care industry are many, and the existence of a government-dependent "medical-industrial-complex" cannot be doubted. Government policy can be seen to influence the growth of the industry and the well-being of its participants in the following ways:

1. Government R&D support supports the development of new devices and techniques.
2. It supports the training of medical professionals who are committed to the practice of heroic medicine at the limits of technological possibility.
3. Its utilization of defense-electronics firms for the development of new devices, and the provision of market advantages through special licensing agreements, ensure their continued domination of the industry.
4. It supports the extension of barriers to entry through the extension of criminal sanctions for unlicensed practice.
5. It provides direct and indirect support for the improvement of medical facilities through a variety of capital improvement grant programs, or through third-party payments for medical services.
6. Existing and proposed expansion of national health insurance schemes will further increase the demand for health care services.

Recent attempts to restrain the inflation in the health care industry through the establishment of government-sanctioned policy boards, and "certificate of need" requirements for the purchase of high-cost items, may be seen to be medical reflections of the Pentagon's efforts to control cost-overruns and inflationary growth in the defense industry.

Because of the great number of ways in which government policy can affect the well-being of the industry, and because of the nature of competing interests within the industry, the policy process is necessarily quite complex and difficult to describe in detail. Unlike the defense industry, the citizen-consumer plays a more direct role in the process; thus the mass media channels assume a greater importance for the delivery of information subsidies related to public policy. In the next section, we discuss the importance of mass media treatment of medical subjects, its role in the transmission of the dominant ideology, and its use by special interests to influence the policy process.

MASS MEDIA AND HEALTH CONSCIOUSNESS

Peter Sandman[9] suggests that the mass media can influence the health consumer in a number of ways:

1. *Need manipulation* through direct advertising appeals. Here we find

attempts to link needs for social acceptance (called "sex appeal") to the more clearly health-related need for regular dental care.

2. *Salience manipulation* where the advertiser attempts to link an existing attitude to a new circumstance, or to suggest the appropriateness of some preferred behavior to an existing attitude. Sandman suggests that "manipulating the salience of an existing attitude is a great deal easier than creating a new attitude."[10]

3. *Reinforcement* of already developed habits and tendencies. Here, promotional appeals provide additional evidence to support those already committed to a product or activity.

More indirect influences include those messages that provide legitimization for current practices and practitioners, help to set the public agenda regarding critical medical problems worthy of national attention, provide models of health behavior to be imitated, and in general, Sandman suggests, "on topics about which people have no strongly developed attitudes in any direction, medical content often determines and disseminates the cultural norms that will influence our behavior."[11]

As we have discussed in Chapter Two, the impact of media content varies with the motivations and expectations of the media consumer. Medical information may be gained through a purposeful search of media channels in pursuit of information about the production and maintenance of health. Information may also be gained indirectly, when media used for some other purpose, such as entertainment, relaxation, or escape, also contain information related to health.

W. Russell Wright [12] reported on a small sample of respondents who were asked to describe the extent to which they made use of newspapers, radio, television, and magazines in search of health-related information. They were also asked whether they made use of dramatic programs for similar information needs. Information about the frquency of use, their recall of specific stories or subject matter, and their evaluation of the relative utility of these sources completed the fairly traditional uses and gratifications study. As expected, newspapers were more important than television or radio as credible sources of health-related information. Nonmedical magazines were identified as being the most important sources of such information, where nearly 65% of the users of these sources described them as being very or fairly helpful. Although use of television was fairly high, less than a third of the users felt that the material was even fairly helpful.

Concern for the accuracy and completeness of medical information is heightened by the consideration of findings reported in two different studies. Robert Bishop[13] examined the relationship between anxiety and the consumption of health-related information. He hypothesized that readership of a story will vary with the level of anxiety present in a reader, which is further dependent upon the extent to which the headlines for the story are characterized as threatening or reassuring. This experimental study made use of measures of health-anxiety and fictional stories with threatening (''Cancer Remains the Silent Killer'') or reassuring (''Two Early Cancer Tests Offer Hope'') headlines. As expected, the encouraging headlines were associated with greater readership, and increased learning of content. Although there were few differences in the patterns of exposure and learning in the low-anxiety group, Bishop found that those who were more anxious read more health-related materials.

In a study of health practices and opinions reported in 1972, National Analysts suggested that persons who were the most anxious about health, who were either fearful of disease, or sought to attain some ''super health'' level, were more likely to be followers of the more questionable health practices. Thus, while they were likely to report that they were actually healthier than most people, they were also more likely to expose themselves to health-related information in a variety of channels, and on the basis of that information, engage in wasteful, if not dangerous, activities.[14]

In contrast with the conclusions reached by General Mills in their study of family health,[15] it is most likely that mass media content *contributes* to heightened medical anxiety, which results in the search for more health-related information and the services of health professionals, and contributes to a willingness to support expansion of government support of medical research and the health care delivery system (Figure 5.1). The treatment of medical subjects in the mass media, combined with the direct and indirect appeals for support of nonprofit, or charitable disease associations, against a background of slickly produced advertisements for nonprescription drugs and health-producing ''natural foods,'' has led to what Aaron Wildavsky describes as a condition where one is ''doing better and feeling worse.''[16] Wildavsky calls our attention to this modern paradox where we find most statical indicators of health status pointing to a general improvement in the nation's health. At the same time we find media channels filled with stories about a crisis in health. Lewis Thomas reflects on the same paradox and refers to our state of generalized anxiety as mass hypochondria where:

> the general belief these days seems to be that the body is fundamentally flawed, subject to disintegration at any moment, always on the verge of mortal disease, always in need of continual monitoring and support by health care professionals.[17]

At the same time we come to believe ourselves in danger, these same media channels are seen to identify the correct solutions to the problems. Ivan Bennett[18] describes the media-generated view of the capacity of modern medicine to respond to and deal with a great variety of threats to our health as the ''Marcus Welby Syndrome.'' Consumers have come to expect that all physicians are as capable, understanding, and readily available as the doctors portrayed in television serials, or highlighted in *Reader's Digest* features. Bennett suggests further that media portrayals tend to reinforce the public demand for high-technology

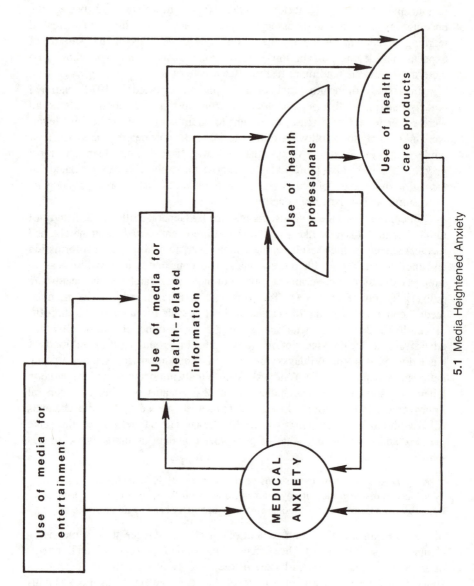

5.1 Media Heightened Anxiety

102

medicine, the kind which serves so well as transitions between scenes, as the camera zooms in on the oscilloscope tracing of the fading heartbeat.

Sandman[19] offers a list of beliefs about medical practice that are likely to be generated or reinforced by even casual attention to the health-related content in the media:

1. That doctors are kind, generous, handsome (male, of course), fearless, and heroic, while sensitive to the personal and psychological needs of their patients (female, of course).[20]
2. That the best, indeed often the only, solution to a host of medical problems is surgery.
3. That access to medical care is quick, non-discriminatory, and apparently costless, since television doctors treat one patient at a time, and never discuss fees.
4. If anyone is at fault in the health production process, it is the patient who characteristically hides vital, perhaps embarrassing, information from the doctor, who has to tease it out finally at the end of a dramatic, tearful confrontation.
5. In those rare instances where radical, experimental surgery or chemotherapy is not the solution to medical problems, the victim is still to be blamed, as the problem is discovered to lie in some psychological problems uncovered by the physician-detective.

Efforts by researchers to demonstrate empirical links between exposure to media portrayals, and public attitudes and beliefs about health have been quite limited. George Gerbner[21] and his associates at the University of Pennsylvania have extended the limits of their cultivation analysis beyond violence and fear to include attitudes about diet and nutrition, smoking, and alcohol use. The authors are quite hesitant, however, to describe their findings as more than preliminary in supporting the conclusion that exposure to television has any influence on health knowledge, attitudes, and behavior. As in the early days of mass communications research, the majority of work in the health field has focused on attempts to describe the health-related content, and merely *assume* the results.

HEALTH-RELATED CONTENT IN THE MEDIA

Numerous studies have described and evaluated the amount, variety, accuracy, and utility of health-related information in the nation's media. Many of these studies have examined both advertising and editorial content in an effort to determine the quality of information made available to the consumer. While the bulk of these studies is concerned with the impact of such content on health beliefs and practices that may be reflected in the health status of individuals, a few studies in recent years have attempted to look beyond the individual, and to link media content to public health policy.

Sorenson and Sorenson[22] studied the relative importance of science content in magazines between 1964 and 1970, and noted that medical subjects received a relatively stable amount of attention over the years studied. As part of a study of media treatment of coronary heart disease, Fisher, Gandy, and Janus[23] identified some 7,177 health-related items published in *Ladies Home Journal, Reader's Digest,* and *Time* magazine. *Reader's Digest* published the greatest number of articles per issue. *Time,* because of its news orientation, tended to be a leader in terms of the periodicals' coverage of heart disease (Figure 5.2). With the exception of 1968, a peak in *Time's* coverage of coronary heart disease occurred the year preceding peaks in the other two magazines. These peaks can be seen to be related to similar peaks in the grants and operations budgets of the National Heart and Lung Institute (NHLI).

Nancy Pfund and Laura Hofstadter examined the treatment of four biomedical innovations that had important policy implications: DES (feared carcinogen), the swine flu program, the artificial heart R&D effort, and recombinant DNA research. In each case, they found a failure on the part of the media to provide sufficient background, or to pay enough attention to the conflict or uncertainty within the medical community. Their analysis suggested that the media took their cues from the mainstream scientific community, such that when it "suggested that there was no cause for debate, reporting of dissident views decreased sharply."[24]

Their findings lend support to our notions about the relationship of dependency that exists between journalists and their sources. The generalized failure of the media's coverage to give sufficient emphasis to the "why" dimension of medical innovations is seen to be a function of media reliance on subsidized information—that contained in press releases, handouts, or presented in formal medical conferences.

They noted the important role played by the scientist-entrepreneurs who provide information to the press because it enhances their reputations and reduces their uncertainty about continued grant support.

> While many of these sources no longer hailed from nonprofit or publicly funded research bases, their representation in the press lost none of the objective and definitive flavor so often reserved for university-based academics and customarily denied to industrial spokesmen.[25]

In fact, they note that for many of the more newsworthy discoveries such as advances in the development of inteferon, these entrepreneurs were the only ones cited in the stories.

Commenting on this tendency, Hillier Krieghbaum suggests that science writers are somewhat less industrious than their other less-specialized colleagues:

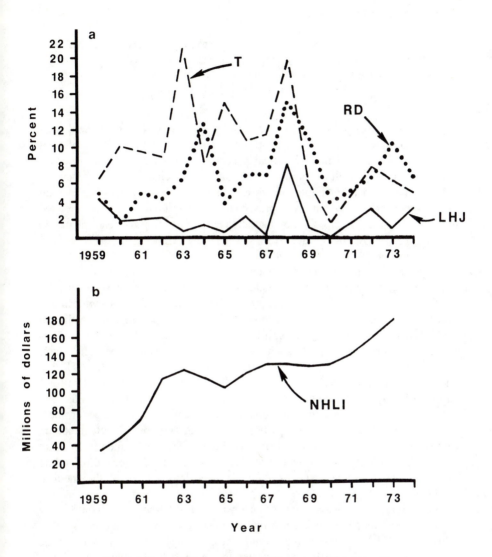

5.2 (a) Percent Coronary Heart Disease in Total Health Coverage. (b) Total Grants and Direct Operations. Abbreviations: RD, Readers Digest; T, Time; LHJ, Ladies Home Journal; NHLI, National Heart and Lung Institute.

While some top-flight science reporters do go out foraging in laboratories and on campuses for news, most spend their time attending science and technical conventions, reading journals, and scanning press releases. More than in most other fields, such as politics, say, the news comes to the science writers.[26]

Laurel Walum[27] suggests that there are problems in the public understanding of science that may result from this approach to reporting. In her analysis of what happened when one of her theoretical papers was seized upon by a writer attending a meeting of the American Sociological Association, she saw science being transformed into "human interest." Although the journalists gave credit to the author, and noted that it was presented at a scientific meeting, most tended to report the study as though they had attended the meeting, or read the paper, when in fact, most of the later stories were drawn from an initial *New York Times* article.

Further evidence of the dependency relationship is found in the cyclical nature of innovation and general health science coverage. Because of the dependence of the press on subsidized, prepackaged material, there is a widespread decline in coverage during those periods when researchers are engaged in clinical trials.[28] While the stories could still be uncovered through the methods of investigatory journalism, reporters tend to wait for their gifts to come in the mail.

The tendency to rely on official sources has also been noted by David Rubin and Val Hendy in their study of the swine flu escapade. The somewhat uniform support of official government policy on the program in its early stages was seen to be the result of a general tendency on the part of the press to rely on government and professional sources. In this particular instance, they found a reluctance on the part of many professionals, many of whom were at least skeptical, if not downright opposed to the program, to "say so in public, for fear of offending the local medical society and breaking with the united front of the medical establishment."[29]

For similar reasons, perhaps, science writers also tend to avoid controversy and conflict. Bruce Cole examined the coverage of scientific conflict in 1951, 1961, and 1971,[30] and reported that while there was a significant increase in the coverage of scientific conflict, science writers were less likely than their general-assignment counterparts to write such stories. He reasoned that science writers, because of their frequent interaction with their sources at conventions or other occasions organized for sharing information, would be less likely to highlight conflict within the community with which they identified. Staff writers, on the other hand, had less of a personal commitment to the science community, and would be less hesitant about reporting conflict (a basic ingredient of good journalism). Cole compared the percent of conflict stories written by full- and part-time science writers and staff reporters assigned to cover science stories. In 1971, 73.1% of the science writers' stories were classified as non-conflictual, while only 58.2% of the staff writer's stories were similarly classified. Sharon Dunwoody's [31] study of the inner circle of science writer lends further support to the notion of consensus-seeking and conflict-avoidance incentives that result in the limited discussion of policy alternatives in the public media.

Dunwoody reports that science writers, as part of a mutually reinforcing community of professionals, diverge from the model of competitive, hard-working, investigative reporters one would expect to find working for major papers or wire services. Instead, science writers in the "inner club" rely on each other to determine what the lead stories are and which ones will be sent back to the home office. These reporters are not above sharing notes and interviews. They help each other by asking follow-up questions if the previous answer was unsatisfactory, and even warn their colleagues when some source is "risky" or unreliable. The end result is homogeneity of content in papers across the nation, particularly when the lead on a story is developed by a writer for one of the wire services.

Health-related stories carried by the AP or UPI are printed in paper after paper, often without inclusion of the science writer's by-line, and frequently without indication that the story is based on a wire release. Very often, the only difference between these stories is their headlines. In an exploratory study of the relationship between characteristics of the community and treatment of health-related issues in the press, it was suggested that even at the level of headlines, there was a tendency toward sensitivity to medical community interests.[32]

A magazine for the nursing profession had completed a survey of some 10,000 of its readers, found some of the results to be startling and disturbing, and prepared a press release. The story was picked up by science writers for the AP and UPI. And, as is generally the case, the AP story by Alton Blakeslee received the greatest response from editors. Copies of several hundred of these stories were compared on several content dimensions.

The stories in these papers were essentially identical, with only slight variations between the morning and evening editions where there was a change in the lead paragraph. However, in those communities where pharmaceuticals represented a substantial portion of the total retail sales in the standard metropolitan statistical area—a condition interpreted as a reflection of the community's health status and dependence upon the medical establishment—there was a greater tendency for the newspapers to use a more reassuring headline for the story.

Irving Page[33] describes the relationship between science writers, physicians, and the public as something of a ménage à trois. The public wants interesting, stimulating stories about valiant struggles against dread disease, or hopeful news of possibilities of a cure for cancer and other ills being just around the corner. This need for media content is matched by the need for publicity and the prestige it brings to the physician-researcher. The "development office" and the press are seen to work hand in hand to meet this public need as long as the prestige-seeker can provide something that at least approaches newsworthiness. Of course, information subsidies designed to meet the organizational requirements of the journalist do not exhaust the routes through which health-related information makes its way into the public media.

George Gerbner and his colleagues have noted the relative popularity of medical themes in prime-time television and the soap operas.[34] They report that medical topics are expected to be treated in a manner consistent with the National Association of Broadcasters (NAB) Code regulations. These voluntary guidelines require realistic settings and require that research claims are based on "the facts" as one could be expected to know them. Because of the code requirements, producers of fictional material can be seen to be faced with a different set of organizational requirements than those faced by journalists. But just as the economic limitations on journalists make them vulnerable to the subsidy efforts of self-interested sources, producers of fictional television can be seen to be dependent upon, and vulnerable to, the interests of the organized medical profession.

John Cooney, reporting in *The Wall Street Journal*[35], described numerous instances of script changes that were made at the suggestion of one of several advisors who make up the American Medical Association's Physician Advisory Committee. In 1977, 19 specialists were assigned to the Committee, and had the responsibility for answering the questions put to them by script writers. Some 20 calls a day are received by this office, which is located in close proximity to the Hollywood production community. Cooney reports that in addition to answering these questions, the Committee reviews some 300 scripts each year for "accuracy and appropriateness." This appropriateness label can cover a variety of sins, as evidenced by the example of a change in a script that was suggested because the reviewer did not think it appropriate for a "doctor to be drinking on the job."

The physicians' committee was joined in 1973 by a similar committee working in the interests of the hospital side of the industry. The American Hospital Association's panel reviews hospital procedures represented in television and motion picture drama, just as the AMA committee looks out for the portrayal of physicians.

There is little wonder then, that Gerbner et al.[36] find that doctors are treated better than other professions portrayed on television. Less than 4% of the doctors in major character roles could be identified as evil. Other professions have twice as many evildoers. As we have suggested, uniformity in the treatment of health and health care professionals may play a role in the public's perception of their own health, and the availability of options for its maintenance. In this next section, we will focus on the formal policy arena in order to see the role of coordinated information subsidies in developing influence over that process.

INFORMATION SUBSIDIES AND PUBLIC POLICIES IN HEALTH

There are numerous examples of efforts by individuals to gain advantages for themselves through self-promotion in the mass media. A few of them have been noted, and, while they contribute to the general coverage of medical research and the nation's health status, we are more concerned here with the efforts of organized interests to influence specific legislation, or to generate public support for their narrow policy goals.

Information subsidies in support of health care policy take some of the same forms as those identified in Chapter Four. Interested groups and their representatives provide information to DMs at all levels of government through a variety of channels. Information is delivered to legislators through: (1) direct personal contact; (2) testimony in congressional hearings; and (3) (indirectly) press coverage of strategically placed media events. The bureaucracy is reached through similar channels, although in addition a well-developed system of advisory panels and policy boards provides access to academic, professional, corporate, and citizen representatives.

Elected officials and bureaucrats themselves seek to influence policy through the use of information subsidies. The politician calls for hearings on science policy or medical fraud in order to call attention to their expertise and concern for the public's welfare. The literature provides numerous examples of jurisdictional battles that erupt when representatives struggle to be associated with a popular issue. Health issues in particular have been guaranteed coverage, and much of the debate over National Health Insurance (NHI) can be seen as attempts by politicians to capture the spotlight by being associated with the effort to help the public with its medical bill.

CANCER AND THE NATIONAL INSTITUTES OF HEALTH (NIH)

The most important sources of policy-relevant information about health are the dozen or so "disease associations," which have as their goal the creation and maintance of broad-based federal support for R&D, and service entitlements for their chosen malady. These associations may be seen to influence the policy environment through direct and indirect means. At one level, the public concern with the status of its health has been linked to the yearly efforts by these associations to raise money for their cause.[37]

Richard Rettig's[38] detailed history of the efforts of Mary Lasker and the American Cancer Society (ACS) to win approval of the National Cancer Act of 1971 provides one of the best examples of an association's role in the policy process. The War on Cancer, like the War on Poverty, was accompanied by a significant shift in the allocation of federal resources. Between fiscal 1970 and fiscal 1980, the budgetary authority for the National Cancer Institute (NCI) increased by more than 470%. The 1980 budgetary authority was nearly twice that of its nearest competitor, the National Heart, Lung, and Blood Institute.[39] The initiation and design of this war effort was seen by many to have been led every step of the way by Mary Lasker and the ACS. And, while cancer is truly a health menace, and worthy of government attention, it is not at all clear that the approach to the problem that seems to be preferred by the ACS should be allowed to dominate federal policy to the extent that it does. Lasker's masterful use of information subsidies provides some insight into how such power is developed and maintained over time.

Lasker, a wealthy heiress to an advertising agency fortune, lost her husband to cancer, and had, therefore, both the reason and the resources to push for a cure. Perhaps as a result of her husband's work in advertising, Lasker also had a greater-than-average appreciation of the power of information. Her association with the American Society for the Control of Cancer, later to become the American Cancer Society, began with her implementation of an information-subsidy program. With her initial gift to the Society, Lasker financed the production of a pamphlet that purported to be the state of the art of cancer research. Later, she arranged for the publication of three brief articles on cancer research in *Reader's Digest*. As a result of these articles, Rettig suggests that Lasker was able to raise $4.2 million for the ACS.

A more important, institutionalized system of information control was the establishment of the Annual Science Writers Seminars under the ACS's sponsorship. In Rettig's view, the seminars were scheduled so as "to encourage national news coverage of cancer research programs a few weeks before each annual ACS fund-raising drive."[40]

Rettig suggests that Lasker's decision to push for an all-out war on cancer was stimulated by a book on cancer research by Soloman Garb. Because Garb's argument for the establishment of a cancer cure as a national goal was so clearly in line with Lasker's own view, and because his ideas were so well organized, Lasker arranged for Garb to testify before Congress. This was just the beginning of her information campaign, which included a full page ad in *The New York Times* telling the president: MR. NIXON: YOU CAN CURE CANCER.[41]

Taking initiative usually reserved for the Chief Executive, Lasker was instrumental in hand-picking a "Panel of Consultants" to direct the war on cancer. Bills drafted on the basis of the initial work of this high-powered panel were introduced by Lasker supporters in the Senate—one year by Ralph Yarborough and the next year by Ted Kennedy. It is suggested that because of the threat Kennedy represented as a presidential contender, Nixon was led to introduce a duplicate bill, although he was not fully in support of the Lasker proposal.

In the hearings on the bill, Lasker's fine hand could again be seen in the scheduling of witnesses. With Kennedy at the helm, the opposition was scheduled to appear first, while Lasker's Panel of Consultants and other advocates would be given a separate day of testimony.

It should be noted that Lasker's proposal was not all that well received by a scientific community that had already developed mutually beneficial relationships within the NIH. The bill would have given the NCI considerable autonomy, and its policy of contract research was seen as antithetical to notions of basic research. Thus, there were information subsidies flowing from that side of the table as well. Rettig notes the heavy coverage given to the public withdrawal of support originally given to the panel by Joshua Lederberg. Once a member of the Panel of Consultants, Lederberg apparently changed his mind, and *Science* published his story, making it even more prominent by outlining it with a bold, black border.[42] Later, 10 prominent scientists were to publish a letter stating their opposition to the latest version of the bill in *The Washington Post,* where it would be most likely to command the attention of Congress.

However, at the Science Writer's Conference, Lasker's subsidy effort was to go into high gear. The president of the ACS issued a statement in support of the Senate bill, which received wide press coverage of the sort the Conference was designed to produce. This was followed up by a letter-writing campaign, which saw a letter by Dr. Garb appear in *The Wall Street Journal.* When Ann Landers published an entire column on the bill, and urged her readers to contact Senator Cranston to express their support, more than 60,000 letters were received in five weeks. When the Landers column was later reproduced in full-page ads in the nation's papers, an additional 250–300,000 letters were generated.[43]

While the Panel of Consultants, with its wealthy and influential participants was of vital importance to the eventual success of the effort, Rettig suggests that the momentum it began would have died without the grass-roots support generated by the Ann Landers' column.[44]

Thus, largely through her uncanny ability to mount a coordinated program of information subsidies, Mary Lasker was able to take on a president and the scientific establishment, and win the approval of a program to "rid the nation of cancer in our lifetime." In the process, she contributed to the institutionalization of a relationship between the ACS and NCI that many consider to be wasteful of resources and limiting with regard to the prevention of many cancers.

Daniel Greenberg and Judith Randal[45] argue that the NCI approach to cancer, which reflects the domination of the Institute's major advisory boards by the ACS members or sympathizers, is outmoded, and occasionally dangerous in its own right. They cite numerous examples of the ACS influence over the development and implementation of the NCI programs, such as the controversial breast screening effort. They suggest as well that the ACS continues to dominate the public's perception of cancer and cancer research through its role as the "NCI's ministry of information for educating the public about cancer."[46] One aspect of the information distributed by the ACS, either directly, or through the NCI publications and information campaigns, is the strict avoidance of consideration of industrial sources of cancer. Instead, the focus reflects the victim-blaming ideology common to the U.S. medical establishment. This dominant ideology defines cancer as the result of bad personal habits like smoking, or failure to have frequent checkups, or failure to pay enough attention to cancer's warning signs, or failure to . . . etc., etc., etc.

THE CORONARY CARE UNIT (CCU)

Coronary heart disease (CHD) has long been considered to be the major cause of death in the U.S. Yet, to date, we have not developed a single "decisive, conclusive technology with the power to turn off, reverse or prevent disease."[47] Instead, what we have is an endless parade of "half-way technologies," which patch up or repair damaged organs, or provide some palliative relief. The CCU is merely a theoretically more efficient and effective method for monitoring and administering care to CHD patients in crises in an effort to reduce the number of in-hospital deaths.

In the absence of reliable evidence of comparable cost-effectiveness, the CCU was introduced into hospitals across the nation in the early 1960s. By 1974, more than 80% of all 300-bed voluntary hospitals had CCUs. And, despite their expense in terms of both capital and operating costs, 18% of the hospitals with fewer than 100 beds had also introduced such a unit. The availability of funds played an important role in the adoption of these units, as indicated by the change in the diffusion rate, which occurred about the time of the passage of Medicare/Medicaid legislation. But, as Louise Russell notes, the devices were already well-diffused in the larger hospitals by this time.[48] Thus, their spread must have been dependent upon other influences.

The government component of the medical-industrial-complex played a supportive role in the diffusion of CCUs because it saw the transformation of the hospital and its staff as just one part of a larger move toward bioengineering. Samuel Fox, in an HEW conference on the impact of CCUs,[49] noted that by that time there was still very little in the way of conclusive evidence of the superiority of CCUs over alternative methods of care. But for the time being, he argued, CCUs were an "attractive concept" that made it easier to bring "possible infarct patients into a protective environment." And even though he recognized that "false alarms" occur in about 50% of the cases of suspected heart attacks, and treatment of suspected arrhythmias would contribute to a substantial increase in medical costs, admission to the CCU was still a good idea. It was a good idea, not only because it *might* save a few more lives, but because it would provide the medical team with the equipment and experience they would need once *the artificial heart* was more fully developed.

It may be that one of the major justifications for the coronary care unit at this time is to prepare the medical team and to provide the architectural circumstances which will be used for the application of mechanically assisted circulation when it is proven a useful therapeutic operation.[50]

This conference, sponsored by the American Hospital Association, was just one of the ways in which information subsidies in support of CCU diffusion were delivered. The popular media were targets of a continual stream of articles about CHD, heart patients, heroic surgery, and the environments that make it possible.

Very few articles in the popular press focused specifically on the CCU, although those that were published reflected a view consistent with that of the medical establishment. *Reader's Digest* published an article by Wolfgang Langewiesche in 1964 that praised the intensive care unit as the "coming thing in hospitals." Langewiesche was advanced in his recognition of the economic issues surrounding the introduction of medical technologies, but his treatment of the issue was still one-sided:

> The nurse didn't say, "This is efficient," or "this is the way to stretch our nursing power"—all of which would have been true. Instead, she said, "This is the nearest thing to old-fashioned nursing."[51]

And, although he noted the difference in cost between CCU and regular ward care, he concluded without equivocation that "there is no doubt that the Intensive Care Unit increases the healing power of a hospital and is a good thing to have in any community."[52]

The CCU was plugged again in a 1968 *Reader's Digest* article condensed from *The Modern Hospital*. In a footnote to this article about external cardiopulmonary resuscitation, readers were referred back to the Langeweische article. As part of the justification for installing CCUs, the article cited Dr. Hughes Day of Bethany Hospital, one of the leaders of the movement to develop CCU use, as suggesting that such units could save approximately 45,000 heart deaths a year.[53] This article failed to mention the considerable debate that was raging about the mixed results in CCU evaluation studies.

A RAND report[54] that sought to summarize the available literature on CCU effectiveness noted several factors that might explain the conflicting and contradictory findings published in the professional literature, and ignored in the popular press. It was suggested that some bias in the results might be explained by the fact that opportunities for carrying out and publishing the results of controlled evaluations were greater in the teaching and research institutions. By the same token, these places were also likely to have better trained, and more experienced CCU personnel, which would result in better outcomes than reported in the non-frontier hospitals. An ideological source of bias may also be seen in the fact that most of the studies that claimed an advantage for CCUs were from U.S. institutions, while those who claimed equal or superior results from alternatives to CCU care were from institutions in England and Australia, where the commitment to hospitalization is not so strong.

Articles that did not focus on CCUs directly can be seen as contributing to the general acceptance of this approach to the care of CHD because the mainstays of CCU care—monitors and defibrillators—were always in evidence in the background. Their presence in the frequent stories of famous patients or famous surgeons in *Reader's Digest* reinforced an image of electronic technology as the norm for competent medical care.

As early as 1962, a *Reader's Digest* piece on "The Man Who Wasn't Allowed to Die" introduced readers to the twins of CCU care:

> His ordeal was not yet over. Twice more within an hour Welsh went into fibrillation and with the aid of the electric defibrillator came back again.[55]

> Minute by minute he watched the greenish light flick across the screen of the cardioscope. The heartbeat began to skip around, and he stepped up the dosage to 400 mg.[56]

Once the race to become the premier specialist in the fine art of heart transplantation was in full swing, readers of *Ladies Home Journal* and *Reader's Digest* had even more examples from which to choose. In 1969, *Reader's Digest* published an article with the incredible title—"The Tragic Shortage of Transplant Hearts," which took the opportunity to give some much-needed publicity to Houston's Dr. Cooley and his artificial heart. Cooley had "demonstrated what could only be done by ultimate trial on a human—that in an emergency an artificial heart *could* preserve human life for at least 60 hours."[57] The year 1972 saw Cooley's competitor for the title of "Supersurgeon," Michael DeBakey given the celebrity treatment in a piece on "A Day in the Life of a Heart Surgeon." In the midst of a description of open heart surgery, the author takes time out to give yet another plug to the DeBakey medical empire:

> On a console beneath the oxygenator are the controls that regulate three DeBakey-designed pumps, the unique mechanical muscle that will substitute for Mrs. Kelley's heart when it must be stilled for the surgeon's knife.[58]

The dramatic scene comes to an end with DeBakey positioning two defibrillating paddles to shock the patient's heart back into normal rhythm.

The federal bureaucracy was itself the source of much of the promotional material included in the approximately 470 articles discussing CHD in *Reader's Digest, Time,* and *Ladies Home Journal* between 1959 and 1974.[59] In September of 1963, *Time* devoted a spread to the inauguration of a new surgical suite at the NIH clinical center. The operating wing, priced at more than $2 million, was described as giving "both surgeons and patients the greatest possible benefits from advances in technology." Center officials, careful to note that the center represented the state of the art in medical as well as instructional technology, were also careful to note that "this setup will be out of date tomorrow."[60] This attempt to make the public aware of the need for continuing its high level of support for biomedical research and development was part of the effort by the NIH to strengthen its hand within the congressional budgetary process. While the NIH had been inordinately successful in boosting its budget from $213 million in 1957 to over $930 million in 1963, they were also coming under increasing pressure from Congress to provide evidence of rational budgetary policy.

Because they chose to take the indirect route to Congress through the grass roots, rather than responding directly to the inquiries of North Carolina's L.H. Fountain, Daniel Greenberg[61] suggests that the NIH may have brought about the dramatic leveling off of federal support in fiscal 1964 and 1965.

All of these efforts to influence the public consciousness about CHD—its incidence, its probable victims, surgery as the penultimate solution, and the electronic-based CCU as the technical norm—contributed to the climate of acceptance that led to the duplication of such facilities. While it cannot be proved, what we know about the power of media coverage to increase the salience of issues, to increase the knowledge of the availability of selected technical options, and to legitimate those options that repeatedly appear in the spotlight, suggests that this impression is correct.

CAT FEVER AND MEDICAL TECHNOLOGY

Although the CCU itself was rarely the primary focus of articles on health care or medicine, such was not the case with the CAT scanner. Anyone who spent any time at all with the popular mass media would have seen one or more representations of the computer-generated images of brain tissue or other internal organs. CAT, for computed-axial-tomography, is the name of the most widely known, and at the same time, one of the most controversial of the new, inordinately expensive medical devices that have diffused throughout the U.S. health care system in recent years.

Working originally on the development of computer algorithms for the recognition of patterns in the written word, G.N. Hounsfield began development work at EMI, Ltd. that was to revolutionize radiology and the practice of medical diagnosis.[62] Hounsfield's device measured the rate of attenuation of X rays as they passed through material of varying densities. With the aid of a computer program, a cross-sectional representation of the varying densities of the material could be produced for interpretation. With encouragement from the British Department of Health in 1970, a prototype scanner for clinical use was built and installed at the Atkinson Morley Hospital. There, J. Ambrose used the scanner to examine a patient under his care who was suspected of having a brain tumor. That suspicion was confirmed by the scanner. Ambrose and Hounsfield presented the results of their efforts at the 1972 meeting of the British Institute of Radiology, and, as they say, the rest is history.

EMI, Ltd. offered the device for sale in 1973, and major centers like the Mayo Clinic, Massachusetts General Hospital, and the George Washington University Medical Center rushed to be the first to put the machine through its paces. By 1974, a growing list of competitors emerged on the scene. By the end of 1975, some 20 firms were said to be developing scanners, with early entrants—EMI, Pfizer, and Ohio Scientific—commanding the greatest share of the market.[63]

Despite the fact that the devices cost between $350–800,000 each, there were always more orders than there were available machines to fill them. With some 1,200 scanners installed in the U.S. by 1977, there were hundreds of orders for machines that were at the time little more than engineering prototypes. This pattern of frenzied, seemingly irrational behavior on the part of normally conservative radiologists was described by Stuart Shapiro and Stanley Wyman as "CAT Fever"—a disease that they said was "transmitted largely through self-perpetuating myths."[64]

Although there was little question that the head scanner provided a noninvasive, relatively risk-free alternative to many of the existing techniques, Shapiro and Wyman argued that mass adoption of the technology should await the results of careful cost analysis. Noting the early results of tests at the Mayo Clinic where scans were replacing radionuclide brain scans, echoencephalograms, and pneumoencephalograms, these early critics questioned the quality of those initial studies. Central to their critique was the failure of analysts to distinguish between need and demand for the scans by physicians. Because physicians controlled demand for diagnostic tests, demand for brain scans would expand to meet the capacity of the machine. When the Mayo Clinic added a second machine, its schedule was immediately filled. Thus, evidence of a reduction in the use of other diagnostic devices was no evidence at all.

It soon became clear that the CAT scanner was going to be responsible for a dramatic increase in the cost of medical care. The scanners, like most of new half-way technologies developed in recent times, tended to add to costs because they made possible the provision of *additional* services that were impossible, too risky, or too expensive at the time. In a review of the experience of The George Washington University Medical Center,[65] the authors attributed 93% of a threefold increase in billings for radiologic procedures to the use of the new scanners. The device was like a hammer in the hands of a child; suddenly *everything* needed a little hammering.

Alarmed by the rising costs attributed to the use of the new scanners, Health Systems Agencies (HSAs) and other planning bodies at the state level sought to develop policies to control the spread of CAT fever. One method of control was the "certificate-of-need" requirement established for the purchase of capital equipment by hospitals. These efforts were severely hampered by the absence of any reliable empirical basis upon which to establish the "need" for scanners independently of the physician's and patient's willingness to have them done.

Delays in HSA action in the provision of these certificates resulted in a phenomenon that became known as "fugitive scanners." Teams of doctors would purchase their own scanner, set it up in some office space convenient to the hospital, and then lease it to the hospital. When the reach of the regulators threatened to extend controls to the physicians themselves, creative entrepreneurs emerged with mobile scanners. By this time, however, the market had been largely saturated, control had been concentrated in the hands of defense-electronics firms, and the innovators were already turning their attention to newer, more challenging, and still more expensive devices.

Several factors can be seen to have contributed to this unprecedented diffusion of a costly medical technology. Clearly, the devices represented an improvement in the state of the art of diagnostic radiology. But, it was more than that; it was also clear that the devices represented a tremendous boost in profits to manufacturers, and revenue for the hospitals and medical centers. The fact that the hospitals were able to charge fees so far in excess of their actual costs, may also be seen to be a *result,* rather than a cause of the machines' popularity. Competition between medical researchers and teaching hospital staffs to become the first to report on a new diagnostic use for the scanners also filled an everwidening pool of scientific and technical publications (Figure 5.3).

Initially, traditional channels for the distribution of scientific and technical information were utilized in the early communications about the technology. However, once the devices were made available as commercial products, traditional channels were bypassed in an attempt to gain the economic advantage that legitimization in the pages of *The New York Times (Times)* or *The Wall Street Journal (Journal)* could bring.

In October 1973, information subsidies for the purpose of self-promotion succeeded in gaining coverage in the *Times*.[66] Scientists at Georgetown University announced that they had developed a scanner that was more advanced than that offered by EMI because theirs would be able to scan the entire body and produce color images of the internal organs being scanned. While the *Times* was the first to cover the technology at any length in its report of the ACTA (Automatic Computerized Transverse Axial Tomographic Scanner) scanner's development, the *Journal* had twice as many articles focused primarily on the scanners or the firms offering them in the American market.

None of the articles in the *Journal* could be described as the result of investigative journalism. Many had their basis in the annual meetings of scientific societies, and several were largely dependent upon press releases by manufacturers of the technology.

Whereas the *Journal* carried a report in advance of the 1977 meeting of the Radiological Society of North America based on the pre-conference announcements of new devices from Ohio Nuclear and EMI,[67] the *Times* carried a post-conference feature that focused on government restrictions on the market.[68] The headline, "The Government Puts a Damper on the Scanner," was reinforced

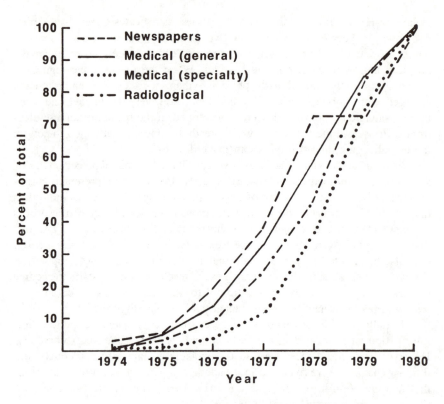

5.3 Distribution of Articles on Computed Tomography in Four Media Channels

with a photograph of a scanner with the legend: "HEW, seeking to pare medical costs, pursues a diagnostic instrument."

Contrary to the expectations of Pfund and Hofstadter,[69] the business periodical did not lead the way in providing its readers with information about such threats to the market. *Times* stories focused on the costs of care as early as October 1975 in their reference to the potential of the devices for raising medical costs.[70] Although it was included in the last paragraph of a lengthy feature story complete with diagrams and pictures of a chest scan, the cautionary note was clear. The *Journal's* first mention of cost considerations came at the end of a front-page feature by Jonathan Spivak on "Super X rays."[71] This December 1975 article described the technology through the eyes of a patient whose life had been saved, and through the comments of numerous radiologists from around the country conveniently gathered in one place.

Many of the pieces in the *Times* and in the *Journal* were based on items originally published in medical journals like the *Journal of the American Medical Association* or the *New England Journal of Medicine*. Occasionally, reporters would follow up with telephone interviews of the authors of those pieces, but generally, their quotes would be drawn directly from the text.

The *Times* and the *Journal* differed however, in their reliance on government and corporate sources. The *Times* was much more likely to include comments by government policy makers, and gave more ready coverage to reports generated by government agencies or related bureaucratic sources. The *Times* gave detailed coverage to the report of the Institute of Medicine's[72] study of the costs of CAT scans. The report was ignored by the *Journal*. This study by the National Academy of Sciences was initiated at the request of Blue Cross, concerned not only about the rising costs of scanner use, but by the installation of such devices in doctors offices and in mobile vans. The report, released in the context of a high-level press conference, recommended that "scanners should be used for diagnoses in doctor's offices and other non-hospital facilities only when placement in a full-service hospital is impractical."

While the *Journal* ignored the Blue Cross-generated report, both papers gave extensive, same-day coverage to a study commissioned by a subsidiary of EMI.[73] Because of the lack of clear guidelines for determining the need for or the relative cost-effectiveness of scanning technology, EMI invested $100,000 in a study of radiological expenditures in nine medical centers. In both cases, the papers reported findings of potential savings in excess of $880 million a year on the basis of comments by an EMI spokesman. Careful reading of the articles would reveal that even though they were printed under the signatures of well-known science writers, neither writer had actually seen the report. Lawrence Altman of the *Times* credited the EMI source as suggesting that:

> the study had been undertaken to counter charges from consumer groups, some doctors and other health care experts who have cited the scanners as a leading example of costly, unproved medical technology that was causing health care costs to soar.[74]

The *Journal* and the *Times* differed as well in their treatment of the controversy in the editorial pages. The *Journal* took the first swipe at government regulators with an editorial in August of 1979.[75] After describing the attempts by government to bring the technology under control as another example of excessive government regulation and the "politicization of medical care," the piece concluded that something was seriously wrong with a system when coercive government agencies lead doctors to resort to "fugitive scanners." *Times* editorials were held off until developers of the technology were awarded the Nobel Prize in October of the same year. The *Times* editorial[76] presented the contradiction represented by a prize-winning technology and government efforts to restrict its proliferation, as a riddle worthy of its own Nobel Prize. Two days later, in an editorial aside, the *Journal* held up the prize as proof of the correctness of medical industry decisions:

> Now let's see the planners explain to us why some communities ready to pay for a scanner shouldn't be allowed to provide one for their citizens.[77]

Overall, the *Times* must be seen as providing the most comprehensive coverage of the technology and the controversy surrounding it. Both papers were heavily dependent upon conferences, conventions, press conferences, and other heavily subsidized channels for information about medical technology. Because of its well-established links with the official bureaucracy, the *Times* was seen as the best route for the delivery of the governmental perspective on cost-containment. The *Journal's* coverage, by and large, was limited to the promotional efforts of companies wishing to announce new models, or of medical centers, hoping to maintain their position in the race to be number one. Occasionally, the *Journal* was the channel through which "coincidence" erased the invisible line between corporate and academic self-promotion.[78]

The articles in the *Times* and the *Journal* must be seen as representing only a select, highly specialized sample of the information available to the general public about CAT scanners and the policy questions they represent. Manufacturers organized their own public relations campaigns aimed at policy makers and the public, and, as we have discovered, periodicals like *Reader's Digest* are much less cautious in their use of such heavily subsidized material for their health-related features.

One approach, which appeared even in a number of *Times* and *Journal* pieces, involves telling the story of an individual whose life was saved because of the avilability of a scanner, or another, whose life was threatened because their hospital had been denied the device by the planning board. The human-interest approach common to *Reader's Digest* makes it difficult for the reader to accept the call for rationality issued by government and insurance agencies as anything other than useless meddling, or heartless materialism.

While the CAT scanner may be fading from prominence in the agendas of the public media, the issue of high-cost medical technology is far from resolved. Reasoned public discussion of the economic, legal, and ethical considerations involved cannot take place when the information channels are clogged with so much interest-laden content. Science writers have a responsibility to their readers to occasionally break away from "the inner circle," to venture out on their own to ensure that the perspectives they offer for our consideration have not been narrowed by the practice of convenience journalism.

CHAPTER FIVE FOOTNOTES

[1] Rich, Spencer. (1981). Medical costs up 15.2% in '80: hit $247 billion. *The Washington Post* (October 30), A1.

[2] Davis, Karen. (1975). "National Health Insurance," pp. 155–157. Washington, D.C.: The Brookings Institution.

[3] Fuchs, Victor. (1974). "Who Shall Live?" New York: Basic Books.

[4] U.S. Department of Health Education and Welfare, Social Security Administration. (1975). "Medical Care Expenditures, Prices, and Costs: Background Book," p. 14. Washington, D.C.: U.S. Government Printing Office.

[5] Ehrenreich, Barbara, and Ehrenreich, John. (1971). "The American Health Empire," pp. 34 ff. New York: Vintage Books.

[6] Stevens, Rosemary. (1971). "American Medicine and the Public Interest," p. 300. New Haven, Connecticut: Yale University Press.

[7] Silverman, Milton, and Lee, Philip. (1974). "Pills, Profits and Politics," p. 77. Berkeley, California: University of California Press.

[8] *Ibid.*, p. 253.

[9] Sandman, Peter M. (1976). Medicine and mass communications: an agenda for physicians. *Annals of Internal Medicine 85,* 378–383.

[10] *Ibid.,* p. 380.

[11] *Ibid.*

[12] Wright, W. Russell. (1975). Mass media as sources of information. *Journal of Communication 25* (No. 3) (Summer), 171–173.

[13] Bishop, Robert L. (1974). Anxiety and readership of health information. *Journalism Quarterly 51* (No. 1) (Spring), 40–46.

[14] National Analysts, Inc. (1972). "A Study of Health Practices and Opinions." Philadelphia, Pennsylvania: National Analysts, Inc.

[15] General Mills, Inc. The General Mills American Family Report 1978–79: Family Health in an Era of Stress. Cited in Gerbner, George, Morgan, Michael, and Signorielli, Nancy. (1981). "Programming health portrayals: what viewers see, say and do." (Paper prepared for "Television and Behavior: Ten Years of Scientific Progress and Implications for the 80's," the National Institute of Mental Health update of the original report of the Surgeon General's Scientific Advisory Committee on Television and Social Behavior).

[16] Wildavsky, Aaron. (1977). Doing better and feeling worse: the political pathology of health policy. *Daedalus 106* (No. 1) (Winter), 105–124.

[17] Thomas, Lewis. (1977). On the science and technology of medicine. *Daedalus 106* (No. 1) (Winter), 43.

[18] Bennett, Ivan. (1977). Technology as a shaping force. *Daedalus 106* (No. 1) (Winter), 125–133.

[19] Sandman, Peter. Page 581 in footnote 9, 1976.

[20] See McLaughlin, James. (1975) "Characters and Symbolic Functions of Fictional Televised Medical Professionals and Their Effect on Children." Master's thesis, University of Pennsylvania.

[21] Gerbner, George, Morgan, Michael, and Signorielli, Nancy. (1981). "Programming health portrayals: what viewers see, say and do." (Paper prepared for "Television and Behavior: Ten Years of Scientific Progress and Implications for the 80's," the National Institute of Mental Health update of the original report of the Surgeon General's Scientific Advisory Committee on Television and Social Behavior).

[22] Sorenson, J.S., and Sorenson, D.D. (1973). A comparison of science content in magazines in 1964–65, and 1969–70. *Journalism Quarterly 50* (Spring), 97–101.

[23] Fisher, June, Gandy, Oscar, and Janus, Noreen. (1981). The role of popular media in defining sickness and health. *In* E. McAnany, J. Schmitman, and N. Janus (Eds.), "Communication and Social Structure," pp. 240–262. New York: Praeger Publishers.

[24] Pfund, Nancy, and Hofstadter, Laura. (1981). Biomedical innovation and the press. *Journal of Communication 31* (No. 2) (Spring), 142.

[25] *Ibid.*

[26] Krieghbaum, Hillier. (1967). "Science and the Mass Media," p. 100. New York: New York University Press.

[27] Walum, Laurel R. (1975). Sociology and the mass media: some major problems and modest proposals. *The American Sociologist 10* (February), 28–32.

[28] Pfund, Nancy, and Hofstadter, Laura. Page 148 in footnote 24, 1981.

[29] Rubin, David M., and Hendy, Val. (1977). Swine influenza and the news media. *Annals of Internal Medicine 87,* 773.

[30] Cole, Bruce J. (1975). Trends in science and conflict coverage in four metropolitan newspapers. *Journalism Quarterly 52* (No. 3) (Autumn), 465–471.

[31] Dunwoody, Sharon. (1980). The Science Writing Inner Club: A Communication Link Between Science and the Lay Public. *Science, Technology and Human Values 5* (No. 30), 14–22.

[32] Gandy, Oscar. (1979). On the use of qualifiers in medical headlines. *The Encoder 6* (No. 2) (Winter), 19–24.

[33] Page, Irving. (1970). Science writers, physicians, and the public—a ménage à trois. *Annals of Internal Medicine 73,* 641–647.

[34] Gerbner, George, Morgan, Michael, and Signorelli, Nancy. Pages 3–5 in footnote 21, 1981.

[35] Cooney, John E. (1977). If the TV script needs a medical checkup, a doctor is on call. *The Wall Street Journal* (November 8), 1 ff.

[36] Gerbner, George, Morgan, Michael, and Signorelli, Nancy. Page 9 in footnote 21, 1981.

[37] Thomas, Lewis. Pages 43–44 in footnote 17, 1977.

[38] Rettig, Richard. (1977). "Cancer Crusade." Princeton, New Jersey: Princeton University Press.

[39] Demkovich, Linda. (1980). Health report. *National Journal* (February 16), 276–280.

[40] Rettig, Richard. Page 24 in footnote 38, 1977.

[41] *Ibid.,* p. 74.

[42] *Ibid.,* p. 165.

[43] *Ibid.,* p. 176.

[44] *Ibid.,* p. 291.

[45] Greenberg, Daniel S., and Randal, Judith E. (1977). Waging the wrong war on cancer. *The Washington Post* (May 1), C1.

[46] *Ibid.*

[47] Thomas, Lewis. Page 38 in footnote 17, 1977.

[48] Russell, Louise B. (1977). The diffusion of hospital technologies: some econometric evidence. *Journal of Human Resources 12* (No. 4), 482–501.

[49] Fox, Samuel M. (1966). Why develop coronary care units? "Proceedings of the Conference on the Impact of a Coronary Care Unit on Hospital, Medical Practice and Community." U.S. Department of Health, Education and Welfare: Heart Disease Control Program. The conference was cosponsored by DHEW and the New York Heart Association.

[50] *Ibid.,* p. 4.

[51] Langewiesche, Wolfgang. (1964). ICU—the latest thing in nursing. *Reader's Digest* (November), 208–214.

[52] *Ibid.,* p. 213.

[53] Deutch, Ron, and Deutch, Patricia. (1966). These hearts need not die. *Reader's Digest* (June), 181–184.

[54] Rockwell, M. (1969). "A Summary of Coronary Care Unit Literature." Santa Monica, California: The Rand Corporation.

[55] Blank, Joseph P. (1962). The man who wasn't allowed to die. *Reader's Digest* (August), 104.

[56] *Ibid.,* p. 105.

[57] Maisel, Albert Q. (1969). The shortage of transplant hearts. *Readers Digest* (August), 73.

[58] Schanche, Don A. (1973). For failing hearts—atomic power. *Readers Digest* (May), 58.

[59] Fisher, June, Gandy, Oscar, and Janus, Noreene. Footnote 23, 1981.

[60] Operating room in the round (quoting NIH director James Shannon). (1963). *Time* (September 13), 85.

[61] Greenberg, Daniel S. (1967). "The Politics of Pure Science," pp. 272–280. New York: The New American Library.

[62] Ambrose, J. (1975). A brief review of the EMI scanner. Abstract, Proceedings of the British Institute of Radiology. *British Journal of Radiology 48*, 605–606.

[63] Banta, David H., and Sanes, Joshua R. (1978). How the CAT got out of the bag. *In* Egdahl and P. Gertman (Eds.), "Technology and the Quality of Health Care." Germantown, Maryland: Aspen Systems Group.

[64] Shapiro, Stuart, and Wyman, Stanley. (1976). CAT fever. *New England Journal of Medicine 294* (April 22), 955.

[65] Knaus, William A., Schrouder, Steven, and Davis, David. (1977). Impact of new technology: the CT scanner. *Medical Care 15* (No. 7) (July), 533–542.

[66] Schmeck, Harry M., Jr. (1973). New cross section x-rays insure high precision. *The New York Times* (October 10).

[67] Technicare, EMI unit announce new models of CT scanner systems. *The Wall Street Journal* (November 22).

[68] Schwartz, Harry. (1977). The government puts a damper on the scanner bonanza. *The New York Times* (December 18), F3.

[69] Pfund, Nancy, and Hofstadter, Laura. Pages 151–152 in footnote 24, 1981.

[70] Brody, Jane. (1975). 3-Dimensional x-ray is tested for new view of body. *The New York Times* (October 22), 89.

[71] Spivak, Jonathan. (1975). A glamour machine is hailed by doctors as a boon to diagnosis. *The Wall Street Journal* (December 10), 1 ff.

[72] Schmeck, Harold M., Jr. (1977). Experts urge controls on device that takes cross-section x-ray. *The New York Times* (May 3), 28.

[73] Bishop, Jerry. (1977). Maker of computerized x-ray scanner says they sharply cut diagnostic costs. *The Wall Street Journal* (July 26), also, Altman, Lawrence K. (1977). Manufacturer says a study shows x-ray scanner can reduce costs. *The New York Times* (July 26), 27.

[74] Altman, Lawrence. Footnote 73, 1977.

[75] Fugitive scanners (editorial). (1979). *The Wall Street Journal* (August 29), 12.

[76] The riddle of the Nobel scanner (editorial). (1979). *The New York Times* (October 15), A18.

[77] Prize for the CAT (editorial aside). (1979). *The Wall Street Journal* (October 17).

[78] Bishop, Jerry. (1977). New x-ray device gives clear picture of beating heart. *The Wall Street Journal* (March 11). The article notes the presentation of research by a Stanford researcher using a high-speed Varian scanner. The report of the Las Vegas conference noted the "co-incidental" nature of a Palo Alto announcement the day before by Varian that an even faster scanner was soon to be made available.

6

The Information Subsidy in Education

The explosion in military expenditures in the early days of the Reagan administration, accompanied by a dramatic reduction in social expenditures may be seen as a final recognition of the truths proposed by Michael Reich in 1973. Reich argued that the U.S. economy was dependent upon military expenditures for continued growth. He disputed those who argued at the time it was possible for social welfare expenditures to replace the defense budget as the principal alternative to increased private aggregate demand in advanced capitalist economies.

> Massive social expenditures would tend to undermine profitability in many sectors of the private economy, remove potential areas of profitmaking, interfere with work incentives in the labor market, and weaken the basic ideological premise of capitalism that social welfare is maximized by giving primary responsibility for the production of goods and services to profit-motivated private enterprises. In short, military spending is much more consistent than is social-services spending with the maintenance and reproduction of the basic social relations of capitalism.[1]

As Reich saw it, social-service expenditures simply did not provide enough opportunities for both profitable and wasteful expenditures. Unlike ships, planes, and rockets, which become rapidly obsolete, investments in facilities for social service (like schools) are generally quite durable, less readily scrapped in favor of a more modern design. Expansion in the social-service sector was seen to be severely constrained by its visibility. Obvious waste in the construction of educational facilities would risk scandals and growing resistance to increased expenditures at the local level. Additionally, he felt that the technology of social services were not "exotic" enough to attract the high-technology firms into the industry.

As we have seen, the health care industry seems to have overcome many of the shortcomings of most social-service expenditures. Its technology is clearly exotic, it has attracted investment by some of the giants of the defense-electronics industry, and it has allowed the private sector to retain control over the production of its goods and services. The attempt to transform the educational sector in a similar fashion can be seen largely to have failed.

This chapter will examine an attempt to transform the educational sector by creating a market for instructional technology that would allow for continued expansion of the defense-electronics industry into non-military markets.[2] To accomplish this transformation, several different requirements had to be met. First, the establishment of an attractive new market required some means to ensure that a sufficiently large population of future consumers had the opportunity to utilize the product under favorable conditions of purchase—either free, or at greatly reduced prices. Second, a committed cadre of advocates, whose own professional interests and fortunes would be served by future product sales, had to be established within the community of potential customers. Third, a program of research and development had to be organized if the new market was not to become prematurely saturated, but instead was provided with a stream of "new and improved" devices and materials. Fourth, a promotional, or market-development campaign had to be established, which would inform consumers of new products and uses. Finally, major firms in the defense industry had to be convinced that this new market held sufficient promise to justify their involvement.

In the pages that follow, we will review the technologies that were adapted for use in education, the defense-electronics firms that entered the field, and the federal programs that helped to finance the purchases and promote their use throughout the world. We then examine the role of information subsidies provided by elected officials, bureaucrats, and representatives of technology producers in establishing the financial and ideological basis upon which this policy was built, and finally abandoned.

INSTRUCTIONAL TECHNOLOGY

In comparison with the highly organized, competitive, R&D effort to extend the frontiers in military technology, the R&D effort in education may be characterized as adaptive scavengery. Very little in the way of capital equipment was developed specifically for use in education. Instead, the educational technology market developed around a variety of devices developed initially for the military or consumer market, and were then modified for use in the classroom.

Motion pictures have had a place in U.S. education almost from the moment of their invention, although films made specifically for instructional purposes were the exception, rather than the rule, until World War II. The 16mm format, generally considered substandard, and not suitable for theatrical projection, became an educational standard after its improvement as part of the war effort. During World War II, 16mm film was used for combat photography, training, and even for screening of copies of theatrical films for the entertainment of enlisted men and women. The Army drafted and commissioned Hollywood actors, producers, directors, and technicians, converted commercial studios for instructional use, and, when necessary, contracted with commercial studios for other instructional films. Charles Hoban reports that between 1943 and 1945 there were more than 4.2 million separate film screenings for soldiers and civilian employees of the Army.[3] The military effort was joined by a smaller scale effort on the part of the education community through the Division of Visual Aids for War Training in the U.S. Office of Education (OE). Here, under the direction of Floyde Booker, the OE produced some 457 sound films to be used in the training of the industrial work force in 1941.[4]

The popularity of the motion picture for instructional uses increased steadily in the postwar period, and its role in the instructional process has not been diminished by the introduction of new instructional devices.

The *filmstrip,* like the 16mm instructional film, was also developed extensively as an aid to the war effort. Although not used as widely as the motion picture, Charles Hoban suggests that the use of the filmstrip in conjunction with special reading materials to train many of the newly drafted but "functionally illiterate" soldiers was probably one of the Army's most valuable contributions to the educational method.[5]

The *overhead projector,* developed by the Bessler corporation under contract to the Navy in 1942, was the only instructional device developed specifically for instructional use. The terms of the contract specified the need for a device that would allow an instructor to project a large, bright image, while still facing the class.[6]

As with the film media, *electronic video technology* was developed for commercial rather than instructional applications. Also, like film, the educational uses of the technology were first explored by researchers in the armed forces. Howard Hitchens reports that the Army and Navy began experimenting with the instructional uses of television as early as 1949. Shortly thereafter, they improved on the techniques available for making films from television images.[7] It was not until some three years after video technology had advanced into the area of color that civilian groups began to explore the instructional uses of television. Educational television came to Hagerstown, Maryland in 1956 with the assistance of the Ford Foundation and the Electronics Industries Association.[8] This and other demonstrations of the feasibility of televised instruction may have done much to stimulate the use of video technology in the schools, although it is more likely that improvements in the technology itself, in pursuit of the consumer market, had the greatest impact on the adoption of the technology by educators.

The *tape recorder,* also developed initially for military use, and adapted for commercial and educational markets, played an important role in language instruction in World War II. According to Paul Saettler:

> Sound recordings were produced in forty languages in the Navy language laboratories, together with accompanying texts containing the romanized transcriptions, and translations. These intensive language training programs developed in the armed services during World War II provided the principal impetus for the development of language laboratories in the postwar years.[9]

Teaching machines, developed to make use of programmed instructional material as a form of mediated self-instruction, have a similar military history. Hitchens credits the Air Force, and the research laboratories it established in the 1940s with providing an important stimulus to the programmed learning movement. Important researchers in the field like "Gagne, Lumsdaine, Crowder, Evans, Homme and Glaser worked in these laboratories. Much of their best thinking and many of their greatest contributions to the programmed learning movement came during their tenure in the Air Force."[10]

The auto-instructional systems provided for (1) individual use; (2) presentation of the material in steps; (3) recording of student response; and (4) response-to-learner decisions, which could serve as reinforcement. The more sophisticated machines could: (1) provide random access and branching; (2) select additional material on the basis of prior learner performance; and (3) provide for interactive communication between machine and learner.[11] While very few of the teaching machines offered by defense-electronics firms in 1962 remain on the market today, the basic instructional paradigm has been incorporated into computer-based systems.

Computer-based instruction includes: (1) computer-assisted instruction (CAI), which uses the computer to present program material for drill, practice, tutorial instruction, and dialogue; (2) computer-developed instruction (CDI), which uses a computer to assist in the design and production of program materials, but does not involve direct learner/computer interaction; (3) simulation, in which the learner interacts with a mathematical model of process, or set of relations as a heuristic aid to learning; and (4) computer-managed instruction (CMI), which uses a computer to regulate student progress and to provide information to the instructor to facilitate tailoring of exercises to suit individual needs.[12]

Of course, the computer had a strong military heritage as well. The development of the computer as a calculating device and the elevation of IBM into a position of leadership in the industry were largely dependent upon the demands of war, and Tom Watson's skill at capturing government contracts. Watson's machines had done government bookkeeping work during the New Deal period, but it was World War II that "propelled the company into really big business with sales leaping from $63 million in 1941 to nearly $142 million in the last year of the war.''[13]

Other computer developments of that time, including what was to become the Sperry-Rand UNIVAC, were similarly focused on the military effort. Even the concept of a stored program core memory, developed by John Von Neumann, was driven by a need to speed the calculations necessary for the development of the atomic bomb by the Los Alamos Manhattan Project team.[14]

In the postwar years, the Department of Defense (DOD) continued to be the primary source of R&D on the instructional uses of the computer.

Early instructional systems, developed with support from the DOD and the National Science Foundation (NSF) were based on a concept of shared use of a large, centralized computer, connected with remote users by phone lines. The PLATO system, developed by the University of Illinois, made use of the greatest number of design features developed specifically for education. However, the TICCIT system, developed by the MITRE corporation, was based on newer, self-contained minicomputers, which provided greater potential for obsolescence, and the requirement for periodic replacement or modification of existing systems on a school-by-school basis.[15]

Electronic distribution systems, including broadcast television, closed circuit television (CCTV), and satellite distribution systems, complete the general classes of instructional technologies appropriate to the creation of a capital equipment market in education.

DEFENSE-ELECTRONICS FIRMS AND THE EDUCATION MARKET

While some of the defense-electronics firms like TRW had been involved in the instructional technology business from its shaky beginnings, most firms entered the field with enthusiasm following the passage of the Elementary and Secondary Education Act (ESEA) in 1965. Many of these new entrants sought to establish a foothold in this promising market through an aggressive program of acquisitions. David Loehwing reports that between 1965 and 1966, there were ''no less than 120 mergers and combines set up to exploit the education market.''[16] In addition to their efforts to acquire expertise through the purchase of educational publishers and other producers of instructional software and low technology delivery systems, many of the defense-electronics firms enticed stars from the government's education bureaucracy through the ''revolving door'' in the hopes that what worked with the DOD would work with the OE just as well.

Among the defense-electronics firms that became active in the instructional technology business, *Raytheon* was probably the most dependent upon defense contracts for its livelihood. Ranked 14th among prime defense contractors between 1960 and 1967,[17] Raytheon was dependent upon government contracts for more than 83% of its income at the time of ESEA.[18] With the brakes being put on defense expenditures in 1964, Raytheon began looking to diversify. In two years, the company invested more than $46 million in an effort to penetrate the education market. It acquired the Dage-Bell Corporation—a manufacturer of instructional television and language laboratory equipment from TRW in 1964. Acquisitions of the Edex Corporation and Macalaster Scientific were capped off with a purchase of D.C. Heath for $40.3 million in 1966. Heath was ninth in sales in an industry composed of more than 100 educational publishers, and was developing a line of audiovisual software. Market analysts at that time seemed to share Raytheon's enthusiasm for the education market:

> One of the relatively untapped business areas is equipment for educational laboratories. The education field is expected to grow at a present rate of $1 billion annually to over $3 billion by 1975. Raytheon's entry into this area via acquisitions has placed the company in an excellent position to share in its growth potentials.[19]

Raytheon's new Education Division did quite well, generating more than $30 million in first-year sales. This new division was headed by Edward L. Katzenback, who came to Raytheon after serving as Deputy Assistant Secretary of Defense for Education.[20] By 1969, however, federal support for instructional technology was being withdrawn, and Raytheon hastily made plans to move back into more dependable markets.

The *Westinghouse Electric Corporation,* considerably more diversified than Raytheon by 1964, took a different approach into the education market, and was relatively more successful as a result. Although Westinghouse was 17th on the list of prime contractors to the DOD, only 13% of its sales between 1960 and 1967 were to the DOD.[21] Rather than following the acquisition path to the market, Westinghouse sought to build its own internal capacity through the development of the Westinghouse Learning Corporation (WLC) with a $12 million base in 1967.

From the beginning, the WLC focused its approach to education on software. The corporation's Central Research Laboratories in Pittsburgh had already developed a CAI system by 1964. Performance contracting by the WLC represented a significant departure from the activities of other defense-electronics firms, but its computer-managed system eventually became profitable in 1972, after many other defense firms had turned their backs on education.[22]

General Electric and Time, Inc. came together to form the *General Learning Corporation* (GLC) in January 1966. Capitalized with more than $37.5 million, the GLC was directed at first by the former head of GE's Defense Programs Division, and later by Francis Keppel, former Commissioner of Education. The firm was only "modestly profitable"[23] until its sale to Scott, Foresman and Company in 1974.

The *RCA Corporation,* also a major defense firm, which was ranked 19th on Seymour Melman's list of prime contractors, acquired Random House in

1966 to add to its not insignificant resources in instructional hardware. Although RCA eventually gave up on their entire computer effort, the Random House Educational Media Division was able to achieve some measure of success in the audiovisual market.[24]

Although the *Bell and Howell* (B&H) Company was never a major defense contractor, defense contracts provided a substantial part of its income. In 1961, defense contracts made up 23% of its business, and into the mid-seventies such government business accounted for between 12 and 16% of total annual sales.[25] The firm was one of the original suppliers of instructional technology to the military. In 1932 B&H introduced a 16mm sound projector (the JAN, for joint-Army-Navy), which was suitable for instructional use. In 1964, it entered the teaching-machine field with its *Language Master* and a companion filmstrip projector.

The links between federal subsidies and industry income is best seen in some of the marked discontinuities in B&H's revenue stream. Following the passage of the National Defense Education Act (NDEA) in 1958, B&H's income rose 186.8%. B&H's earning took another dramatic leap in 1966, following the passage of ESEA. In 1966, earnings increased approximately 50%, and in the next eight years, during which B&H took the education market more seriously, it enjoyed a 204.2% increase in before-tax income.[26] By 1974, B&H considered itself the world leader in "Learning Systems and Materials."[27] Other firms with varying amounts of success in penetrating the education market include IBM, which offered its model 1500 as a computer-based instructional system; TRW, which was one of the pioneers of programmed instructional and language laboratory systems; McGraw-Edison, which developed a "talking-typewriter"; and the Xerox Corporation, whose acquisitions of publishing and information-processing subsidiaries placed it in a strong position to compete in the emerging information-systems markets.

LEGISLATIVE SUPPORT

Several education bills, including Title III of the National Defense Education Act (NDEA), the Educational Broadcasting Facilities Act, and Title VI-A of the Higher Education Act, provided funds specifically for the purchase of instructional technology. Other titles of these bills provided for salaries of instructional media specialists, financed regional media centers, and special institutes for the training of hardware-oriented professionals.

The need for product development was served initially through Title VII of the NDEA, Title III of the Elementary and Secondary Education Act (ESEA), and finally, through the R&D contracts managed through the National Institute of Education (NIE). R&D in education, traditionally the province of the universities and colleges, had been extended through the contract system to include the defense-electronics firms and their "not-for-profit" cousins as increasingly unequal competitors. Products developed in university-related R&D centers under government contract were then integrated into the commercial market through license agreements.

The promotional, information-subsidy effort involved an extension of the R&D responsibilities of participating institutions and firms to include *dissemination*—a euphemistic label for a program that seeks to stimulate the adoption of the products of R&D. Demonstration projects, travelling seminars and junkets, and the publication of handbooks, guides, and evaluation reports were all provided for in the NDEA, ESEA, and NIE enabling legislation.

As the first of the bills explicitly committed to the transformation of U.S. education, the NDEA of 1958 was the most direct in its focus. In order to meet the "crisis" in education underscored by the launch of the Soviet *Sputnik,* the NDEA funds provided for matching grants not to exceed 50% of the expenditures at the state level. Title III of the Act specifically forbade the purchase of textbooks with the NDEA funds.

Title VII of the NDEA was designed primarily to meet the information requirements of the transformation effort. It was the intention of Title VIII's backers that research conducted under contract with the Office of Education (OE) would produce "evidence" to support their contention that "AV was good for education." Part A of the title, concerned with Research and Development, empowered the Commissioner of Education to enter into contracts that foster the development and evaluation of instructional media projects. The approach of the title was not to determine which were the most effective means available for improving science and mathematics instruction, but rather to determine the most effective *capital equipment-based* methods to improve instruction. Furthermore, the R&D effort was directed toward finding uses for existing equipment, rather than developing technology for existing *needs.*

The patterns established under the NDEA titles were reinforced in later legislation. The Elementary and Secondary Education Act (ESEA) provisions brought the effort under more direct federal control. Where local agencies had been allowed some flexibility under the NDEA's guidelines, the ESEA represented a major shift in decision-making power toward the federal bureaucracy. Because the areas of educational innovation covered by Title III of the ESEA were so broad, it is difficult to determine precisely how much of the annual allocations went for the promotion and adoption of capital technologies. Title III was, however, an important source of support for computer-related projects funded by the OE.

Title IV of the ESEA provided for the establishment of a network of regional education laboratories whose principal purpose was the development and dissemination of applications for technologies developed elsewhere in the R&D system.

The NDEA, ESEA, Educational Broadcast Facilities, Higher Education

Act, Corporation for Public Broadcasting, and Ford Foundation monies allocated between 1958 and 1975, which can be clearly identified with the effort to transform U.S. education through the introduction of capital technologies, total more than $4.2 billion.[28]

At the same time that this portfolio of entitlements sought to spur the development of a domestic market, similar legislative efforts lent support to the creation of an export market. It is this foreign market, concentrated in the less-developed and dependent nations, that continues to show the greatest potential for growth in sales of instructional technologies.

The same approach that provides free or discounted equipment, assistance in the development of pro-capital cadres, and diffusion through demonstration projects can be seen to characterize the international marketing strategy.

Educational technology supports in the overseas market had their beginnings with an Information Media Guarantee Program begun in 1948. With the assistance of the U.S. Information Agency (USIA), U.S. publishers were assisted in their efforts to sell materials in countries with nonconvertible currencies. The International Education Act passed in 1966 expanded the role of the U.S. Agency for International Development (USAID). Although the promotion of instructional technology has not been the primary concern of the USAID, through its grants to research centers like the Institute for Communication Research at Stanford University and the Academy for Educational Development, the USAID remains the dominant force in the promotion of high-technology systems for education abroad.

THE EDUCATION MARKET

The impact of the legislative program can be seen in several areas. Increased resources and the special training programs developed to improve the use of instructional materials also contributed to the development of a group of instructional media specialists. Although their numbers were not reported as a separate category by the National Center for Educational Statistics (NCES), they are included in the category of "instructional perrsonnel," which is separate from that of "classroom teacher." Their number per 1,000 students increased from 38.9 in 1955–56, to 49.9 in 1972–73.[29] Measured somewhat differently in a Brookings study, the number of pupils per "other instructional employee" dropped from 325 to 160 between 1959 and 1971.[30]

Average expenditures per student more than kept pace with inflation as a result of the shift in resources from defense into education. Between the 1959–60 and 1971–72 school years, expenditures expressed in terms of 1971–72 purchasing power increased by 88.3%.[31] Although the NCES statistics do not provide any reliable way of estimating what percentage of those expenditures was for instructional technology as we have defined it, the reports of industry observers suggest that it was substantial.

The Hope Reports and the *Education and Media Supplements* provide the best statistical measures of the growth in the instructional technology market. In 1975, a 15-year review of the audiovisual industry (historically linked to the NDEA) concluded that:

> America's schools continue to be the single largest market for audiovisual products in spite of the drop in federal aid over the past two years. In terms of direct dollar expenditures, schools spend more than half a billion annually. When administrative, in-plant production and educational television are added in, the total market is one of $1.2 billion.[32]

Later in that report, it is estimated that between 1959 and 1973, a total of $7.2 billion was spent for instructional media, 24% of which was paid for out of federal funds. Figure 6.1 shows the striking relationship between the sales of audiovisual materials and NDEA and ESEA funds. The dramatic increase in sales following the passage of the ESEA began a trend that continued long after federal support was withdrawn.

Unfortunately, at least for those who hoped for a more complete transformation of the educational production process, most of those sales were for relatively inexpensive, low-technology items. The market for CCTV saw sales volume more than double between 1966 and 1969. By 1974, sales had begun to decline because of a lack of funds at the federal and local levels. The picture for broadcast distribution systems was even more gloomy, with school systems opting for the greater flexibility in small-format video tape.

Growth in the CAI market was also much slower than anticipated. While there was an increase in the use of computers for administrative purposes, instructional use remained quite limited by 1975.[33]

The value of continued federal support for the use of audiovisual devices declined even further as competition from Japan saw the electronics industry transformed in all but the most advanced technologies.[34]

THE INFORMATION SUBSIDY IN EDUCATION

A system of financial and bureaucratic support for the transformation of the educational process does not just happen; it does not spring forth full-blown, or even develop gradually without the assistance of an organized promotional effort. In describing the role and influence of formal and informal participants in this effort, we will pay particular attention to their attempts to influence the policy process by subsidizing the information-gathering activities of other participants.

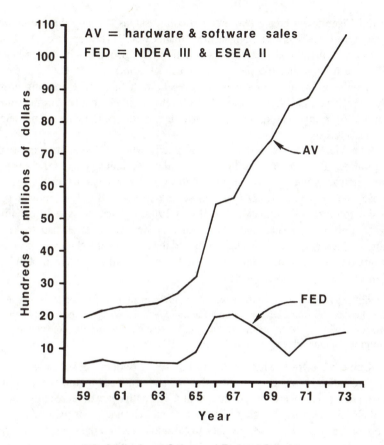

6.1 Audiovisual Sales and Federal Subsidy

THE WHITE HOUSE

As we have noted in Chapter Three, the President and White House staff play a major role in the process at the stage of problem definition and the generation of proposals for its solution. This was not always the case. Prior to the passage of the NDEA in 1958, the responsibility for initiating federal educational programs rested with the Congress, and that body had successfully resisted most presidential efforts to modify its favorite patronage vehicles. Eisenhower made use of the special Presidential Commission or Task Force to take the policy initiative as many would do thereafter. However, Eisenhower's efforts lagged behind the efforts of the scientific technical committee which won public attention through hearings of the Joint Atomic Energy Committee in 1956. Only then did Eisenhower create two national commissions to study the problem of shortages in scientific and engineering "manpower." The report of the Committee on Scientists and Engineers was delivered to Congress in November of 1957—one month after the successful launch of *Sputnik*.

In light of Eisenhower's expressed reservations about the growing power of the "military-industrial complex," it is highly unlikely that he was the source of an approach that would help to finance the capture of the educational sector by these interests.

John McHale suggests that it was Kennedy who first began to explore the possibilities of redirecting the focus of the defense industry toward the social sector. It was Kennedy's expansion of the Eisenhower budget in the area of defense and aerospace R&D that had served to spark the development of a cohesive military-industrial complex. But by 1963, signs of stress in the economy and the policy suggested that growth in defense expenditures had to be restrained.[35] Kennedy and McGovern proposed the creation of a National Economic Conversion Commission, arguing that defense expenditures were robbing the nation of productive investment.

> In his proposals for converting weaponry investment into "peace" growth he invoked all the strategies for the now familiar war on poverty: schools, hospitals, mental health facilities, urban transit systems, recreation, and the conversion of military training sites to vocational colleges.[36]

Kennedy's efforts to further define the "new frontiers" of social investment were forestalled by his assassination, but the shock caused by the event allowed Johnson to move forward even more quickly. The cutback in defense expenditures was dramatic. Defense Secretary McNamara had eliminated or reduced in scale the operations of at least 600 military installations around the country by 1964. Without the benefit of new or renewed defense contracts, unemployment in the industry rose almost immediately. The slack in the economy had to be taken up somewhere, and the War on Poverty was the answer.

Lyndon Johnson took the policy initiative with his domestic battle plans, and established a record of information management not to be matched by any modern president. Johnson made frequent use of advisory commissions and task forces. As many as 12 formal task force reports on education were prepared for Johnson's review,[37] but very few of them were ever made public. It was Johnson's practice to try to achieve consensus prior to introducing a bill, and:

> the secrecy of the task forces was one of their most important operational characteristics. In the eyes of President Johnson and his staff, secrecy was crucial for it enabled them to ignore proposals that were politically infeasible. Recommendations could be adopted or rejected without having to expend political resources defending the choices made.[38]

The most famous of the "secret" Johnson task forces was that headed by John Gardner, then president of the Carnegie Foundation, and later to become

Secretary of HEW. Formed in the summer of 1964, the Gardner Task Force was responsible for much of the philosophy and language that would emerge as the ESEA. James Guthrie suggests that the Task Force did not actually *produce* any innovative ideas, but merely pulled together some of the ideas in currency in intellectual circles.

> In assembling a variety of educational ideas, weaving them together in a coherent fashion, and elevating them to the level of presidential visibility, the Task Force performed a necessary and valuable function.[39]

One function of the task forces was clearly legitimization—providing the president with articulate, highly credible statements of justification for already well-developed policy positions. Still, many of the Task Force's suggestions, such as the establishment of supplementary education centers, and the expansion of the R&D effort through a network of regional laboratories, found their way into the education bill that Johnson eventually sent to Congress.

Nixon, whose educational policy was based in part on a lack of confidence in the educational establishment, simply buried task force reports that were inconsistent with that view. A case in point was the report of the Hester Task Force delivered to Nixon in 1970. Chester Finn reports that because most of its members were college presidents, their natural inclination was to recommend increased federal expenditures.

> Once released, the Hester Report would strengthen the hand of those whose main goal was bigger appropriations and who faulted the administration for spending too little on education. Hence not only was the report ignored . . . it was actually suppressed for a time, not being published by the Government Printing Office until August, long after the Administration's proposals were public.[40]

Of course, ideas that are incorporated in presidential policy initiatives may come from a variety of sources. Where Johnson and Kennedy made regular use of the advisory system, and their dependence upon the expertise of organized client groups was consistent with a policy of expansion, Nixon's policy of retrenchment had to rely on the guidance of a hand-picked White House Staff. The expansion of the Executive Office of the President under Nixon reflects an attempt to bypass a resistant, occasionally hostile bureaucracy with policy advisors whose interests were more closely in line with those of the president. Indeed, special assistants were selected on the basis of their commitment so that they could generate the kind of policy the president would have written, if he had a fully developed interest in that area.

Educational policy development in the Nixon administration was concentrated in the hands of a working group dominated by Daniel Patrick Moynihan, and inspired by the analysis of James Coleman. Coleman's historic analysis of the status of U.S. education had concluded that school resources, including audiovisual media, made little independent contribution to what students actually learned. Thus, there was little justification for pouring additional funds into education without evidence of effectiveness.

Finn's analysis of events leading up to Nixon's Education messages in 1970 and the passage of the Education Amendments in 1972 points to the importance of this internal working group as a selective filter, which screened out ideas and recommendations inconsistent with their dominant policy idea.[41]

The Office of Management and Budget (OMB) had been established as a key policy center long before David Stockman turned the OMB into a household word. As a political appointee, the director has generally had ready access to the president—a link to power that at times exceeded that of many cabinet officers.

> All proposals from the cabinet departments are submitted to OMB for clearance, where they are judged against presidential ideology, and within that context, judged against priorities as expressed in the annual presidential budget.[42]

Harry Summerfield also suggests that the OMB also controls the information flow, serving as an administrative censor, and "strikes out clandestine or inadvertant public statements that could commit the administration to a non-priority course."[43]

Not only was the director of the budget in Johnson's time concerned with stimulating budgetary growth, but on occasion, when money would not be spent quickly enough, the Bureau would insert special incentives into the proposals.[44] On the advice of the budget director and other advisors, the president determines the advisability of applying the veto, impounding funds, or otherwise bringing educational expenditures in line with current fiscal policy.

THE CONGRESS

While several other committees have been influential in the past in generating ideas and approaches to the problems of education and human resources, principal responsibility for the policy adoption phase of the educational policy process rests with the two education committees of the Congress. The House Committee on Education and Labor and the Senate Committee on Labor and Public Welfare have traditionally provided strongly contrasting images of the legislative process. Where committees of the House have tended to be contentious, with struggles to establish a public image as a defender of the public interest, educational policy in the Senate finds less competition between senators for dominance.

Because education is rarely high on the public agenda, it provides few opportunities for senators to gain valuable publicity. Summerfield suggests that education hearings in the Senate are poorly attended, and often the subcommittee chair is the only member in attendance. Beyond an occasionally heated debate between opponents, the meetings are generally friendly, and serve as opportunities for advocates to enter a plea for their particular program, or on behalf of their constituents. These "record-building" hearings occasionally provide the opportunity for the senator to register opposition to an administrative proposal, and an executive-branch bureaucrat may be taken to task as a proxy for the president.[45]

In the House, responsibility for education is divided among three subcommittees, and their chairs are often in competition for control of a particular bill. John Brademas and Edith Green struggled continually over a variety of issues that culminated in her eventual success in reestablishing the power of the states in the control of Title III programs.

In building her assault on the OE, Green began with a broad investigation of the geographic and institutional biases in the OE's use of consultants and advisors. The Bureau of Research used over 200 consultants in the previous year, but 49% came from four states and the District of Columbia. The advisory committees were similarly unrepresentative, in that 25% of the states had no representatives, and 53% of the advisors came from six states.[46] In Green's view, there was a Washington-dominated elite that was making educational policy, and imposing it upon state education agencies.

Whereas Green was focusing her efforts on returning discretion to the states, John Brademas sought to rekindle interest in, and support for, instructional technology. Where Green's subcommittee investigated the shortcomings of the OE, Brademas extended the reach of a commission on educational broadcasting to produce a document supporting all instructional technology. *To Improve Learning* was released in March of 1970, to accompany Brademas' own Educational Technology Act (H.R.-8838).[47]

On occasion, joint committees of the Congress may be seen to play critical roles in defining policy options. As noted previously, the Joint Committee on Atomic Energy sounded the alarm about limitations in "scientific and technical manpower" in 1956, which was to result in the NDEA in 1958. Subcommittee chairman Melvin Price can be credited with starting the "scientist race" with the publication of his study of the comparative supply of engineers in the U.S. and the Soviet Union.

After convincing Clinton Anderson to publish his report as a Joint Committee document, Price was able to call his own subcommittee into hearings the following month, fully mindful of the information subsidy provided by the exercise:

> A major role of this hearing is to develop greater public awareness of this important problem and perhaps to reach some tentative conclusions as to the directions our efforts should take.[48]

It was during these hearings that the first push for instructional technology was heard in the context of educational competition with the Soviet Union. M.H. Trytten of the National Academy of Sciences entered an article into the record written by former Senator William Benton. Then publisher of "Encyclopaedia Britannica," Benton called for a 16mm projector in every U.S. classroom.

Hearings organized in 1966 by the Joint Economic Committee sought to collect information about the status of the education market. The first witnesses called by Wright Patman's Subcommittee on Economic Progress were from "Encyclopaedia Britannica," Xerox, and McGraw-Hill. The witnesses on the next day were from the educational research community, and each was a well-known supporter of instructional technology. On the third day, educational administrators, both inside and outside of the government, were called to help build a record of support. Only the testimony of Norman Kurland, of the New York State Education Department, could be interpreted as raising any serious questions about the capitalization effort. Kurland's concern was that oft-expressed by representative Green, that the state's power was being usurped by the federal government.

When a representative takes the time to attend these meetings, and the slate of witnesses is overwhelmingly in support of some particular policy, the only recourse left to a critic like William Proxmire is to ask a few difficult questions, or make a personal plea.

> It would be tragic if control of curriculum and the content of courses were to pass by default into the hands of large corporate producers in the "hardware" or "software" end of the business. Teaching aids and devices should be developed to meet explicit educational objectives and needs, rather than to broaden markets for particular products.[49]

Although the subcommittee expressed some concern about the shape of the newly developed market, they seemed to have little doubt that it would continue to grow, and require increasing amounts of federal assistance.

ADMINISTRATIVE AGENCIES

The U.S. Office of Education (OE) had primary responsibility for the implementation of federal policy in education, although in the best of times it controlled only 39% of all government expenditures for education.[50] Of course, the OE's power to influence policy was not limited to the implementation stage, as the bureaucracy plays an important role in the formation and adoption of policy as well. The Commissioner of Education and the various bureau chiefs served on presidential task forces and advisory panels, and were called upon on numerous occasions to provide advice and counsel to executive staff and others throughout the HEW bureaucracy.

Outside government, agency officials are frequent speakers at meetings of corporate suppliers of the bureaucracy. As luncheon speakers at meetings of educational publishers, the OE representatives would outline plans for future research efforts, warn executives about expected changes in the education budget, and provide advance warning of changes in bureaucratic orientation, such as Louis Bright's suggestion that the emphasis in the future would be on instructional *systems* rather than supplementary media.[51]

Testimony before congressional committees is an important opportunity for agency representatives to create a sense of confidence about the widespread public and professional support for the agency's mission, and the competence of its administrators to pursue those goals. While the general tendency in appropriations committees has been toward generosity to education, the image of the agency created in those hearings can make the difference between stability and substantial gains in budget obligations. Thomas Wolanin suggests that:

> analysts in the executive branch and postsecondary education are treated with substantial skepticism by congressmen and their staffs . . . to them, analysis is often perceived as an analytical trap . . . . This is particularly true as the questions and analytical techniques become more abstract and are cast in terms of statistical procedures and simulations.[52]

Thus, when a department head fails to tailor the testimony to fit the needs and expectations of the committees, the agency may suffer.

A recent history of the beginnings of the NIE provides numerous examples of the importance of well-planned testimony:

> It is possible that NIE might have fared better had its first director been more of a politician. Glennon was a researcher, and his forays into the political arena, particularly his first budget testimonies were not very successful. His answers to congressional questions were discursive, rather than crisp. His explanations were abstract, practically devoid of examples or anecdotes. And, he did not always have ready answers for specific questions.[53]

To make matters worse for the NIE in its first years, it did not have the same kind of well-staffed public affairs office to handle such key opportunities for information management. The director of the NIE's external affairs unit was a former school administrator with no Washington experience, but he was responsible for congressional liaison as well as press relations. As a result, media channels were devoid of the kinds of favorable publicity that might have served to isolate the NIE from the bad press being heaped on the OE.

While agency representatives are generally sent forward to carry the messages of the administration in power, there are occasions when they may have agendas of their own, or have to mobilize outside pressure to bring professional bureaucrats within their own organization into line. Leon Lessinger, as Associate Commissioner in the Bureau of Elementary and Secondary Education, is cited as an example of just such an end runner in the Nixon administration. Lessinger visited with representatives on both sides of the House and set up a series of tours and speaking engagements ''gradually building grass-roots support for his position.'' When one of his pet projects hit the front page of *The Wall Street Journal,* he won an audience with Moynihan, and many of his ideas ultimately found their way into Nixon's 1969 education messages.[54]

When these bureaucrats have the kind of discretionary funds that allow them extended travel, many choose to provide small grants for demonstrations that are consistent with their policy goals. Summerfield suggests that:

> If a USOE commissioner or the director of NIE "lets it be known" that USOE or NIE is interested in researching a certain idea, many individuals or institutions will offer a proposal to do the work. Thus, an idea favored within USOE or NIE will receive research and public dissemination. *The power to decide what the money will be spent for is the power to encourage particular ideas* (emphasis added).[55]

Within the area of implementation, an agency's influence flows from its control over the issuance of guidelines and regulations for the administration of legislative enactments, and from its control over the contracts for educational R&D. While agency regulations have the status of law, *guidelines* do not, and need not follow any uniform format. Despite the somewhat tenuous basis for the authority of these agency guidelines, students of educational policy would agree that the issuance of guidelines is the primary instrument of policy available to the directors of the various divisions of the OE.

Doris Kearns suggests that it is in the area of guideline preparation that policies that could not be supported openly in the political arena find their way back into the policy structure.[56] Thus a single note in the ESEA legislation offering support for "school library resources" could emerge in the guidelines to include virtually everything available. Where previous guidelines might restrict support for devices for presentation and display, revised guidelines might allow for the purchase of production equipment.

To the extent that the coordination of the research, development, and dissemination activities of the educational community is an important aspect of information management, the contract and grants mechanism under the control of the OE and the NIE may have been more important than either regulations or guidelines. Obligations for R&D controlled by the OE grew from $10 million in 1960 to over $100 million in 1966, and much more slowly thereafter to $175 million in 1976.[57]

INFORMAL POLICY ACTORS

Interest groups outside government enter the educational policy process at all three stages through their well-cultivated access to all of the key DMs. Three Washington-based associations played major roles in the formation, adoption, and implementation of the capitalization policy: The National Audio Visual Association (NAVA), the Association for Educational Communications and Technology (AECT), and the National Security Industrial Association (NSIA).

The NAVA has earned a position of prominence within any analysis of the education-policy process. Their visibility on a variety of education bills of interest to their members is unmatched by any organization of similar size. Until he left the association in 1972, Donald White was their chief "lobbyist," and one of the designers of the federal capitalization policy. Back in 1956, when the discussions in the Capitol were focused on the shortages in scientific expertise, White convinced the Chicago-based association that the time was ripe for the passage of a federal school aid bill. At his insistence, the NAVA financed the establishment of a Washington office, and White moved in.[58]

In addition to organizing important industry witnesses for House committee hearings on the NDEA, White and Hank Rourke, the NAVA's education officer, wrote the draft of Title VII in about half a day. This title actually replaced an original Title X, which favored the use of television to distribute educational materials to schools "free of charge." White not only prevailed with Title VII, but he succeeded in having Title III, which was initially to provide only for scientific laboratory equipment, modified to support the purchase of audiovisual hardware.

When the educational subcommittee was working on the ESEA under the leadership of Adam Clayton Powell, White's friendship with Powell put him in the position to once again provide draft copies of the legislation. In one case, it was the night before the bill was to be reported out of committee that Powell gave White the draft copy to review, and instructed him to make any changes he thought were necessary. White reported that he made at least 28 key changes in the bill that would ensure that audiovisual materials and equipment could be purchased with the ESEA funds.

The AECT in 1975 was an association of between 8,000 and 10,000 members, and was affiliated with the National Education Association. Its executive director was Howard Hitchens, who had come to the AECT after 26 years of service in the Air Force, the last 10 of which were spent as director of instructional media programs for the USAF Academy.

While considered a relatively minor force in the education policy environment, Hitchens was a regular witness at congressional hearings where instructional technology was on the agenda. Hitchens would often come to the hearings armed with slide, filmstrip, or 16mm examples of the kinds of uses to which the technology might be put. The response of committee members was generally positive:

Senator Young: Doctor, I think your showing of the film and your presentation is the best argument I ever heard for having this kind of equipment in the schools. The film on the use of narcotics in itself would well justify the money spent. This has become a serious problem, and to me this film would be more impressive on the students than maybe a half dozen pages.[59]

The AECT, and its predecessor, the Department of Audiovisual Instruction (DAVI) have played an important information role throughout the history of federal aid to education. As a neighbor to the OE, with many members moving back and forth between agency and association through the revolving door, it is suggested that the association's power may have been greater at the implementation than at the policy-formation or adoption stages of the process.[60] As producers of many publications on instructional technology, many of which have been distributed through the OE, the association maintained an important influence over the definition and evaluation of instructional technologies.

With the War on Poverty, and the effort to move defense firms into the education market, the National Security Industrial Association (NSIA) came to play a somewhat minor role in the formation of educational policy outside the military. In 1966, the Department of Defense (DOD) invited the NSIA and the departments of Education and Labor to join forces in the educational area. This new association was to concentrate initially on military training, but its attention soon turned to public education. The NSIA was asked to organize a conference on the "systematic application of technology to education and training." The outcome of that conference was to be the establishment of good working relations between suppliers and consumers of instructional technology. This new relationship was to be guided by an annual symposium, organized under the acronym ARISTOTLE (Annual Review of Information and Symposium on the Technology of Training and Learning and Education).

The conference organizer, Eugene Ferraro, Deputy Under Secretary of the Air Force (for Manpower), noted the similarities between the defense and educational supply structures:

> The emerging education industry appears to be following a pattern similar to that evolution of the defense industry in the late 1940s and early 1950s. Education research efforts are being discussed; the contract system and its management techniques are beginning to be used by several federal agencies . . . . Federal dollars for education affect the decisions of both the producers and the consumers of industry's services and new technologies. Therefore, there is a need for direct communication between Government agencies at all levels and industry.[61]

Because ARISTOTLE's organizing committee was top-heavy with defense-industry representatives, newly merged into the education business, and had only limited participation by the academic research community, the project soon faded from view. In commenting on ARISTOTLE's demise, Robert Seidel questioned whether the "model of research, development and operational utility for industry is compatible either with the education profession or that of government."[62]

Other interest groups active in promoting the introduction of instructional technology in the schools include the private foundations. The Ford Foundation has been the most active and influential member of this community where policy has involved telecommunications. Its role in the development of educational broadcasting goes back to 1951 when it helped to form the Fund for Adult Education and the Fund for the Advancement of Education.[63] Other associations started with Ford Foundation grants, which have been active and influential in the subsidy effort, include the Joint Council on Educational Television (JCET), and the National Association of Educational Broadcasters (NAEB).

Together, the JCET and NAEB formed the leading edge of an effort to win reserved frequencies for educational broadcasters. Successful there, the Fund for Adult Education then disbursed some $3.5 million in matching grants to aid in the activation of some 30 stations by 1959.[64]

The foundation funded a number of major demonstration projects to produce "evidence" of the value of television as an instructional aid. From Hagerstown, Maryland, to American Samoa, foundation dollars subsidized the national diet of information about educational television.

Beyond the foundations, informal participants in the policy process who play a vital role in the provision of information relevant to the deliberations of formal participants would have to include the academic experts. Researchers like Wilbur Schramm and Ithiel de Sola Pool, because of their reputations and the sheer volume of their writing, can influence the thinking of policy makers. It is not clear, however, whether these scholars influence, reinforce, or merely provide legitimate expression for policy conclusions already reached.

IN CONCLUSION

The policy to establish a system of fiscal, bureaucratic, and ideological support for the transformation of education at home and abroad was accomplished through the involvement of elected officials, appointed and career bureaucrats, and a variety of organizations representing producers of educational goods and services. Their influence on the formulation, adoption, and implementation of the overall policy was delivered primarily through efforts to provide information subsidies through selected channels of communication. Presidential messages, congressional testimony, speeches, films, research reports, and press releases all contributed to the creation of a climate supportive of instructional technology. When the pressures on the economy as a whole made it clear that education could not absorb surplus industrial and technical capacity at a sufficient rate, Lyndon Johnson, and then Richard Nixon took the lead in returning the responsibility to the defense establishment.

At no stage in this process was the average citizen seen to have any identifiable role.

CHAPTER SIX FOOTNOTES

[1] Reich, Michael. (1973). Does the United States economy require military spending? *In* H. Weaver (Ed.), "Modern Political Economy," p. 358. Boston, Massachusetts: Allyn and Bacon.

[2] This chapter is based on my doctoral dissertation: Gandy, Oscar. (1976). "Instructional Technology: The Reselling of the Pentagon." Stanford University.

[3] Hoban, Charles. (1966). "Movies That Teach." New York: Dryden Press.

[4] Saettler, Paul. (1968). "A History of Instructional Technology," p. 106. New York: McGraw-Hill.

[5] Hoban, Charles. Footnote 3, 1946.

[6] Saettley, Paul. Footnote 4, 1968.

[7] Hitchens, Howard. (1971). Instructional technology in the armed forces. *In* S. Tickton (Ed.), "To Improve Learning," Vol. II. New York: R. R. Bowker.

[8] Saettler, Paul. Footnote 4, 1968.

[9] *Ibid.*, p. 171.

[10] Hitchens, Howard. Page 703 in footnote 7, 1971.

[11] Finn, James, and Perrin, Donald G. (1962). "Teaching Machines and Programmed Learning. A Survey of the Industry, 1962." Washington, D.C.: U.S. Department of Health, Education, and Welfare.

[12] Siebert, Ivan. (1975). "Educational Technology. A Handbook of Standard Terminology and a Guide for Recording and Reporting Information About Educational Technology," pp. 104–105. Washington, D.C.: U.S. Government Printing Office.

[13] Rodgers, William. (1970). "Think. A Biography of the Watsons and IBM," p. 162. New York: New American Library.

[14] *Ibid.*

[15] Williams, Erik D. (1975). "Report of Progress for the Field Test of the University of Illinois PLATO System of CAI"; also "Report of Progress for the Field Test of the TICCIT system of CAI." Washington, D.C.: National Science Foundation.

[16] Loehwing, David A. (1966). The learning industry. *Barrons* (October 3), 10.

[17] Melman, Seymour. (1970). "Pentagon Capitalism: The Political Economy of War." New York: McGraw-Hill.

[18] *Wall Street Transcripts* (November 15 1965), 5922.

[19] *Ibid.*

[20] Raytheon Company. *Annual Report,* 1966.

[21] Melman, Seymour. Footnote 17, 1970.

[22] Westinghouse Electric Company. *Annual Report* for the years 1964, 1966, 1970, 1971, 1973, 1974.

[23] Time Inc. *Annual Report,* 1971.

[24] RCA Corporation. *Annual Report* for the years 1969, 1970, 1971, 1973, 1974.

[25] Bell and Howell. *Annual Report,* issues between 1961 and 1973.

[26] Bell and Howell. *Annual Report,* 1971.

[27] Bell and Howell. *Annual Report,* 1973.

[28] Page 32, Table II in footnote 2, 1976. Total compiled from numerous Office of Education and National Center for Educational Statistics publications reporting educational expenditures or allocations.

[29] *Ibid.*, p. 152, Table I. Figures compiled from numerous National Center for Educational Statistics publications.

[30] Schultz, Charles. (1972). "Setting National Priorities. The 1973 Budget." Washington, D.C.: The Brookings Institution.

[31] Scott, Geraldine. (1975). "Statistics of the State School Systems. 1971–1972." Washington, D.C.: U.S. Government Printing Office.

[32] Hope Reports, Inc. (1975). "AV-USA. 1973–1974. Current Hope Reports." Rochester, New York: Hope Reports, Inc.

[33] Bukoski, William, and Lorotkin, Arthur. (1975). "Computing Activities in Secondary Education. Final Report." Washington, D.C.: American Institutes for Research.

[34] Electronic Industries Association. (1974). "1974 Electronic Market Data Book." Washington, D.C.: Electronic Industries Association.

[35] McHale, John. (1965). Big business enlists for the war on poverty. *Trans-Action 2* (No. 4), (May/June), 3–9.

[36] *Ibid.* citing McGovern's comments in support of legislation to establish the Commission.
[37] Summerfield, Harry L. (1974). "Power and Process." Berkeley, California: McCutcheon Publishing Corporation.
[38] Thomas, Norman. (1975). "Education in National Politics," p. 24. New York: David McKay.
[39] Guthrie, James. (1968). "The 1965 ESEA: The National Politics of Educational Reform," p. 74. Ph.D. dissertation, Stanford University.
[40] Finn, Chester E. (1977). "Education and the Presidency," p. 56. Lexington, Massachusetts: D.C. Heath.
[41] *Ibid.,* pp. 73–74.
[42] Summerfield, Harry L. Page 119 in footnote 37, 1974.
[43] *Ibid.*
[44] Halperin, Samuel. (1970). ESEA: five years later, submitted in the testimony of Congressman Leeds. U.S. Congress, House. *Congressional Record 116* (No. 23), 30916–30919 (September 9).
[45] Summerfield, Harry L. Pages 90–92 in footnote 37, 1974.
[46] U.S. Congress, House, Subcommittee on Education, Education and Labor Committee. (1967). "Study of the United States Office of Education." Washington, D.C.: U.S. Government Printing Office.
[47] Carpenter, C. Ray. (1970). Commission on Instructional Technology and its report. *Educational Broadcasting Review 4* (No. 2) (April).
[48] U.S. Congress, Joint Committee on Atomic Energy, Subcommittee on Research and Development. (1956). "Shortage of Scientific and Engineering Manpower," p. 1. Washington, D.C.: U.S. Government Printing Office.
[49] U.S. Congress, Joint Economic Committee, Subcommittee on Economic Progress. (1966). "Automation and Technology in Education," p. 11. Washington, D.C.: U.S. Government Printing Office.
[50] Finn, Chester E. Page 15 in footnote 40, 1977.
[51] Bright, R. L., associate commissioner for research. (1968). Statement at a meeting of the American Educational Publishers Institute. *Publishers Weekly* (January), 35–38.
[52] Wolanin, Thomas R. (1976). Don't trouble me with the facts: Congress, information and policy making for postsecondary education. *In* S. Gove and F. Wirt (Eds.), "Political Science and School Politics," pp. 105–106. Lexington, Massachusetts: D.C. Heath.
[53] Sproul, Lee, Weiner, Stephen, and Wolf, David. (1978). "Organizing an Anarchy," p. 92. Chicago, Illinois: University of Chicago Press.
[54] Summerfield, Harry L. Page 49 in footnote 37, 1974.
[55] *Ibid.,* p. 160.
[56] Kearns, Doris. (1969). The growth and development of Title III, ESEA. *Educational Technology 9* (No. 5) (May), 7–14.
[57] U.S. Office of Management and Budget. Special Analyses. (1976). "Budget of the United States Government for Fiscal Years 1974–76." Washington, D.C.: U.S. Government Printing Office.
[58] Much of the history of NAVA was gathered in an interview with White in the fall of 1975. Through interviews with others active in educational policy, including Samuel Halperin and Howard Hitchens, confirmation of White's role was readily available.
[59] U.S. Congress, Senate, Committee on Appropriations. (1970). "Office of Education Appropriations," p. 517. Washington, D.C.: U.S. Government Printing Office.
[60] Lembo, Diana, and Bruce, Carol. (1972). The growth and development of the department of audiovisual instruction: 1923–1968. *Audiovisual Instruction* (March).
[61] Ferraro, Eugene. (1967). Project ARISTOTLE. *Defense Industry Bulletin* (March), 22.
[62] Seidel, Robert J. (1970). Resource allocation to effect operationally useful CAI. "Proceedings of a Conference on the Application of Computers to Training," pp. xxx–11. Washington, D.C.: National Security Industrial Association.

[63] The Network Project. (1971). "The Fourth Network." New York: The Network Project. See also Bailey, Stephen. (1975). "Education Groups in the Nation's Capitol." Washington, D.C.: American Council on Education.

[64] The Ford Foundation and the Fund for the Advancement of Education. (1959). "Teaching by Television." New York: The Ford Foundation.

7

Science and Technology

At the core of the economic system, where they serve as the principal force governing change in the production and distribution of power and resources, science and technology have come to depend upon the coordinated action of the state. Science and technological innovation are said to have been responsible for some 45% of the nation's growth between 1929 and 1969. Technology-based industries grew faster, employed more people, and were substantially more profitable than less technology-intensive industries between 1957 and 1973. Yet, planners in the Department of Commerce were concerned that the U.S. was losing its technological edge over other competitors in the international marketplace.[1] The U.S. share of patents was down, both at home and abroad. Fewer high-technology firms were beginning each year than was traditional in the past. Industrial productivity was growing well below its historical trend, and the balance of trade in products produced by technology-intensive firms was equally "disquieting."

Commerce analysts were unsure of the true causes for this decline in the global competitiveness of the U.S. economy, but they were sure that the solution lay in a "coherent national technology policy," which would "promote private sector investment in technological innovation." Proposals to remove the "regulatory and social barriers to innovation" were largely focused on problems of scientific and technical information (STI), and the need to increase public awareness of and support for technological innovation.

Questions of science and technology were not always so high on the public agenda. Daniel S. Greenberg argues that prior to 1940, pure research as distinguished from applied research and technology was treated pretty much as an orphan child, and scientists were allowed to pursue knowledge without regard for its utility. The growing war in Europe changed all that:

> in a period of months, patterns that had more or less prevailed for 150 years were cast away and replaced; with astonishing speed, the aloofness was destroyed, and science, fed by government subsidy, was linked to government purpose.[2]

The same process also linked the universities to the government R&D effort. Initially, because of scientific egos and the mistrust of military decision making, scientists recruited for the war effort balked at the idea of working under military direction. Instead, the Los Alamos Scientific Laboratory was organized as an adjunct of the University of California, the Radiation Laboratory with MIT, the Metallurgical Laboratory at the University of Chicago, and the Applied Physics Laboratory at Johns Hopkins.[3] To this day, these universities remain inextricably tied to the federal purse, although their research is no longer limited to the development of atomic weaponry.

The scientific community was not anxious to give up the benefits of government financing and notoriety after the war was over, and Vannevar Bush saw no reason why it should. Bush's Office of Scientific Research and Development (OSRD), which was responsible for developing most of the war-related contracts with the universities, set the tone for the continuing relationship in a special report—''Science, The Endless Frontier.'' This report, supposedly requested by President Franklin Roosevelt, but actually recommended by Bush himself, set the stage for federal support of basic and applied research in the physical sciences. It carefully avoided including the social sciences because of a fear that the topics explored by the social scientists were likely to arouse the interest of politicians.[4] Because the proposed National Science Foundation (NSF) was so well protected from the political system, President Harry Truman vetoed the first bill presented to him, and did not approve this new relationship until 1950.[5]

While scientists were content to focus their attention on matters of esoteric interest, Congress was generally willing to pay the bills for a larger and larger chunk of scientific R&D. However, with the rapid escalation in expenditures occasioned by U.S. participation in the space race, the bill for R&D soon topped the $15 billion mark and Congress began to take a more active role in seeking justifications for these expenditures. Whereas in the past, the scientific community, through a system of peer review and consultation, largely determined the scientific policy agenda, and controlled the distribution of resources, a newly aroused Congress began to impose its own system of accountability. Science policy would have to become government policy, and political concerns and incentives would take a more active part in setting the goals of scientific research.

With this somewhat reluctant emergence into the light of public debate on the merits of scientific endeavor, the scientific establishment joined other participants in the process who sought to produce influence in any way they could. Scientists, whether based in universities, research centers, or profit-seeking firms, are all *producers* of a commodity, the demand for which is ultimately dependent upon government policy. And while the scientific establishment occasionally gives the impression that its interests are being ignored more and more these days,[6] that could not be further from the truth. It is merely that science policy has become more contentious in the post-Vietnam era when critics of business as usual have turned their attention to the business of science as well.

Although basic science remains somewhat insulated from the tinkering of politicians by virtue of its incomprehensibility, changes in the sophistication of congressional staffs is ensuring that more and more dimensions of scientific work are discussed in the public forum. Where policy in the past was concerned with the relative efficiency of the scientific effort, today's debates frequently evolve around issues of social impact. Technology assessments initiated by congressional action are frequently based on the currently popular belief that science is as much the cause as the solution to many problems in society.[7]

When the science/government partnership began in the development of civilian applications of atomic energy, there was little concern for the negative consequences that might flow from the use of the technology. Scientists had been given a technical challenge, the industry had been shown the possibility of profit, and that was all that mattered. Scientists attracted by the promise of fame and fortune, went ahead with all deliberate speed to transform a submarine power source, much increased in scale, but otherwise unfettered by considerations of special civilian needs. Problems of cooling associated with the necessity of a ready supply of water that were nonexistent in normal submarine operations, but highly critical in land-based operations, were largely ignored.

Also ignored were problems of the tail end of the nuclear cycle, the problems to be inherited by future generations:

> Chemists and engineers were not interested in dealing with waste. It was not glamourous; there were no careers; it was messy; nobody got brownie points for caring about nuclear waste.[8]

Today, with the aid of scientist/activists, estimates of the potentially harmful impacts of some new technique, process, or procedure are at least considered in the formulation of public policy involving science and technology.

Responsible scientists, concerned about the potential dangers associated with genetic experimentation, were successful in temporarily halting experimentation with human deoxyribonucleic acid (DNA). Fearful that cancer research involving human bacteria might result in an epidemic, cautious scientists called for an investigation of the potential danger; at the same time, they issued a warning to the public at large.[9] Because genetic engineering involved considerably more than the threat of cancer, and was indeed, linked to basic moral questions about the creation of new forms of life, the issue attracted broad public attention, and eventually brought about action by the political and bureaucratic system to impose controls over laboratory conditions. Unfortunately, what occurred with atomic energy also transpired in genetic engineering—commerical interests took over where academic scientists left off, and for the time being corporate policy will be the source of public consequences.

Some of these scientific whistle blowers, or the "visible scientists" as they are called by Rae Goodell,[10] play an important role in the assessment of new technologies. It is likely, however, that most of their influence is indirect, having the greatest effect on public opinion and confidence in science and government, and only a marginal impact on the decision making of the legislators and bureaucrats who ultimately set policy. Goodell suggests that popular science figures like Barry Commoner and Linus Pauling are called to testify in congressional hearings for the publicity and media attention they bring wherever they go, rather than for their specialized insight into any particular technical debate. For serious, credible information, politicians and bureaucratic policy makers are more likely to turn to the traditional establishment sources.

The National Academy of Sciences (NAS) is supposed to be a "Supreme Court of final advice" on matters of scientific controversy. Studies by the Academy are done at the request of Congress, or at the suggestion of organized interests who expect to benefit from the added weight or scientific credibility. Because of its dependent relationship to the government maintained through contracts for its investigations, the Academy is seen by some as being overly cautious about issuing many critical reports which might offend sponsors in Congress or the bureaucracy.[11] The NAS is also limited to a supportive role by the nature of government requests for an investigation:

> Federal officials can set policy without bothering to consult the Academy; they can then ask the Academy to help advise them on the best way to carry out that policy; and the Academy generally pitches in to help without worrying about whether the policy is misguided.[12]

Because of its reliance on government money, there is less evidence of corporate influence on Academy investigations. However, the National Academy of Engineering (NAE), because of its close relations with the defense industry, was seen to be much more sensitive to direct corporate influence. Many of the advisory committees of the NAE have been headed by representatives of corporations with a direct stake in the outcome of the Academy's investigation.[13] It is suggested further that the academic member, thought to be independent because of his institutional base, is even more susceptible to influence because of the nature of contract research.

Within the bureaucracy, scientific advice is often routed through a number of advisory committees, where superior resources tend to give industry representatives the upper hand in most investigations. In an examination of the role played by citizen groups in the Atomic Energy Commission's (AEC) resolution of reactor siting controversies, researchers concluded that:

> the weight of influence, talent, money, power, policy and decision making lies with government and industry. As a result citizen groups are usually restricted to raising questions about matters concerning which they possess little knowledge or expertise.[14]

Citizen groups that might appear before an AEC committee generally cannot afford to hire scientific expertise, so they are often represented before the Commission by graduate students. If these groups were successful in raising sufficient funds to hire an expert consultant—a scientist with enough credibility to have any impact on the proceedings, and who would not buckle under the attack of industry attorneys—they would face yet another barrier. Because virtually all funding for nuclear reactor research came through the AEC, very few scientists with any experience in the field would be willing to testify on their behalf, and risk future contracts and grants. Those that might be supportive of citizen positions are limited to expressing that support in secret, or off the record. Most often this support came in the form of leaks of sensitive documents, which would provide petitioners with some marginal assistance in raising questions or disputing industry testimony.[15]

The lack of information upon which to make appeals to the reason of government policy makers leaves the citizen consumer in a weak position in the science policy arena. The lack of information in a usable form is complicated by the traditions of science reporting, which finds journalists likely to avoid conflict in preference for the more promotional output of sources in science. Hillier Krieghbaum suggests that the traditional media are capable of providing the consumer with *awareness* of science, but understanding is very rarely achieved.[16]

June Goodfield has suggested that the special problems of reporting science and scientific controversy are inherent in the nature of the news media:

1. Newspapers and other commercial media are constrained by the need to make a profit, thus there is a built-in need to find "interesting" stories. Science may not always fill the bill.
2. Journalistic practice utilizes an inverted pyramid form of organization, so that paragraphs may be added or deleted from the end of the article in response to changing demands for space. This cannot work where the goal is understanding because a series of "bridges" have to be built before the latest fact or contribution is introduced. None of the bridges can be eliminated without a failure of understanding.
3. The news media, and television in particular, are enamoured with the *new,* or the fashionable.
4. There is a tendency to rely on authorities, experts, as safe sources.

> It is presumed that the higher in the hierarchy a person is, the more he knows. If you want an eminent quote, such a person is worth significantly more than somebody working lower down, even though the latter may be doing all the research and knows infinitely more about the subject.[17]

Not unexpectedly, Goodfield does not suggest that interest in the outcome of policy deliberations causes scientific sources to seek out journalists, by either direct or indirect means, with the intention of introducing policy-relevant content into the public-information stream.

We have already discussed the preference shown by journalists and science writers alike for the least costly, low-risk opportunities for usable material afforded by scientific meetings. While these meetings are by no means free of attempts by interested sources to influence the newsgathering process through a well placed subsidy, they are presently an alternative to the products of corporate or university information offices. However, with the emergence of a new relationship between business and universities, and one that is likely to accelerate under the influence of Reaganomics, scientific meetings will become less productive sources for content distinguishable from corporate news releases.

Where scientific advances were once presented at meetings of research societies for the benefit that derived from peer review and discussion, the economic value of new discoveries these days is apparently so high, and the professional standards so low, that a cloak of secrecy has begun to envelop the scientific community. Many scholars have given up their freedom to discuss their work in exchange for consultant fees; others have their freedom given away for them when their university enters into an exclusive contractual relationship with a commercial firm, or decides to pursue the benefits of the market on its own behalf. Donald Kennedy, president of Stanford University, has been identified as sharing a growing concern that:

> the university biology department is one place that people might turn for information and the opinions of scholars without having to worry about the corporate conflict of interest that taints a scholar's opinion. That may no longer be true.[18]

The impact of commercial interests on the flow of scientific and technical information (STI) is seen as well in the growth of commercially sponsored technical literature. Marquis and Allen note that the technical literature is different from the traditional scientific journals in several important ways. There is less of a tendency in the technical literature to cite other sources; where it occurs at all, citation is generally cited to an earlier work by the same author. However, because the technical journals are generally more intelligible to the nonscientist DM, they are more likely to be used than the more heavily documented journal articles. Thus, "the net result is that the most widely used formal written channels of communication are no longer under the control of the professionals who use them. Control has passed to a group of businessmen (publishers and advertisers) who exercise editorial power over the journal's contents."[19] Although the authors do not suggest the possibility, the control exercised by those advertisers may be to restrict the flow of negative content, while increasing the flow of content supportive of sponsor interests.

Although conference after conference has been organized to discuss the problems of STI, most have concerned themselves with the availability of information technology to facilitate access to the exponentially growing body of scientific information.[20] Very few have addressed the far more serious problem of the inaccuracy or incompleteness[21] of some of the information in those advanced systems, and the possibility that the errors are nonrandom and purposive. A brief look at the role of information in the formation and implementation of the U.S.'s energy policy may provide some sense of the seriousness of the problem.

ENERGY POLICY

> When one reads the protracted legislative debate on natural gas pricing, it becomes apparent that the main reason legislators are unable to do anything useful in this realm is that they do not know what they are talking about.[22]

This abysmal ignorance that Tom Bethell ascribes to politicians is neither accidental nor a recent phenomenon. The oil and nuclear wings of the energy establishment have joined hands with their brethren in the energy bureaucracy on numerous occasions in the past in order to ensure that national energy policy lurches along from crisis to crisis without ever threatening the profitability of the major firms in the industry.

While it would be absurd to suggest that OPEC's four-fold increase in the price of imported oil had no impact on inflation, and the recession of 1974, its impact on the U.S. economy must also be seen as having been conditioned by several decades of industry-managed, domestic energy policies.[23] Oil depletion allowances kept profits high and prices low by reducing the tax liabilities of domestic producers. Other tax policies allowed sweetheart agreements between the oil majors and the resource owners to treat royalties as taxes, which robbed the tax payer of $1.5 billion in tax revenues each year. Policies that favored highways and high-powered automobiles over mass transit systems increased vulnerability to sudden changes in energy prices.

Even the failure to consider all of the environmental costs associated with the production and utilization of energy tends to lower the direct costs to users. These low prices contributed to excessive consumption and demand, which only heightened the pain of withdrawal when prices eventually reached the point of equilibrium. But at every step of the way, despite the occasional theatrics and political rhetoric, government and industry actors in the policy process cooperated to create the systematic ignorance that inflicts most participants in the energy policy arena.

In 1977, when Jimmy Carter fired the first rhetorical shot in his "moral equivalent of war" against the public's already weakening demand for imported oil, he was engaging in a classic attempt to pull synthetic wool over the eyes of the U.S. consumer. While with one hand he was going to remove the controls on domestic oil prices to allow the pressures of the pocketbook to stimulate voluntary conservation, he needed to create a diversion with his other hand to keep the public from examining his windfall profits scheme too closely. Carter played his role to the hilt, stunning even the editors of *Time* with the sting of his mock assault:

> the single most surprising aspect of Carter's entire message was its harsh indictment of the oil industry. More than just populist politics with a dash of down home demagogy, the President's assault was a bold—perhaps desperate gamble to out-flank industry lobbying efforts in Congress and rally public opinion behind the profits tax.[24]

The public had come to believe that the energy crisis was phony, that the shortages were the result of industry restriction of supply designed largely to win decontrol of domestic prices. So as not to confirm the public view, as he was planning to do just that, Carter had to create the impression that the industry would not benefit from decontrol, but the tax money would be used to develop alternative sources of energy. He sought to capitalize on public mistrust by aligning himself with them, and asking for grass-roots support in convincing a weak- and special-interest-dominated legislature to let him have his way.

What he did not tell the public was that his windfall tax proposal was also a phony. As Howard Metzenbaum noted in arguing against decontrol, the industry was already investing its record profits in other industries unrelated to energy, and the proposed tax was in reality a deductible business expenses—just like advertising, which would mean that the 50% tax would actually be reduced to something less than 12% at a time when the extra profits would top $14 billion.[25] By describing this extra tax on the U.S. consumer as a tax on Big Oil, Carter sought to involve the public actively in its own exploitation.

This bit of fiction was not the only example of presidential slight of hand in the promotion of energy policy under the Carter administration, and it was by no means the worst. Barry Commoner tells of some attempts at statistical manipulation that ultimately brought about the departure of Carter's Energy Secretary, James Schlesinger.[26] In preparation for his major energy address, Carter assigned Schlesinger the task of developing a National Energy Plan and an accompanying *Fact Sheet* easily digestible by the press. In contrast with most such proposals, the Plan was largely devoid of supporting statistics. The 103-page document had only two pages of tables, which none of the Department of Energy (DOE) representatives were able to interpret to the satisfaction of questioners. The difficulty was not lack of familiarity with the figures as one excuse went, but it was that the statistics were the product of a statistical model that had been tampered with to such an extent that it was impossible to evaluate its projections.

It seems that the Project Independent Energy System (PIES), which was developed under fairly objective conditions during the Nixon administration, had been tinkered with to make it support Carter's energy proposal. Some 21 changes in the model resulted in a sizeable increase in the projected impact of unfettered energy demand.

> This manipulation is reminiscent of bargaining in a bazaar, where a merchant might quote a $25 price on an item that he is prepared to sell for $16 or less, so that when the item is finally sold for $14 the buyer will think that he has won the bargain.[27]

Commoner suggests that because of this tinkering, the logic of the model was no longer indentifiable, and the predictions were no longer defendable. Thus, the administration never engaged in debate about the projections upon which the policy was proposed, and eventually approved in Congress.

While Carter was partially successful in creating an impression of a genuine adversarial relationship between the White House and Big Oil, Schlesinger and the DOE came under repeated fire for being overly responsive to industry needs, and relying too heavily on industry-supplied information about the nature of reserves and investments.

In Senate hearings in 1978, representatives of the American Petroleum Institute (API)—the major informational arm of the energy lobby—reported numerous instances when the DOE staff provided the API with advance information about energy proposals. In Metzenbaum's opening statement in these hearings, he pointed to the impact of such aid:

> Anyone who is at all familiar with the regulatory process can well appreciate the advantages associated with its receiving advance notice of, or private access to, proposed agency regulations and internal studies. Not only are parties that receive this information given advanced lead time to prepare rebuttals or offer counter proposals, but they are permitted to secretly influence the drafting of public decisions, which have tremendous economic consequences for both producers and consumers.[28]

Neither Metzenbaum's comments nor the special hearings were directed at influencing any particular bit of legislation; instead, his effort was directed toward the grass roots. Just as Carter sought to create the impression of distance, even aloofness from sources of influence, Metzenbaum was concerned with public perceptions of government. Without public confidence in government management of energy resources, appeals for conservation could only go so far.

> I say to you that until you get your house in order, until people are convinced that the Department of Energy is their Department of Energy and not the oil industry's Department of Energy; until such time, you are not going to get the cooperation of the American people . . . . We are talking about an agency's credibility and

an agency's integrity and an agency's reputation; and we are talking about a national energy plan that still hasn't been enacted, because there is no public hue and cry for it and because there is a question even there as to whose side the Department of Energy is on.[29]

The DOE's dependence on industry consultants and former employees was the principal focus of Senate hearings on government use of consultants. In the words of an early witness, the situation was such at the DOE that "were the identity of its contractors made public, it would appear that the DOE has chosen to employ the energy industry rather than to regulate it."[30]

Many of the consultants to the DOE serve in a similar capacity with major firms in the industry, and although there is little evidence of direct corporate influence over the recommendations made by those consultants to the DOE or to the Energy Research and Development Administration (ERDA), when the statement of work virtually hands over the policy-making responsibility to the consultants, the temptation must be very great.

> Prepare materials as required for the Annual Report to Congress including strategy statements, special issue analysis, program implementation plans, objective statements and milestones . . . prepare long-range strategy and guidelines related to industrial developments, institutional and resource constraints for fossil energy development.[31]

Even without intentional manipulation of the DOE's information-gathering process, the selection of industry-qualified sources increases the probability that an industry, rather than a consumer, orientation will emerge in the recommendations.

Such a conclusion might easily be drawn from the conviction with which the DOE pursued investigations of industry culpability in the case of gasoline shortages in the summer of 1979. Carter is reported to have asked the DOE to "conduct a vigorous investigation" in order to determine the causes of a gasoline shortage which were not experienced by any other nations. In record time, the DOE reported the investigation was complete, and there was no evidence of any wrongdoing on the part of the industry. Critics of that report revealed, however, that "DOE's 'investigation' had depended mainly on industry-supplied information, taken no sworn testimony, subpoenaed no data and conducted no audits of company books."[32]

In the case of nuclear energy, the degree of cooperation between government and industry was rarely the subject of question. Indeed, the relationship between the Atomic Energy Commission (AEC) and the fledgling industry was often pointed to with pride. The AEC not only had the responsibility for overseeing the development of the industry through its support of nuclear research, development, and demonstration, but was also primarily responsible for creating public acceptance of nuclear power.

Eric Barnouw describes the AEC's tight control over media access to nuclear installations. Before any documentary crew would be given the right to film, the AEC would review the script and shooting plan to ensure that only the best side of the "marvelous atom" was shown to the admiring public. When GE and Westinghouse moved to assume leadership positions in the new industry, both became active producers of AEC-approved films and cartoons screened in schools and on television. Barnouw reports that the AEC released more than 100 films on the peaceful uses of atomic energy and "almost all described atomic energy as safe, clean, cheap and absolutely necessary to meet surging energy 'demands' which were meanwhile being manufactured via television and other media."[33]

When the petroleum industry firms moved into nuclear energy, they joined in the production of promotional films. Barnouw concludes that until the end of the 1960s, virtually everything the U.S. public had a chance to see about nuclear energy had been produced by a source with some personal investment in the success of the industry. Because the technology was new, and relatively unknown to journalists, there was little reason for them to question a technology marked by such a high degree of government and industry support and cooperation. Barnouw suggests that the information shield developed a leak only after responsibility from the industry was turned over to the Nuclear Regulatory Commission and the ERDA.

In 1976, two GE engineers resigned with considerable fanfare, claiming their consciences would not allow them to continue the charade of nuclear safety. This jolt was followed by another in 1977 when public television's *Nova* series highlighted an accident at an Alabama reactor. While public television's audiences might have had some advance knowledge of the dangers of nuclear energy, an NBC documentary, *Danger—Radioactive Waste* brought the issue before the U.S. public as it had never been addressed before. Later that year, mass demonstrations would vie for public attention in an attempt to raise the public's consciousness about the potentially catastrophic results of a serious accident, which became increasingly likely as the number of nuclear installations grew. Some 2,000 people demonstrated in Seabrook, New Hampshire at the site of a new plant, and by the end of the year, there had been more than 100 anti-nuclear demonstrations around the country. In 1978, the second Seabrook demonstration attracted more than 20,000 demonstrators, and some credited the demonstration with defeating the reelection bid of New Hampshire's pronuclear governor.[34] The pendulum of public opinion was just beginning to swing.

THREE MILE ISLAND

On March 28, 1979, the inevitable came to pass. Malfunctions in the cooling and monitoring systems of one of Metropolitan Edison's (Met Ed) nuclear reactors on Three Mile Island (TMI) began a series of events that would come to dominate media channels and public attention for eight days.[35] Although Met

Ed's public relations (PR) staff had been trying since 1965[36] to promote a public image of safe, clean, economical power, delivered by competent responsible management, its campaign of press releases, advertisements, radio spots, pamphlets, and special billing inserts mailed to its customers in the Harrisburg area was neutralized in less than a week by the force of objective reality.

Press coverage of the TMI event, as well as the behavior of the official sources that dominated that coverage, was the subject of a special task force investigation, organized as part of a presidential commission formed to study the accident and its management. The special task force concluded that the public was not well served by either media or public officials. Although most of the errors in the published reports could be traced to their source in officialdom, the investigators concluded that the reporters "compounded these errors through a general ignorance of nuclear technology and the language of radiation."[37]

Much of the confusion and uncertainty about the extent of danger associated with the release of radioactivity into the atmosphere and into the Susquehanna River, or the possibility of a "meltdown," could be traced to issuance of contradictory reports by a variety of seemingly official sources. In the case of possible damage to the core of the reactor, Nuclear Regulatory Commission (NRC) sources in Pennsylvania were still saying that there had been no damage long after NRC officials in the Bethesda headquarters had admitted that damage had occurred.[38] Official versions and the truth diverged on several other points as well. Operator error, now recognized as having played an important role in the mishap was vigorously denied in the press at the same time as it was being confirmed to the NRC officials. Differences of opinion within the NRC resulted in the unattributed release of estimates of the probability of an imminent explosion associated with the hydrogen gas bubble said to be forming in the reactor's dome. By April 1, official NRC spokesman Harold Denton was reporting that there never had been any danger of explosion. The amount of contradictory information declined rapidly after the NRC won an agreement that it, rather than Met Ed, would be the source for any future statements about TMI.

The impact of the incident's coverage in the press was dramatic, but temporary. The nuclear industry commissioned a special study of public opinion for a year following the TMI accident in order to estimate the impact of the negative publicity on the future of nuclear energy.[39] The dramatic rise in the proportion of Americans surveyed who were opposed to nuclear power plants soon gave way to a steady decline between April and September, rising again only briefly around the time of the release of a Kemeny Commission Report on the TMI accident. It would be a mistake, however, to assume that the public is merely foregetful, and that the normal state of public consciousness is one of support for nuclear energy. While the science writers may have turned away from questions of nuclear safety, the nuclear industry's image makers merely moved into higher gear after TMI to help repair the damage to public opinion.

One week after the accident, Met Ed hired Hill and Knowlton to help repair the damage to the firm's credibility, and to help prepare its officials to make a creditable appearance under the bright lights of congressional investigations.[40] Other members of the industry began to take their collective responsibilities more seriously, and mobilized to defeat a House proposal to impose a six-month moratorium on plant construction.[41] The fact that the NRC imposed its own de facto moratorium does not erase the fact of renewed industry efforts to influence policy through a subsidy effort.

More than a dozen nuclear firms were reported to have established Washington offices since TMI. Since many of the battles being fought by the industry take place in local jurisdictions, where local public utility commissions (PUCs) must decide the fate of plans for new construction, the Edison Electric Institute holds a series of seminars and strategy sessions for representatives of the nuclear industry.

Another member of the industry team is the American Nuclear Energy Council, which recieves membership fees from industry leaders like Westinghouse Electric, General Electric, and Bechtel Power Corporation, to pursue a variety of bills impacting on the nuclear industry. In its effort to defeat the moratorium proposal, it repeatedly called attention to what would be generally perceived as negative consequences of such an act: (1) the "Ayatollah factor," described their emphasis on the danger of vulnerability to a cutoff to oil imports; (2) the environmental dangers, like "acid rain," which might accompany switching to alternative fuels like coal; and (3) the impact of a moratorium on employment in some representative's district.[42] Yet another group, the Committee for Energy Awareness, was organized to provide the industry with a variety of designs for information subsidies to counter the fairly well-organized efforts of the anti-nuclear activitists.

By early 1981, observers agreed that the future of nuclear energy in the U.S. seemed very uncertain. TMI had not only underscored the importance of safety considerations, but investors were made increasingly aware of the risks involved in pursuit of an industry that had become so highly politicized. Part of this increased risk came to the forefront when several PUCs ruled that it was the stockholders rather than the consumers who should bear the cost of investments in nuclear projects that were not completed as planned. When the Bank of America announced a policy of avoiding nuclear investment, the rest of the investment community took heed.[43]

It is important to recall, however, that TMI would not have had the effect it did on the energy policy arena if there had been no organized anti-nuclear movement. Just as the anti-war demonstrations put the costs of the Vietnam War on the national agenda, and made them the basis for the nation's eventual withdrawal,[44] the salience of nuclear energy as a public issue was dependent largely upon the efforts of a small group of dedicated activists. It is suggested that the Seabrook occupation was the critical point in the movement's history when the "handful of lonely voices had been transformed into a full-blown social movement.''[45] While earlier nuclear mishaps, like the 1966 accident at the Fermi reactor in Detroit went virtually unnoticed, TMI added momentum to an existing movement, and reinforced aspects of its claim that nuclear energy was unsafe.

Of course, the struggle over energy policy is far from complete. Where Jimmy Carter somewhat grudgingly accepted the need for a continued nuclear role, while rejecting the breeder reactor as both too expensive and too risky in terms of the potential for nuclear proliferation, Ronald Reagan appears less hesitant. Indeed, apparently with support from the administration, the DOE was reported to have embarked on a multimillion dollar ''propaganda campaign'' to generate public support for the nuclear industry. In a memorandum leaked to the press by Rep. Richard Ottinger, the DOE had plans to utilize PR consultants to (1) organize public appearances for department officials; (2) finance a $200,000 study by a pronuclear alternative to the Union for Concerned Scientists; (3) request that the U.S. Surgeon General ''certify the negligible effect of nuclear power reactors''; (4) recommend a number of sympathetic columnists who might interview department officials; and (5) identify a number of industry-based organizations that could distribute commissioned articles and other ''educational materials.''[46]

Information subsidies are expected to play a similar role in the Reagan administration's effort to dismantle the federal bureaucracy, and reduce the role of the state to the bare essentials—highways and defense. In the next chapter we will examine how information subsidies prepared the way for our first lesson in *Reaganomics*.

CHAPTER SEVEN FOOTNOTES

[1] U.S. Department of Commerce. Office of the Secretary. U.S. Technology Policy. Draft study. (1977). *Federal Register* 42:65 (April 5), 18121–18124.

[2] Greenberg, Daniel S. (1971). ''The Politics of Pure Science,'' p. 81. New York: New American Library.

[3] *Ibid.*, pp. 83–84.

[4] Kash, Don E. (1972). Politics and research. *In* S. Nagi, and R. Corwin (Eds.), ''The Social Contexts of Research,'' p. 105. New York: Wiley Interscience.

[5] Greenberg, Daniel S. Pages 120–121 in footnote 2, 1971.

[6] Abelson, Philip H. (1979). Power in Washington. *Science 203* (No. 4376) (January 12), 129.

[7] La Porte, Todd, and Metlay, Daniel. (1975). Technology observed: attitudes of a way public. *Science 188* (No. 4184) (April 11), 121–127.

[8] Wilson, Caroll L. (1980). What went wrong? *In* E. F. Oatman (Ed.), ''Prospects for Energy in America,'' p. 76. New York: H. W. Wilson.

[9] Hilts, Philip J. (1981). Gene splicers fear recedes, awe remains. *The Washington Post* (November 4), A1 ff.

[10] Goodell, Rae. (1975). ''The Visible Scientists.'' Boston, Massachusetts: Little, Brown & Company.

[11] Boffey, Phillip M. (1975). ''The Brain Bank of America.'' New York: McGraw-Hill.

[12] *Ibid.*, p. 61.

[13] *Ibid.*, p. 68.

[14] Ebbin, Steven, and Kasper, Raphael. (1974). "Citizen Groups and the Nuclear Power Controversy: Uses of Scientific and Technical Information," p. 1. Cambridge, Massachusetts: MIT Press.

[15] *Ibid.*, p. 211.

[16] Krieghbaum, Hillier. (1967). "Science and the Mass Media." New York: New York University Press.

[17] Goodfield, June. (1979). Communicating science: the special problems of reporting scientific enquiry in the media," p. 15. (Paper presented to the annual meeting of the International Institute of Communication, September.) (ERDS ED 182 774.)

[18] Hilts, Philip J. (1981). The gold rush of companies into biotechnology is waning. *The Washington Post* (November 3), A10.

[19] Marquis, Donald, and Allen, Thomas. (1966). Communication patterns in applied technology. *The American Psychologist 21*, 1052–1062.

[20] Hersey, David F. (1978). "Information resources and the growth of science and technology in the United States." (ERDS ED 180 436.); and Parker, Edwin B. (1973). "Information and society: a report to the national commission on libraries and information science." Washington, D.C.: U.S. Office of Education (DHEW).

[21] Sullivan, Walter. (1981). Data sources map the way in labyrinths of information. *The New York Times* (August 23), E9.

[22] Bethell, Tom. (1979). The gas price fixers. *Harper's* (June), 105.

[23] Council of Economic Advisors. (1978). "Economic Report of the President." Washington, D.C.: U.S. Government Printing Office.

[24] Use less, pay more. (1979). *Time* (April 16), 67.

[25] Metzenbaum, Howard. (1980). The case against oil price decontrol. *In* E. F. Oatman (Ed.), "Prospects for Energy in America," pp. 50–51. New York: H. W. Wilson.

[26] Commoner, Barry. (1979). "The Politics of Energy." New York: Alfred A. Knopf.

[27] *Ibid.*, p. 15.

[28] U. S. Congress. Senate. Committee on Energy and National Resoucres. (1978). "The relationship between the Department of Energy and energy industries," p. 2, 95th Congress, 2nd Session, June 16, July 10. Washington, D.C.: U.S. Government Printing Office.

[29] *Ibid.*, p. 29.

[30] Statement of Daniel Guttman in U.S. Congress. Senate. Subcommittee on Civil Services and General Services. (1979). "Federal Government's use of consultant services," p. 25, 96th Congress, October. Washington, D.C.: U.S. Government Printing Office.

[31] *Ibid.*, p. 29.

[32] Miller, James Nathan. (1980). Who has the facts? *In* E. Oatman (Ed.), "Prospects for Energy in America," p. 32. New York: H. W. Wilson.

[33] Barnouw, Eric. (1978). "The Sponsor," p. 164. New York: Oxford University Press.

[34] Commoner, Barry. Page 46 in footnote 26, 1979.

[35] Krieghbaum, Hillier. (1979). Three Mile Island: a crash course for readers. *Mass Communications Review 6* (No. 2) (Spring), 2–10.

[36] Friedman, Sharon M. (1981). Blueprint for breakdown: Three Mile Island and the media before the accident. *Journal of Communication 31* (No. 2) (Spring), 116–128.

[37] President's Commission on the Accident at Three Mile Island. (1979), "Report of the Public's Right to Know Task Force," p. 13, Washington, D.C.: U.S. Government Printing Office.

[38] Stephens, Mitchell, and Edison, Nadyne. (1980). Coverage of events at Three Mile Island. *Mass Communications Review 7* (No. 3) (Fall), 3–9.

[39] Mazur, Allan. (1981). Media coverage and public opinion on scientific controversies. *Journal of Communication 31* (No. 2) (Spring), 112–113.

[40] Luxenberg, Stan. (1979). Image industries thrive on crises. *The New York Times* (July 29), Sec. III, 9.

[41] Lanouette, William J. (1980). Under scrutiny by a divided government, the nuclear industry tries to unite. *National Journal* (January 12), 44–48.

[42] *Ibid.,* pp. 45–46.

[43] Haines, Pamela, and Moyer, William. (1981). "No Nukes" is not enough. *The Progressive* (March), 24–42.

[44] Burnstein, Paul, and Freudenburg, William. (1978). Changing public policy: the impact of public opinion, anti-war demonstrations, and war costs on Senate voting on Vietnam War motions. *American Journal of Sociology 84* (No. 1), 99–122.

[45] Haines, Pamela, and Moyer, William. Page 35 in footnote 43, 1981.

[46] United Press International. (1981). Memo urges PR drive for nuclear power. *The Washington Post* (October 12), A11.

8

Reaganomics

THE MANUFACTURED MANDATE

The Reagan economic program, which won victory after victory in both houses of Congress, was made possible by a widespread belief that the conservative president had the nation on his side. Bumper stickers on a few cars in Washington, D.C. reflected the power of this myth: "What this nation needs is a few Democrats with guts." With few exceptions, Democratic legislators had turned aside partisan interests and fell in line with the steamroller of proposals streaming out of the president's budget office. It was only near the end of the first year of the Reagan administration, when the evidence of failure was piling up like snowdrifts in a blizzard, that any form of opposition began to develop in the Congress.

It had been said that the nation was becoming increasingly conservative, and the election of Reagan was just the culmination of a gradual process. Paletz and Entman[1] mark the beginnings of the media's use of this theme with the series of articles by David Broder in *The Washington Post* in 1975. For some unexplained reason, journalists writing for largely liberal publications had misinterpreted the public opinion polls reported between 1968 and 1978. Paletz and Entman note that a smaller percentage of Americans identified themselves as conservative in 1978 than did so in 1968. At the same time, the proportion of Americans who believed that business operated in the public interest had fallen from 70 to 15%. While they noted some positions on social issues had moved to the right, many more moved in a decidedly liberal direction. And, most important, in terms of the content of the Reagan economic program, the majority of the people said they would prefer to cut defense expenditures, rather than cut funds for education or health care services.

Following the election, and after the smoke had cleared from the administration's flurry of budgetary maneuvers, a few voices were raised to question the validity of the election results as evidence of a national commitment toward conservative political change. A collection of studies based on the CBS and *New York Times* exit poll data[2] concluded that there was no conservative mandate. Most folks who voted for Reagan did not consider themselves to be conservatives, and actually disagreed with the candidate on a number of key issues. What they did agree was that Jimmy Carter was simply not up to the job, and there was a need for a change—in personnel, not in philosophy. Analysis of the more detailed and more carefully sampled opinions gathered by the University of Michigan's Institute for Social Research (ISR) pointed to similar conclusions.[3]

The tax cut proposal, which could not have been foreseen as being so clearly aimed at the upper and middle classes, was not supported by more than a third of the Democrats, and less than half of the Republicans voting for Reagan. Voters apparently favored an increase in educational spending, and continued to support most social programs with which they were familiar. Arthur Miller concluded that:

> the administration's repeated claims to "mandates" can thus be seen as a part of its attempt to in fact create such a consensus today, either by inventing popular wishes or using selective evidence to support its case.[4]

But, despite its absence in fact, the press treated the myth as reality. Paletz and Entman suggest that once the ball had begun to roll, and the patterns of "pack journalism" were established, reporters began to *seek out* conservatives as knowledgeable sources about this new political trend.

"Who sought whom?" is an empirical question. The dramatic increase in the resources available to the conservative think tanks and "educational foundations" from corporate supporters suggests that representatives of the New Right did not wait to be asked. The American Enterprise Institute (AEI) saw its budget increase tenfold in as many years to the point where its full-time and contract researchers were able to churn out hundreds of reports and analyses pointing to the wisdom of the new economics.[5] The growth of conservative ideas in the press was less of a reflection of public opinion than the return on the investment of firms that were expected to add an additional $60 million to an AEI endowment fund in less than three years.

Dividends on the corporate investments were being paid long before the election of Ronald Reagan. The intellectual contributions of the AEI and the other conservative policy research centers could be seen during the waning days of the Carter administration. Robert Zevin notes that changes in the Carter

Cabinet came in the summer of 1979 when monetarist Paul Volcker was appointed to head the Federal Reserve System. Earlier in February, the Joint Economic Committee, despite its having a Democratic majority, issued an annual report with some 42 recommendations that were indistinguishable from those in the Republican platform. Zevin notes that:

> the report denounced wage and price controls, excessive regulation, and govern-ment inefficiency; emphasized the primary importance of fighting inflation rather than unemployment; advocated monetary restraint, tax restraint, and spending restraint; endorsed special incentives for savers and investors.[6]

Conservative economists, nurtured in the warmth of AEI fellowships, and kept in shape by a series of special seminars, were already fairly well distributed throughout the Carter bureaucracy, and were a major force on many legislative staffs. Economics as a basic tool of policy making was by then already familiar to most legislators, and had largely replaced the more humanistic guidelines of justice and equity. Within regulatory agencies like the Federal Communications Commission (FCC), conservative economists led the charge to substitute the rule of imaginary markets for the will of the Congress.

With Reagan's election in November, the AEI and the other conservative resource groups began to prepare the way for a total and dramatic reorganization of the federal bureaucracy. With guidance from the Heritage Foundation's how-to-do-it manual—*A Mandate for Leadership*—and a virtual army of certified conservatives, the work began in earnest.

THE REAGAN BUDGET

Although there was much ideological work to be done, such as removing the vestiges of "favoritism toward labor or consumers,"[7] the most important item on the Reagan agenda was the preparation of a budget proposal. Throughout the presidential campaign, reporters and commentators presented Reagan as something of a "lightweight," as being far from the intellectual equal of either Carter or Anderson. His answers to complex questions were simple, homey, and very often wrong. As the conservative standard bearer, his grasp of conservative or any brand of economics was quite weak. The somewhat mystical quality of his projections led Republican opponents to label his approach "Voodoo Eco-nomics." Because of his weakness in the fiscal area, and because it was generally his style of leadership, Reagan the candidate and Reagan the president relied very heavily on his advisors and staff to take care of the fine details, while he concentrated on the ideological bottom line.

Bringing about an unprecedented reduction in the government's share of the GNP by reducing the growth in the federal budget was one thing. Doing it at the same time he was "closing the window of vulnerability" through an explosion in defense spending and attempting to stimulate personal savings and corporate investment through massive tax cuts was something else again. Balancing the budget at the same time would be nothing short of alchemy. Yet, this was the charge he laid before David Stockman, his choice to head the Office of Management and Budget (OMB).

Young, bright, articulate, and a certified true believer, Stockman had the responsibility not only for spinning gold from straw, but he was also expected to sell this fool's gold to the Congress and the U.S. public in very much the same way that he sold himself to the Reagan transition team. Stockman's skill as a performer and intellect had come to Reagan's attention at the time of the presidential debates. It was his responsibility to act as a stand-in for Carter and Anderson as Reagan practiced his disarming smile, and his look of naive innocence. His budgetary knowledge and conservative credentials were made known through a carefully planned and coordinated information-subsidy effort. Conservative columnists and Stockman admirers, Evans and Novak provided frequent lauditory mentions in their column. Through a series of well-timed leaks, his memorandum on Reagan's forthcoming "economic Dunkirk" was given prominent display in both *The Washington Post* and *The New York Times*.[8] His academic publications on the wastefulness of federal social programs were given broad circulation among Reagan's political advisors.

Even though he was not trained as an economist, and was something of a recent convert to the doctrines of supply-side theory, Stockman began the process of building a budget in fairly traditional fashion. Before constructing a model of his new economic system—based largely on an untested theory about the nature of human expectations—there would be a need for a strong statistical base upon which to mount it defense. Unfortunately, the numbers generated by the OMB computer were a long way from those he needed to gain support for his truly "revolutionary" proposals. When the computer runs kept predicting 1984 deficits in the neighborhood of $116 billion, Stockman simply called together a few like-minded souls and reprogrammed the computer until it produced numbers more in line with what supply-side logic would demand.

The newly educated computer finally reported that the good life for all Americans could be had if Stockman would get a $40 billion cut in federal spending in the first year, and was thereafter favored with declining interest rates and prices, at the same time that productivity, employment, and investment reached new heights.[9] All these things were the promise of the new economics, and they would depend on a dramatic shift in public expectations of the future.

Stockman's sleight of hand with the computer might have been able to snow the ill-informed and largely unmotivated members of Congress who were unwilling to look beyond the neon lights, but the investment community had computers of its own, and what their forecasts revealed was a lot closer to the numbers that Stockman had just banished from his realm.

With new figures in hand, Stockman rushed through the budget preparation phase in record time in order to take advantage of the element of surprise. Armed with his proposals and Reagan's approval for most of them, Stockman waded into the new Cabinet members before they had time to review the proposals thoroughly, or to make use of counterproposals suggested by the subsidy efforts of their bureaus, clients, or constituents. In one example, Stockman reports getting the upper hand at the Cabinet level in deliberations over his proposed cuts in the funding for the Export-Import Bank.

After engaging in what seemed like an interminable argument with Commerce Secretary Baldridge about the need to assist U.S. firms in competing against state-subsidized firms from Germany or Japan, Stockman triggered the release of his undercover subsidy by asking if anyone had any *facts* that might be used to resolve the issue. It just so happened that he had provided the Deputy Secretary of the Treasury with a list of the top 50 firms that were the principal beneficiaries of the export subsidy. The leading firms were some of the most heavily dependent corporations in the nation (Boeing, Lockheed, General Electric, Westinghouse, etc.). After the list was produced, Stockman appealed to Baldridge, with all the theatrics the moment required, to consider how it might *look* for the president to be asking for everyone to sacrifice, while Boeing received a subsidy.[10]

As a backup or reinforcement for his direct subsidy efforts, Stockman made sure that his victories received broad press coverage. This would ensure against backsliding, and it would also serve as a warning to others at different levels of the government. A key part of the Stockman strategy was to make it seem unconscionable for any legislator or bureaucrat to appeal on behalf of her own constitutents' interests while everybody elses' were being threatened. They were given to believe, from the steady publicity that the budget director's skirmishes were receiving, that they would be seriously damaged by their identification as one who would not go along with the Reagan mandate, and was instead aligned with the special interests.

Stockman's leverage for this "we're all in this together" approach to legislative management was weakened quite early in the game. Because of his perceived need to gain the support of powerful leaders like Howard Baker, Stockman choked up on his axe when it came time to chop the breeder reactor boondoggle at Clinch River.[11] His efforts to maintain an image of evenhandedness were dealt a more serious blow by Reagan himself. Stockman had a second group of budget items that he called "Chapter II." These proposals were directed mainly at closing the loopholes that primarily served the oil industry and other corporate interests. Reagan rejected the proposals, supposedly on ideological grounds, although it is just as likely that he feared the reaction of the Business Roundtable members who were responsible for his being in the White House. Instead, he went along with some of the more symbolic "mansion cap" recommendations, which would establish fees for private boats and aircraft. As partial payment, perhaps, W.R. Grace and Company took out a full page ad in the *Post:*

WE SAY REAGAN'S TAX CUTS DON'T FAVOR THE RICH. THE WASHINGTON POST SAYS WE'RE WRONG.

YOU BE THE JUDGE.

The ad contained a copy of a previous *Post* editorial that criticized an earlier Grace ad based on Stockman's magic numbers. Through neatly written comments in the margins, they proceeded to pick apart the *Post's* editorial line by line.[12] The ad concluded with an appeal for grass-roots action:

We are not alone in this argument. It affects all of us. And so we ask others who care—the business community, the press, and the people at large—to take an interest in this debate and be heard.

Write to your Congressmen today and tell them you support the Administration's efforts to lower our tax burden and cut government spending.

By May, Stockman and his magic budget had been promoted through every available media channel, and he was backed up by a direct appeal to the American Newspaper Publishers' Association (ANPA) convention. Warning that the debate over the Reagan budget was going to heat up very quickly, Stockman appealed to the publishers to keep their representation of that debate at a "high standard of balanced coverage." As an example of what he wanted them to guard against, Stockman proceeded to criticize the Congressional Budget Office (CBO) projections that demonstrated that a disproportunate penalty would fall on the poorer segments of society. Knowing full well that his own budget projections were purposely distorted, he actually claimed that some of the poor would enjoy a measurable increase in spendable income, and "at worst, 4% of the families would suffer a significant adverse shift." But even this group, he added, was not really poor as "60% have total incomes over the poverty level."[13]

In order to justify his proposals for cuts in Social Security, an area known to be politically sensitive, Stockman conjured up a set of statistics different from those he used in support of other parts of the budget. When Senator Moynihan decided to break the silence and challenge the crisis figures, Secretary Schweiker was forced to admit that the administration was using "worst case" figures for unemployment and inflation to show how the Social Security system would be stretched, while at the same time it was "officially projecting a much more favorable economic scenario for the rest of government."[14] When supporters of the National Science Foundation social science programs mounted their own subsidy effort to save their primary source of income, they suggested that there was a contradiction at hand when an administration that depended so heavily on economic statistics for its budgetary projections was at the same time proposing to wipe out those programs that provided the statistics.[15] What these critics failed to realize was that neither Stockman nor his chief congressional opponent, Jim

Jones, had any faith in the numbers they were using to bolster their arguments. William Greider quotes Stockman as admitting that:

> none of us really understands what's going on with all these numbers . . . . You've got so many different budgets out and so many different base lines . . . people are getting from A to B and it's not clear how they are getting there. It's not clear now we got there, and it's not clear how Jones is going to get there.[16]

For Wall Street analysts who had taken a much closer look at Stockman's statistics and the output of their own computers, it was already becoming clear that it simply was not possible to get to some of the imaginary savings Stockman was projecting. The financial pages were filled with talk of growing deficits, and the market fell into a steep decline. Rather than invest in productive ventures as the supply-side theory would predict, investors moved to take advantage of the record interest rates being offered on the money market. Eventually forced to face the growing doubts about the believability of their projections, the administration began to revise their estimates of 1981 deficits upward. While denying that a recession rather than a boom was the likely prospect, Treasury Secretary Donald Regan admitted that the summer might bring another "temporary" business slowdown.[17]

By this time, the element of surprise had been spent, and Stockman's ability to dazzle his opposition with statistical illusions was beginning to wear thin. At the last moment, Reagan went on national television to appeal to the U.S. public with some rhetorical tricks of his own. Those in the Congress who had begun to doubt the strength of Reagan's popular appeal immediately fell back in line once the flood of calls and letters were registered by their office staffs. Once again, Congress would suspend belief in the facts at their command, turning instead toward the fantasies being promoted by the White House.[18] The bedazzlement could not last.

Reagan was called upon more and more to use his personal appeal on the members of Congress. Democrats and Republicans alike were called into the Oval Office for a one on one with the president. Martin Schramm observed that Reagan's style differed markedly from the hard sell approach favored by Lyndon Johnson. Reagan was a listener. He conveyed the impression that he sympathized with the problems faced by legislators ill-equipped to defend the cuts in the programs that promised to weigh so heavily on their constituents, and were believed to favor the wealthy and powerful. Reagan would agree it was a problem, and indicate to an advisor to make a note of that problem so he could look into it. His charm was so complete that most legislators failed to notice his skilled use of index cards, keyed to the various parts of the Stockman budget plan likely to be the subject of questions or complaint. When there were not any answers to be found on the cards, Reagan would respond: "I just have faith it will work out all right."[19]

Perhaps becoming a bit overconfident with the success of his direct subsidy approach, Reagan failed to prepare sufficiently for a press conference in June, and took a rather severe beating at the hands of journalists who were declaring the traditional honeymoon was over. Despite the need for his support behind his tax cut, and the second round of budget cuts, Reagan avoided the conference room for more than 15 weeks. When he was forced to return in October, he was well-rehearsed and supplied with the props appropriate for the illusion he was hoping to create. When he was asked if he had succeeded in winning the confidence of Wall Street, he magically produced a letter that supposedly made it so.[20]

For those moments when the questioning got too heavy, and it was clear that his answers were growing dangerously thin, Reagan was able to turn to his right and direct the next question to come from a collection of "known friendlies" that his staff had assigned to the front-row seats. Schramm notes a particular example where the pressure of questions about the persistent high interest rates led the president to call on the vice president of RKO General Broadcasting. Clifford Evans took the cue smartly, and asked the president what were his thoughts about traveling to China.[21]

By the end of October, however, the Reagan forces were revealing considerable dissension in the ranks. This was different from the somewhat juvenile flaps that occurred when Secretary of State Alexander Haig tried to assert his authority over matters of foreign policy. Economic policy was at the core of the Reagan administration, and there were signs that it was coming apart at the seams. Stockman was no longer limiting his statements to the press to off-the-record leaks. He had gone on the offensive in an effort to capture the confidence of the financial markets while trying to convince Reagan's political advisors that even more difficult cuts would have to be made.

The internal debates taking place within the administration were moved onto center stage in an analytical piece by Caroline Atkinson in the *Post*.[22] Stockman had gone public with his call for a reduction in the tax cut—an option rejected by Reagan. He needed to drive home the seriousness of the rising deficits, which it was no longer in his interest to hide, or explain away.

Whether it was by coincidence, or had been timed to maximize its impact on the debate, William Grieder's article on the "Education of David Stockman" was released to the public. The reaction was immediate. Here was the architect of Reaganomics being quoted as saying that supply-side economics was "trickle down theory" in disguise; here was the dazzling light of congressional testimony admitting that his figures were as phony as the theory they were meant to reflect; and here was the insider describing the politics of tax reform as akin to hogs at the feeding trough. For those unable to get a copy of the *Atlantic Monthly* article, which had been sold out almost immediately, the *Post* ran a lengthy abstract with some of the more damaging quotes.[23]

Perhaps because the Greider article merely linked its source to things that Stockman had been leaking regularly to the press,[24] or because he knew that this sorcerer had no apprentice with whom he could be replaced, Stockman's offer of resignation was refused. However, because his credibility had been so seriously damaged by the revelations made in the article, Treasury Secretary Regan would assume much of the responsibility for the public defense of the administration's economic program. From Stockman's point of view, it was probably just as well, as the president seemed unwilling to follow his advice, and continued to resist proposed cuts in defense, social security, or a reduction in the promised tax cuts.

By December, virtually all of Reagan's advisors were trying to get him to face up to reality, and admit the impossibility of his meeting his budgetary goals. Failing in the direct approach as Stockman had before them, Reagan's advisors increased the volume of leaks to the press. Cabinet members, faced with additional cuts in their budgets, began to go on the offensive to protect their programs.[25]

In an almost desperate attempt to demonstrate that he was still in charge, despite all the evidence to the contrary, Reagan staged a showdown with Congress over the continuing resolutions that were generally necessary to sustain the government until final budgetary details had been completed. In his veto message, Reagan attempted to shift the responsibility for the failure of Reaganomics to the shoulders of the Congress:

> By refusing to make even this small saving to protect the American people against overspending, the Congress has paved the way for higher interest rates and inflation and the continued loss of investment, jobs and economic growth.[26]

Reagan shut down the government and sent the "nonessential" workers home for the day over a difference of less than $2.5 billion—an insignificant amount when the budget deficit was expected to top $100 billion.[27] *The Washington Post* cited "senior officials" as admitting that "the president needed a vehicle to reaffirm his enthusiasm for budget cutting, even if he has to abandon his recent objectives." If the Congress defeated the president on this relatively insignificant issue, those sources felt that it would be impossible to win congressional support for additional cuts that he would have to propose in February 1982. Although he had won that symbolic battle with the Congress, Reagan appeared to be losing the struggle within the White House.

Reagan's economic advisors, in a dramatic bit of heresy, reported to an audience at an AEI seminar that deficits really did not matter. William Niskanen, member of the President's Council of Economic Advisors, made the most detailed comments on the issue:

> Controlling for the other obvious conditions that affect inflation rates in a more complex model, you also find no effect of deficits themselves on the inflation rate. . . . So we shouldn't worry about a direct relationship between deficits and inflation. It just is not in the data, and it isn't consistent with at least monetary theory, and it is not something I think there is any special reason to be concerned.[28]

That might be something that an academic economist could say to a group of graduate students peering over a mountain of computer output; but this was the purest heresy for all but the strictest Republican monetarists. Secretary Regan was quick to appear before a special breakfast held for key journalists, and reassert the administration's line that the president was "not soft on deficits."[29] At the same time that Regan was trying to put out the fire on the matter of deficits, he made his own contribution to a growing sense of disarray within the administration.

As part of his evidence that the president wanted to reduce the budget deficit, and eventually achieve a balanced budget, Regan implied that the president was now willing to impose a windfall profits tax as a condition for further decontrolling the price of natural gas. This was in direct conflict with promises that Reagan had made to one of the "boll weevil" Democrats in order to ensure his vote on the reconciliation bill. Representative English was expected to hold the president to his promise; and the noose drew tighter still.

By the end of the year, conservative columnists Evans and Novak were describing Reagan as a prisoner of his advisors. The president apparently could not be counted on to stick with the script on economic matters. As a result of the extremely high degree of staff control and responsibility in the White House, "Reagan has only a tiny window to receive and transmit information beyond the confines of his elite staff—contacts with Congress, the news media and a few friends."[30] Following his press conference of December 17, 1981, when the president reiterated his resolve not to raise taxes, he was reminded that his latest proposal to Congress included $22 billion in "revenue enhancements"—newspeak for taxes. As had been done throughout his campaign, and at several points during his first year, Reagan's press secretary was obliged to "set the record straight" about what the president *actually meant to say*.

REAGANOMICS AND REALITY

As noted in Chapter Three, objective social conditions may be both cause and result of significant changes in public policy. The Reagan economic program began with an attempt to redefine the nature of economic and political reality. Capitalizing on a media-generated belief in a transformation of national political consciousness, the Reagan team defined its policies as the crystallization of this nascent conservativism. Long before the new budget was actually introduced, the information-subsidy effort focused attention on the efficiency and ideological commitment of the Reagan transition team. The budget itself was introduced with a media blitz of uncommon proportions. However, Stockman's magic numbers, and his unrealistic assumptions about the nature of economic behavior, provided the Congress with a view of the world that simply could not be sustained.

While the publication of Stockman's confessions was a damaging blow to the credibility of administration pronouncements, it was the grim reality of the economy itself that raised the costs of supporting Reaganomics. It soon became clear that the people who mattered—those in the investment community—simply did not believe it was possible to maintain necessary growth without the continued stimulation of government spending in the social sector.

In one sense, Reaganomics was an attempt to swim against the tide of economic reality. If the "new conservatism" was as well developed as the Reagan forces claimed, then it might have been possible to maintain a broad commitment within the Congress despite the sharp downturn in the economy. But because this mandate was as artificial as Stockman's budgetary projections, it was swept away with the first strong breeze. The lesson of Reaganomics is that truly conservative notions of competition and rugged independence of action are incompatible with the needs of the transnational corporations at their present stage of development.

While members of the Business Roundtable may have initially lent their support to the Reagan program, this support was based primarily on the expectation that the benefits of Reaganomics would come in the form of reductions in the costs of regulation—tax cuts and related incentives for investment. Threats to effective consumer demand for their products was not part of the bargain. Following a period of readjustment, we can expect the voice of corporate America to begin singing a somewhat different tune about the responsibilities of government, and once again we may find ourselves humming its catchy but somewhat elusive melody without remembering just where we heard it . . .

We'd like to teach the world to sing in perfect harmony, . . .

CHAPTER EIGHT FOOTNOTES

[1] Paletz, David L., and Entman, Robert M. (1981). "Media Power Politics," pp. 196–212. New York: The Free Press.

[2] Wilson, James Q. (1981). Does Reagan have a mandate? *The New York Times Book Review* (June 7), 3 ff.

[3] Miller, Arthur H. (1981). What mandate? What realignment? *The Washington Post* (June 28), D1 ff.

[4] *Ibid.*, p. D5.

[5] Stone, Peter H. (1981). Conservative brain trust. *The New York Times Magazine* (May 3), 18 ff.

[6] Zevin, Robert B. (1981). The new economic faith. *The Atlantic Monthly* (April), 25.

[7] Brown, Warren. (1981). Donovan to reorganize the Department of Labor. *The Washington Post* (July 10), A3.

[8] Kaiser, Robert G. (1981). High visibility and higher stakes. *The Washington Post* (February 5), A1.

[9] Greider, William. (1981). The education of David Stockman. *The Atlantic Monthly* (December), 32.

[10] *Ibid.*, p. 35.

[11] *Ibid.*, p. 36.

¹² Grace, W.R. & Company. (1981). We say Reagan's tax cuts don't favor the rich (advertisement). *The Washington Post* (March 24), A7.

¹³ Jones, William H. (1981). Stockman: clash of old and new. *The Washington Post* (May 7), B1.

¹⁴ Rich, Spencer. (1981). Plight of Social Security is being exaggerated Democrats charge. *The Washington Post* (July 8), A3.

¹⁵ Hilts, Philip J. (1980). White House uses social sciences, but cuts funding for research. *The Washington Post* (June 29).

¹⁶ Greider, William. Page 38 in footnote 9, 1981.

¹⁷ Pine, Art. (1981). $60 billion budget deficit likely. *The Washington Post* (May 7), B1.

¹⁸ Schramm, Martin. (1981). Reagan tax lobbyist: an artist at work. *The Washington Post* (August 13), A3.

¹⁹ *Ibid.*

²⁰ Schramm, Martin. (1981). A safe performance. *The Washington Post* (October 13), A11.

²¹ *Ibid.*

²² Atkinson, Caroline. (1981). Supply side: is the bubble bursting? *The Washington Post* (November 9), A1 ff.

²³ Grieder, William. (1981). What David Stockman said. *The Washington Post* (November 22), C1 ff.

²⁴ Kaiser, Robert G. (1981). Those embarrassing words have a familiar ring. *The Washington Post* (November 13), A1 ff.

²⁵ Atkinson, Caroline, and Kaiser, Robert G. (1981). Administration deeply split over further cuts in budget. *The Washington Post* (December 6), A14.

²⁶ Reagan, Ronald. (1981). Stopgap bills are "budget-busters." *The Washington Post* (November 24), A5.

²⁷ Kaiser, Robert G. (1981). Probably good politics, but budget problems remain unresolved. *The Washington Post* (November 24), A6.

²⁸ Niskanen, William. (1981). Comments before American Enterprise Institute seminal. *The Washington Post* (December 12), F6.

²⁹ Broder, David S. (1981). President is not soft on deficits, aides say. *The Washington Post* (December 10), A9.

³⁰ Evans, Rowland, and Novak, Robert. (1981). The president's taxphobia. *The Washington Post* (December 21), A21.

9

Information
Inequality

Christopher Jencks' radical egalitarianism[1] will find no ready ear in a time of Reaganomics. His call for equality of outcome or results, instead of equality of opportunity was even a bit too much for the liberal forces enrolled in the War on Poverty.[2] Jencks' analysis had demonstrated that the causes of income inequality were many, and in contrast to the proponents of victim-blaming solutions, he rejected the possibility and the ultimate utility of equalizing schooling or the cognitive skills it is supposed to produce. We face a similar problem in trying to reduce the inequality in the distribution of information and the power to put it to use.

Fritz Machlup[3] identifies five different types of knowledge as viewed from the perspective of the knower. We are concerned here with practical knowledge—the information one has that can be used in one's work, in making decisions, and in taking actions, which may include actions to influence the decisions of others. The distribution of practical knowledge in this society is *at least* as distorted as the distribution of income. Unequal access to practical information tends to be self-reinforcing, and over time, the inequality tends to grow. Just as access to education does not automatically result in a narrowing of the income gap, access to information does not result in a narrowing of the gap in knowledge or power. Indeed, many have suggested that an increase in the flow of information only widens that gap.

THE KNOWLEDGE GAP

There are a great many explanations for the inequitable distribution of practical information, but these three factors are most often seen as reinforcing this pattern: (1) information systems, including the mass media, tend to distribute information in a form most familiar to users with more education; (2) information users with more education and more highly developed communication and analytical skills have a greater variety of uses for available information; and (3) information users in the upper classes have more interpersonal contacts where policy-relevant information often serves as social currency.[4] Stated another way, the poor have come to see very little utility in much of the information that is available to them in society, either because it is too complex or difficult to understand, or because they cannot see how they might put it to use to improve their present condition.

Evidence of media's tilt toward the upper classes is available from a number of sources. Findahl and Höijer have focused on television news in Sweden and suggest that the traditional organization of broadcasts tends to fragment the stories so that members of the audience get only bits and pieces of information, and very little understanding of events at home and abroad.[5] Comprehension is diminished further when the stories are about unfamiliar places, events, and circumstances, and the broadcasters fail to provide enough contextual material for the viewer to make the necessary personal association—''where does this information fit with what I already know about the world?'' Because of the bias toward the already initiated, many stories for the average viewer are nothing but ''words, words, words.'' In a series of experimental investigations, Findahl and Höijer found that the more highly educated were able to recall more stories and more detail about those stories than those with less education. They concluded that:

> the failure to describe background factors in many items meant that they were only understood by people who already knew something about the news event and could thus place the information offered in context on their own.[6]

Whatever communication there was taking place, was between broadcasters and the already well-informed members of the audience.

Through her studies of Finnish workers, and their perception of their social problems, Elina Suominen concluded that:

> the media use primarily the language and terminology familiar to the highly educated section of the population, the terminology which those with less education have not completely mastered. They talk about issues so abstract that they do not reach the audience and in a manner shunned by the working class.[7]

She noted, as well, a tendency for ''serious'' subjects, discussions of history, politics, and economics—content at the heart of public affairs—to be covered only by those media favored by the educated classes.

Stauffer, Frost, and Rybolt[8] determined that the language used by news-writers was at a fairly high level of difficulty, which might serve as a barrier for "functional illiterates" in the U.S. audience. In their study of learning and recall from television, they compared adult nonreaders with college students and found significant differences in the expected direction. The ever-widening information and knowledge gap can be seen clearly to be linked to the fact that those who rely most heavily on television news for their public-affairs information are likely to derive the least amount of information from that source.

Clarke and Fredin[9] have provided additional evidence from a well-constructed analysis of media use and public-affairs knowledge. They assumed that an informed voter should have *reasons* for an expressed preference for a political candidate. The number of reasons that respondents could provide was taken as an index of the extent to which they had been informed by media or other sources of information. As expected, those who relied more heavily on television news for their public-affairs information were less likely to have detailed reasons for candidate preferences. Even when education and interest in political issues were statistically removed as influences, reliance on newspapers helped, whereas reliance on television news actually worked against rational political decision making.

There are, of course, even class differences between newspapers, and depending upon which newspapers one chooses, one can expect to be more or less well informed. Readers of *The New York Times* were significantly better prepared than readers of the *Daily News* or *The Washington Post*. These studies and others seeking to document and understand the knowledge gap phenomenon suggest that even when the poor and the poorly educated attend to the news, they learn less because of the manner in which public-affairs issues are treated in the media they prefer.

The difficulty in comprehension that is associated with the complexity of the issues and the lack of familiarity or experience with them lead to an avoidance of such stories, or those media channels characteristically presenting such material. There are even differences among the elite leaders of the society in terms of their willingness to expose themselves to more difficult or unfamiliar material on a regular basis. Carol Weiss's investigation into "What America's Leaders Read"[10] revealed that business and political leaders were likely to rank *Readers Digest* and *U.S. News and World Report* very high on their list of magazines read regularly, while intellectuals and managers of the mass media were likely to place these sources near the bottom of their list. Conversely, the *New York Review of Books* was ranked second, next to *The New York Times Magazine* for the intellectuals, but sixteenth and seventeenth for the economic and political leaders, respectively.

Perceived utility is the most important quality of information in determining the amount of time, money, or energy any potential user will invest in transforming that information into practical knowledge. People tend to seek information when they see both the need and the *possibility* of meaningful action on their part. People who have accepted their circumstances as unyielding can have no incentives for seeking additional verification of that fact.

It is suggested that the poor are less likely to see their problems as having a basis in information. Brenda Dervin's work with low-income users of public services revealed that the poor tended to identify fewer situations as problematic; of those they identified, they tended to see those problems as being less complex, involving fewer people or influences. They also tended to see fewer connections between their situation and other events taking place in their environment. Their responses to problematic situations were seen to be less complex, in that the poor used a narrower range of tactics in overcoming difficulty, and in general, they sought less information than their wealthier counterparts.[11] The objective conditions faced by the poor people in Dervin's sample were apparently such that they did not evaluate information with the same criteria used by the general population. Social support and encouragement rather than problem resolution, or even the possibility of resolution, were all the poor had come to expect from others, and the information they might provide. Since they rarely expected to be helped in planning strategies of action, information was rarely sought toward that end. It would make little sense, therefore, for such persons to invest time and energy in the pursuit of information that was unlikely to provide support and encouragement.

Perceived utility is not limited to estimations of the effectiveness of the information. The salience or relevance of the issue to individuals also determines the amount of personal investment they will make in gathering information. When asked what information they wanted, or thought they needed, Suominen[12] found that people wanted more information about things in their immediate, day-to-day experience—information about the availability of food, receipes for preparing it, changes in old-age pensions, etc. There was no expressed interest in current affairs, things that would ultimately have an effect on the quality of their lives. Their subjective estimation of their need for information had been conditioned over time so that it diverged consistently from an objective need to know more about issues and events that impact on their lives.

It is clear, however, that when there is substantial interest and by inference some perceived utility to be derived from knowledge about some event or issue, some of the mass media can result in a narrowing of the knowledge and information gap. Genova and Greenberg's preliminary[13] investigation into the relationship between interest and knowledge suggests that there are differences associated with the way that interest is defined. Self-interest is defined as a function of the "event's influence on their own life, their job or that of someone close to them, the cost of living, and their general satisfaction with things around them." Self-interest so defined was not as good a predictor of gains in factual or structural knowledge as a measure of what they defined as social interest. The extent to which one talked about an issue or event with friends, family, or co-workers was a better predictor of how much people learned about the National Football League strike, or the Nixon impeachment proceedings. The distinction between self-interest and social interest may be valuable as a concept, but it is unlikely that most viewers would be able to identify how either event would have an impact on their personal lives. And, because it is the nature of broadcast news to treat most *stories* as just that—dramatic events displayed in their broad outline, with conflict and resolution in 30 seconds—there is rarely any suggestion of any public role or responsibility, or any incentive for a viewer to get involved. It is only when familiarity with those stories—not substantially different from one's familiarity with a soap opera, or a recent movie—is useful in maintaining social contact that one is likely to invest the time and effort necessary to learn more of the details.

ACCESS, COMPREHENSION, AND COMMUNICATION COMPETENCE

Information inequality is not limited to the receiving end of the communication process. Just as there are differences in the incentives and resources necessary for one to use information to reduce one's own uncertainty, there is substantial inequality in the ability to produce uncertainty in others, or to reduce their uncertainty in ways that are personally beneficial. Just as lack of familiarity with the language and analytical approaches common to certain media channels serves as a barrier to their ι ? by the poor and the poorly educated to solve their own problems, their inability to translate their ideas and insights into forms appropriate to those channels will limit their utility as a means of influencing others.

Robert Meadow sees strikes, riots, demonstrations, and "terrorist activity" as the "language of the inarticulate."[14] Those who are relatively less articulate, in terms of their ability to utilize political language appropriate to the courts, the legislature, or the evidentiary hearing, are seen to turn to less traditional forms of political communication.

Differential access to mass media channels has also been noted by several observers of the U.S. press. Edie Goldenberg's "Making the Papers" is perhaps the most comprehensive attempt to describe the imbalance in a single metropolitan area.[15] After noting that mass media channels are used by groups as an alternative to direct access to government officials, Goldenberg provided support for a number of propositions about the likelihood of gaining access. She noted a tendency in the press to prefer simple, easily verifiable, nontechnical issues, and a tendency to avoid those issues that required analysis and interpretation. Thus, if the concerns of a community group surrounded historical relationships, or underlying issues like racism or sexism, there was great difficulty in having those issues covered in the press.

Groups that were well-organized, and had sufficient resources to allow them to prepare detailed, "factual" reports and analyses were more likely to have their perspectives on the definition of problems and solutions given regular display in the media. However, the number of "outgroups" with such resources was seen to be quite low. For the resource-poor groups to be defined as newsworthy, something unusual must occur, whereas "the newsworthiness of someone prominent is virtually ensured by his or her prominence."[16] Goldenberg and others note the barrier that routines or "beats" represent for the resource-poor or underrepresented groups. Bureaucratically organized sources can be counted on for usable material on a regular basis, and they need not make a special effort to attract the attention of the press. Each day a reporter will make her way down to city hall, where news is bound to happen. Another reporter will go to the courts or the police district. In order to get the reporter to depart from those routines, some special event or disturbance in the routine must be planned.

Mark Fishman provides an example of the kinds of barriers faced by the inarticulate, even when they happen to be part of a routine news event. He describes a non-event as "something which cannot be seen under a certain scheme of interpretation but can be seen under a different one."[17] This particular non-event was a woman who had come to testify in a public hearing, but her comments and suggestions did not fit sufficiently well within the parameters of the issue as defined by the officials. Because she did not represent any group with standing in the debate, there was no incentive for the press or the board to make any effort to understand how her concerns were part of the proceedings. As a result, her intervention in the proceedings was little more than an embarrassing pause, and because it did not appear on the evening news—it did not happen.

Goldenberg suggests that there are countless other characteristics and procedures of news work that work against the interests of resource-poor groups in gaining access. Even when it may be possible for a group to gain favor with a particular reporter who may wish to support them in their cause, the organizational requirements for rewrite, editorial conferences, professional standards, and a preference for authoritative sources may combine to weaken the influence of any single reporter. In summarizing her observations in the Boston metropolitan region, Goldenberg concludes that:

> resource-rich sources enjoy certain advantages that place them in a much stronger position to bargain with reporters and to manage the news than resource-poor groups. These advantages stem from conventional criteria of newsworthiness applied in newspapers, from the structure of the beat and the specialist systems, and from the capabilities of rich sources to ease the reporter's job in collecting the news.[18]

Thus, the ability to subsidize the information-gathering efforts of a reporter, and through him, that of the ultimate target in the policy arena, is seen to vary directly with wealth or resources. Herbert Gans takes a similar position on the relationship between journalists, sources, resources, and power:

> Given the journalists' insatiable appetite for story ideas and stories, sources which are able to supply suitable news can overcome deficiencies of power. Even so, the ability to be newsworthy itself requires resources and skills, many of which go hand in hand with economic power, at least, and are possessed by only a few.[19]

Occasionally, as in the case of the Students for a Democratic Society (SDS), media coverage is not originally pursued, and later attempts to influence news-making are taken more as a means of self-defense than a means of producing influence over public policy. Todd Gitlin's[20] reconstruction of the battle between movement and media for self-definition is a story of attempts to beat the media system at its own game and losing badly. A grass-roots, person-to-person organization, based on an intellectual and philosophical tradition of resistance and democratic participation, was transformed into a loosely coordinated national movement that had lost sight of its original purpose.

Gitlin suggests that other opposition movement groups learned from the experience of the SDS, and some, like Common Cause and Ralph Nader's consumer groups have even achieved a degree of legitimacy:

> Ralph Nader and other public interest lawyers have become respected celebrities, often interviewed for response statements, photographed in suits and ties and sitting squarely behind desks or in front of bookshelves, embodying solid expertise and mainstream reliability. They have learned how to make the journalistic code work for them.[21]

In spite of the alleged legitimacy that reduces the costs they face in managing the news, public-interest or consumer-oriented sources are still relatively poor when compared with the information power of government and industry.

Common Cause, perhaps the most successful of the consumer organizations in terms of its ability to generate consistently favorable coverage of its activities, and accurate transmission of its perspective on a variety of public policy issues,[22] has a budget in the neighborhood of $5 million, and nearly a third of that amount is spent each year in an effort to recruit and retain members.[23] General Motors, on the other hand, spent that much in 1976 just for its own dues payments to a variety of trade associations.[24] Ralph Nader's organization, Public Citizen, ideologically committed to grass-roots participation, has been forced to seek more well-heeled supporters, through a $1,000-a-plate fund-raising dinner.[25] Corporate America, on the other hand, can spend whatever it wishes on the production of influence, and has most of those expenditures treated as legitimate business expenses.

IRS AND THE BUDGETARY CONSTRAINT

Since 1962, Income Tax Regulations issued by the Internal Revenue Service (IRS) allow corporations to deduct the expenses they incur in efforts to mobilize public opinion. The inequity of a law that allows the corporation privileges denied to citizens is no longer the point of debate; instead, corporate attorneys are seeking to remove even this last barrier from the corporate roadway. In 1980, the IRS proposed a series of rules to determine whether the fine line between direct and indirect information subsidization had been crossed.[26] In 1978, congressional hearings based on a survey by the Congressional Reference Service (CRS) revealed widespread disregard for existing IRS guidelines regarding "grass-roots lobbying."[27]

Out of 467 firms surveyed, only 268 responded, and only 170 of those could be considered to be reasonably complete. Many of the firms simply replied that "their records and accounts were not kept in such a manner as to enable them to respond partially or fully to the questionnaire."[28] But, there was some evidence that the Business Roundtable, the American Gas Association, The U.S. Chamber of Commerce, and the National Association of Electric Companies wrote their membership suggesting that only the most limited response was required, as most doubted that the CRS had the authority to require compliance with its request.

The CRS teams suggested that many of the firms that engaged in grass-roots information campaigns did so out of ignorance of the law with regard to such indirect subsidies. They found, for example, 20 firms that reported that they did not attempt to influence legislation through appeals to the public, but then enclosed examples of messages doing just that. Annual reports to shareholders were widely used by corporations to express positions on legislative matters, or in support of broad ideological positions. Other routes to the public not often considered in discussions of advocacy advertising include the practice of manufacturers, especially those in the automotive industry, to send special messages to their customers, dealers, suppliers, and others likely to have a common interest in automotive safety or energy legislation. Electric companies and other public utilities include messages to their users with the monthly bill.

After estimating the business efforts to influence public opinion probably exceeded $1 billion a year, S. Prakash Sethi concluded that the public was essentially helpless to counteract this massive subsidy:

> Even if a group were able to counteract the information presented in a specific advocacy advertisement through a paid advertisement of its own, or if a newspaper were to carry a story or an editorial correcting any false impression created by a particular ad, no group, no paper, no TV station is in a position to continuously match the efforts of a corporation for the duration of an advocacy campaign.[29]

The IRS proposals were in no way meant to serve as a means of redressing the balance between the public and the corporate interest. Instead, the proposed guidelines were meant to clarify the rules so that corporations and voluntary associations would no longer confuse legitimate and exempt means of producing influence.

The regulations proposed three criteria that would determine whether a particular information subsidy would constitute "an attempt to influence the public with respect to legislation."[30] The proposed criteria leave a tremendous amount of room for the management of public opinion at public expense:

A communication will be treated as an attempt of that sort only if it— (1) Pertains to actions by a legislative body; (2) Reflects a view on that legislative action, whether explicitly or implicitly; and (3) Is distributed in a manner so as to reach individuals as voters or constituents.[31]

The responses of corporate, association, and foundation executives filled volume after volume of IRS files.[32] The American Association of Advertising Agencies, whose members' incomes would be affected by any restriction on the eligibility of advocacy ads, sent the IRS a 19-page response. Leonard S. Matthews, president of the Association, argued that the regulations allow firms to deduct "all the ordinary and necessary expenses" that they incur in carrying on trade or business, as long as it is appropriate and has the promise of being useful. It was only reasonable that attempts to influence the public with regard to legislation be seen as similarly ordinary and necessary.

The Mobil Oil Company, widely recognized as the leader among firms directing their messages toward the public, devoted most of their response to what they saw as inequities in the way the regulations are applied. Because of Mobil's running battle with the networks over their refusal to carry some of the firm's more controversial advertisements, their attorney was quick to point out the contradiction in the policies that support or even require editorializing by media corporations, but impose restrictions on the editorializing by other firms. The letter complained as well about the tricks used by organizations to bypass guidelines for the use of "nonpartisan analysis, study or research." Citing Energy Action as an example, Mobil suggested that so-called educational foundations were really fronts for lobbying organizations, and the research reports they released were really efforts to influence the grass roots.

Mobil's concern for improvement in the IRS's administration of tax laws can only be seen as posturing in light of the corporation's own behavior with regard to accuracy in reporting subsidy expenditures. In 1977, Mobil is reported to have spent $4 million on advocacy ads. The corporation is not registered as a lobbyist, and the seven individuals who did register and listed Mobil as a client reported spending less than $800 between them on Mobil's behalf in the first nine months of that year.[33] While Mobil was suggesting that public interest organizations ought to be more forthright in reporting their expenditures, its Board of Directors was recommending against similar disclosures to its stockholders. A religious order in Milwaukee that owned some 2,000 shares of Mobil stock had offered a resolution requiring the corporation to "summarize all expenditures in fiscal years 1979 and 1980 on lobbying and advertising. Include separate accounting for expenditures on the Washington, D. C. public affairs office, outside counsel, and indirect lobbying to convince stockholders and the public of our company's positions."[34]

In recommending against passage of the resolution, the Board of Directors argued that:

> Mobil, like every other company involved in efforts to affect the course of governmental actions relating to its business, files regular reports as requested by law on its lobbying activities. . . . Further reporting as requested by the proponent of this proposal would serve no useful purpose. Mobil considers the efforts it makes in this area crucial to the welfare of the corporation and its shareholders because of the economic impact that governmental regulation can and does have on its business affairs and profitability.[35]

Yet, Mobil was among the respondents to the CRS inquiry that denied being involved in any grass-roots lobbying activities, and only provided a pro forma response of the type recommended by the Business Roundtable.

The IRS is unlikely to take any action to improve its own administration of existing tax laws. The 1980 proposals came only after a series of well-publicized congressional hearings, and the response from the corporate community was so immediate and so well coordinated that only a series of public scandals two orders of magnitude more serious than Koreagate could pressure the newly appointed commissioner to take action on these proposals. In addition, because they are limited to only a small part of the total of subsidized information, strict adherence to existing regulations would do very little to redress the balance of power.

Neither existing nor proposed regulations would apply to attempts to influence the actions of administrative or executive agencies. Even though such agencies have the responsibility of interpreting the intention of Congress in their administration of the laws, attempts to influence *those* regulations would be deductible as legitimate business expenses . . . unless of course, you were not *in* business, but merely employed by one.

For the briefest instant in the history of regulatory action, public participation in the rule-making process had been subsidized by the agencies involved. Under the leadership of Michael Pertschuk, the Federal Trade Commission (FTC) led the way in offering support to consumer and small-business representatives wishing to testify before the Commission.[36] Critics of Pertshuck's activism in pursuit of his version of the public interest suggest that Pertschuk and his assistant, Tracy Westen, used these funds to "stack the deck" against the corporate position in a number of investigations.[37] They were particularly incensed by the fact that most of the groups compensated for expenses related to delivering testimony were actually based in Washington, and their principal activity was seen as lobbying the government. Agency representatives were quite willing to admit that the funds were useful in helping them to hold their ground against overwhelming industry power:

It's just not an equal match when the hearing record is dominated by business alone. Nor is it fair and reasonable to have a GS-14 from our agency negotiating with some high-powered corporate lawyer from Arnold and Porter. We need the counterpressure that the public-interest groups provide.[38]

However, even before the budgetary squeeze of the Reagan administration had begun to be felt throughout the bureaucracy, the system had already started to correct the distortions introduced by its more liberal wing. The Ford Foundation announced that it would withdraw its support from the public-interest law firms that its $21 million in grants had brought into existence. At about the same time, traditional Democratic supporters of public participation agreed to leave provisions of financing for such participation out of their regulatory reform proposals.[39] With the almost total withdrawal of federal and foundation support for public representation before administrative and judicial bodies, inequality of information promises to spread at an alarming rate, and the mounting pressure to ''deregulate'' the information industry can only add to that trend.

INFORMATION UTILITIES AND THE INFORMATION POOR

The popular mythology that sees the avalanche of new information technologies as heralding a new democratic, egalitarian age is little more than a cruel hoax—the product of marketing hype, or self-delusion. What we know about the relationship between the flow of information and its utilization by different segments of society can only lead to the conclusion that the gap between the haves and the have-nots will widen even further until the slender thread that binds these ends together snaps with the most distressing consequences.

Nolan Bowie is among those who reject the dominant view of information technology as a liberating force in a capitalist society. In his comments on the promise of the new technologies for service in the public interest, Bowie offers three propositions: (1) that the distribution of benefits flowing from the new technologies will widen the information gap between the rich and the poor; (2) that the new technologies, despite their number and supposed variety, will not result in more diversified viewpoints, better programming, or greater access by potential communicators; and (3) that minority audiences will remain of marginal interest, and will have limited input into the development of systems, or in the design of content.[40] The primary support offered for these pessimistic forecasts is the recognition that the transformation of information into a commodity traded in an unregulated marketplace will mean that the poor will simply not be able to afford access to most of the new technologies or their software.

The resource constraint faced by the poor in making use of the new information technologies is not limited entirely to considerations of economic resources. Presently, there is a boundless supply of information available without cost in the nation's libraries. This information is not utilized by the poor in large measure because of the personal costs in terms of time and effort to glean practical information from systems organized to serve the needs and interests of the middle and upper classes. Edwin Parker suggests that it is "unfair" to compare the poor's use of library resources with their use of television and other entertainment because "much more money is spent (by advertisers) to subsidize television than is spent (by government) to subsidize libraries. Television has more incentive to work hard at attracting audiences."[41] He suggests further that:

> the only way one can maintain the argument that information would not be used is to assume that information will continue to be as expensive to obtain as it is now or to assume that the information will be irrelevant to the needs and interests of those not now benefiting from existing information resources.[42]

In an era of Reaganomics no other assumptions make sense.

Parker and others who make reference to the rapidly declining costs of information seem to confuse the cost of information technology with the cost of information. There is no question that the cost of computing power has dropped dramatically, and will continue to drop as large-scale integrated-circuit technology advances. Costs of information transmission are also dropping rapidly, and may have already beaten the costs of first-class mail.[43] Personal computers, many capable of gaining access to computerized information banks, are also less expensive than when they were when originally introduced. But at some point, these declining curves will level off, and scale economies will cease to operate. This leveling off point is a long way from zero. Walter Baer estimates that the basic information utility capable of receiving cable signals, displaying teletext graphics, complete with video recording and display capacity will cost more than $1,000 for equipment alone[44]—to say nothing of the costs of the information these systems are designed to display. Because of the cost of such systems, only 16.8% of the experts polled expected that 25% of U.S. homes would have a telecommunication center by 1985, and less than 60% thought that a quarter of the population would be so served by the year 2000.[45]

But once the new systems are installed in the homes of this already narrow segment of the population, the true nature of the information market is revealed. The value of the new digital systems is that many of the problems with information as a commodity have been overcome, and that access to information may be denied to those who have not signed an agreement to pay for its use. Two-way systems make it possible to charge for each message received. With a viewdata system, users would be charged for each page of information used, in addition to the basic charge for access to the central computer. Additional costs would be incurred if the user wanted to have a hard copy of some particularly valuable information—perhaps to use for future reference.

All these added costs are the costs of input, transmission, reception, and display. There is very little being done in the way of generating *new* information.

Current users of commerical data sources are paying for access to information that was produced for other users, and then shared with the computer hobbyist at a price appropriate for the pleasure of being the first one on your block able to quote the closing price of Xerox, or the time of the last flight out of Dallas. Thus, in the near term, at least, the diversity available to the general public via the new technologies is not likely to improve measurably beyond that which is already available. In the words of Mary Jones, vice president for consumer affairs for Western Union:

> Even market place information and documentation about most public policy issues, such as nuclear energy, energy conservation, environmental costs and benefits, carcinogen and other health hazards in foods, drugs, pesticides and the like have not regularly been made available by the traditional information providers in our current society. There is no reason to believe that this situation will change drastically if these same sectors of society remain the information providers under the new technologies.[46]

The same information, already rejected by the poor as being of little use when it was available in the library, would still be useless or irrelevant when received in the home; the only difference would be that it would cost substantially more. It is also highly likely that the skills necessary to carry out an efficient search of a computerized data base are not well distributed throughout this population.

Thus, even if we could imagine a time when a corporate subsidy might make it possible for every poor adult to have access to a computer terminal, and a federal subsidy would provide a monthly allotment of "information stamps," these users are bound to be frustrated by what they produce with their unaided searches. As the amount of information in data banks grows, a number of data services have developed to help the business and professional community find their way through the labyrinths,[47] but this guidance is unlikely to be covered by the quite meager allotment of information stamps. After a while, the poor citizens of tomorrow will do as the poor citizens today, and invest their time and energy in the entertainment channels.

But of course, that imaginary future is highly improbable. What we are more likely to see are more specialized services designed to meet the needs of the major corporations able to pay the cost, and write it off as a legitimate business expense. One proposed service, marketed as a rival to the Central Intelligence Agency (CIA), plans to charge corporate users fees ranging from $20,000 to $200,000 for access to its computer in Crystal City, Virginia.[48] Calling itself IRIS (International Reporting and Information Systems), the firm will use only information that would be generally available to the public, or to enterprising reporters. Noting that much of the CIA's information comes from similar sources, the prospectus claimed that the service would actually "surpass the CIA in scope and accuracy of its forecasts." These forecasts would involve

"CIA-like analyses and 'scenarios' of political and economic risks that insurance companies, banks, other business and governments might encounter in various parts of the world."[49] While poor citizens might not be able to afford access to computer information systems, there is every reason to believe that those systems will contain quite a lot of information about them.

Authorities polled by Joseph Pelton in an attempt to specify the limits of the foreseeable future in information technology were generally in agreement that "there would be an integrated data base on virtually all U.S. citizens."[50] More than 55% of those polled felt it would be accomplished by the year 2000. Questions of privacy and the probability that commercial and political interests would be aided by the introduction of the new technologies into the U.S. household have been raised by numerous observers.

Because of the necessity for accurate records of information purchases, so as not to over- or undercharge the consumer, computers will record each purchase. In order to provide advertisers with reliable estimates of the size of the audience for each of the 100 or so channels available in the home of the future, that computer will poll each user terminal at least once a minute to record which channel has been selected. In order to provide information for accurate utility billing, gas and electric meters will be polled each day, and for those who subscribe to the "energy saver" program, outlets in each room, and at each major appliance will be polled more often so as to aid the consumer in making more efficient use of energy resources. Given the increasing threat of violence and intrusion by burglars, the same computer will interrogate each ultrasonic sensor strategically located inside and outside the house. Smoke detectors will be polled almost as often in similar fashion.

While all this is going on, the middle-class family will be taking part in a little "electronic democracy," waiting for the computer to read their terminal and record their vote on a resolution favoring the decriminalization of illiteracy. All this information might be stored in a single central computer; and for a price, some enterprising businessperson might make that information available to the highest bidder. This scenario is no more "blue sky" than those predicting that average users will utilize their computer system for the purpose of continuing education. And, given what we already know about the value of information about consumers, it is considerably more probable.

Armed with information about family tastes, habits, and opinions on a variety of issues of public concern, interested parties with sufficient resources would be better equipped to prepare specially tailored information subsidies. The computer has already been useful in promoting market segmentation among the readers of the *Louisville Courier-Journal*. After determining that many of the readers of the *Courier-Journal* were also readers of *Time*, and were willing to have the magazine delivered each week along with their newspaper, the management put the computer to work.

The demographic profile of every subscriber is held on-line, and *Time* magazine offers four separate editions to cater to four different class and economic groupings. The *Courier-Journal* gets the right copy to the right reader.[51]

If it were not for some of the difficulties associated with printing different specialized editions of the paper, targeting would be much more advanced with the print technology. With the electronic technology, targeting is much less of a problem. Indeed, consumers may be willing to pay a premium to have the computer select those stories that they have indicated an interest in, or have demonstrated an interest by voluntary selections from listings in the past. Computer programs could "learn" to please the information consumer. Computer programs could just as easily be taught to teach the consumer.

Ben Bagdikian offered what he saw as a possible solution to the more obvious kinds of invasions of personal privacy that are made possible by the new information utilities:

> Each query about a person should automatically record the origin of the inquiry, and when the inquiries form a particular pattern approaching private and potentially harmful information—on medical and psychiatric history, for example—the file should be locked automatically and notification sent to the subject that someone is asking these questions of the computer, identifying the inquirer.[52]

Of course, such sophisticated safeguards would only be available at an added cost, and much of the information that might be used in developing an economic or political profile would not be seen as sensitive on an item-by-item basis. It is only when the information about the daily habits of thousands of people are examined that analysts are able to develop reliable profiles. It is much more likely that the information users of the future will make a great deal of information about their personal lives available to the central computer in order to improve the ability of the company to "serve" them. Or, alternatively, consumers may trade information about themselves in exchange for reductions in their monthly charges.

So, the information poor and the relatively poor are likely to be limited in their ability to retrieve any more useful information from these new systems than they do from existing systems. In fact, it is likely that in *relative* terms, they will be getting even less than they do today from media that serve a more heterogenous audience. The poor and the not-so-poor will also be somewhat more vulnerable to influence because those with the resources will be able to utilize information about them to prepare more efficient, specially tailored subsidies. What promise do the new technologies hold for the poor as communicators, as sources of their own information subsidies?

Ownership of the new delivery systems is simply out of the question. Low Power Television systems, which might be turned on at a minimum cost of $50,000 in the first year, were immediately seized upon by middle-level firms that sought to combine the stations into pay networks, interconnected via satellite. What was then seen as an opportunity for minority-group, community, and even public-interest group ownership was soon bogged down in a bureaucratic quagmire because the Federal Communications Commission (FCC) was ill-equipped to handle 6,000 applications.[53]

Other more potentially profitable forms of media enterprise have been dominated by corporations with tremendous resources. Cable television services are dominated by firms that hold franchises around the country. The top five multiple system operators (MSOs) have more than 40% of the total number of subscribers currently enrolled by the top 50 MSOs.[54] With the rural markets already well developed, the majors are engaged in heavy, and occasionally illegal, competition to win franchises in major metropolitan areas. Citing costs ranging from $50 to $100 million to build a competitive urban system, witnesses appearing before a House Subcommittee on Minority Enterprise seemed to agree that there was little possibility for minority ownership. A single black entrepreneur, hardly a member of the under class, was able to put together $300 million in financing for a bid for a Queens, New York franchise.[55] Percy Sutton, owner of station WBLS, rated number one in the nation, was also sufficiently well-heeled to afford the $14 million bid for access to a single transponder on a commercial satellite.

Beyond cable, the financial requirements are prohibitive for all but the largest corporations. COMSAT proposed to spend three quarters of a billion dollars for its direct-broadcast satellite system; the proposal by RCA was in the same neighborhood at $760 million.[56] With those possibilities clearly beyond the reach of the average citizen, or even the Mom-and-Pop entrepreneur, what are the possibilities for access to the new information channels as a programmer or information provider (IP)? Here, the opportunities are somewhat greater. With so many channels to fill, these new systems have been leasing time to programmers with a great variety of messages to deliver. Religious organizations have become some of the more successful of the alternative program suppliers, but in order to gain access to a larger share of the television audience, religious broadcasters have begun to imitate the format and style of commercial programs—including the somewhat racy plots of the daytime serials.

Todd Gitlin,[57] in his recent evaluation of the new video technology, seems to agree that the growth in media outlets will result in something akin to greater diversity. But he suggests that video diversity will be like the diversity one finds on the magazine racks in bus stations and shopping malls. Narrow special interests served by special-interest magazines. In reminiscing about the loss of the general-interest magazines, Gitlin concludes that the video ''narrowcasting'' will make no noticeable contribution to ''public enlightenment and democratic political dialogue.''

The audience fragmentation is bound to work against the voices of opposition who wish to move against the ideological grain. While the multiplicity of channels will make it possible for a highly motivated but resource-poor citizen to gain access to an audience numbering in the thousands, it will be a very special audience, one that is also likely to favor ideas and perspectives on the margin of mainstream thinking. Only those with access to budgets running in the millions can demand (pay for) access to an audience numbering in the millions. And because the smaller audience is now available, there is no longer any responsibility for the mass-audience channels to provide access to the unendowed. It is the multiplicity of channels made possible by the introduction of new technologies that is held up as a justification for eliminating the Fairness and Equal Time provisions of the Communications Act.

It is too early, of course, to predict how the newer information services will evolve, and how they will respond to attempts to gain access. The commitment of system resources to the commercial or marketing imperative must mean that it will select those messages, and message producers best able to attract the highest dollar volume—even if that volume is a fraction of that required for success in traditional mass media. A broadcast teletext system with only 100 pages available to any IP is going to find the price for access to those pages being bid up higher and higher as the value of the pages is realized. In a more complex and potentially more specialized videotext system where access to a computer is provided over telephone lines, the need for promotion adds costs and begins to make possible differentiation among IPs. A catalog or "information about information" becomes necessary to entice users to purchase information from source A rather than source B.[58] With the possibility of self-promotion comes the probability of advantage in the competition for access to audiences.

It is difficult to predict what changes in technology will mean for the traditional mass media as well. Anthony Smith describes some fairly clear changes taking place in the nature of professional responsibility and the definition of authorship in the modern newspaper equipped with a computerized system. *The Washington Post* system introduces layer upon layer of decision makers between the reporter and the final printed page. In the computer age, the production of news is truly industrialized. At one point during coverage of the 48-hour siege involving a Hanafi Muslim sect, nearly 100 different employees were involved in producing copy about the event for the *Post:* 28 reporters, 21 newswriters, 35 editors, and 12 people who took dictation.[59] More and more on major stories, the *system* takes over, and "the text no longer hangs upon the name of an individual writer." This industrialization reduces the importance of individual elements of the system in a way that reinforces the importance of ideology as a barrier to unusual, peripheral, oppositional content—raising the costs faced by sources trying to influence the flow of public information, and reducing the costs faced by sources trying to accelerate movement along a well-established path.

James Carey's comments on the promise of modern communications would seem to suggest that despite the seemingly revolutionary changes we have seen in the nature of information technology, very little of substance has changed:

For all the vaunted capacity of the computer to store, process and make available information in densities and quantities heretofore unknown, the pervasive tendency to monopolize knowledge in the professions and the databanks continues unabated . . . it seems at the moment reasonable to conclude that electrical communication has up to this time served to consolidate and extend the cultural hegemony and social forms that first appeared in the wake of the printing press.[60]

CHAPTER NINE FOOTNOTES

[1] Jencks, Christopher, Smith, Marshall, Acland, Henry, Bane, Mary Jo, Cohen, David, Gintis, Herbert, Heyns, Barbara, and Michelson, Stephen. (1972). "Inequality." New York: Harper-Colophon Books.

[2] Aaron, Henry. (1978). "Politics and the Professors: The Great Society in Perspective." Washington, D.C.: The Brookings Institution.

[3] Machlup, Fritz. (1962). "The Production and Distribution of Knowledge in the United States." Princeton, New Jersey: Princeton University Press.

[4] Donohue, George A., Tichenor, Phillip J., and Olien, Clarice N. (1975). Mass media and the knowledge gap. A hypothesis revisited. *Communication Research 2* (No. 1) (January), 3–23.

[5] Findahl, Olle, and Höijer, Birgitta. (1981). Studies of news from the perspective of human comprehension. *In* G. C. Wilhoit and H. de Bock (Eds.), "Mass Communication Review Yearbook," Vol. II, pp. 393–403. Beverly Hills, California: Sage Publications.

[6] *Ibid.*, p. 401.

[7] Suominen, Elina. (1976). Who needs information and why? *Journal of Communication 26* (No. 4) (Autumn), 117.

[8] Stauffer, John, Frost, Richard, and Rybolt, William. (1978). Literacy, illiteracy, and learning from television news. *Communication Research 5* (No. 2) (April), 221–232.

[9] Clarke, Peter, and Fredin, Eric. (1978). Newspapers, television and political reasoning. *Public Opinion Quarterly 42* (Summer), 143–160.

[10] Weiss, Carol H. (1974). What America's leaders read. *Public Opinion Quarterly 38* (Spring), 1–22.

[11] Dervin, Brenda. (1977). "Communicating with, not to the urban poor." New York: ERIC Clearinghouse on Urban Education (August) (ED 150 240).

[12] Suominen, Elina. Footnote 7, 1976.

[13] Genova, Bissy K. L., and Greenberg, Bradley. (1979). Interest in news and the knowledge gap. *Public Opinion Quarterly 43* (No. 1) (Spring), 79–91.

[14] Meadow, Robert G. (1980). "Politics as Communication," p. 30. Norwood, New Jersey: Ablex.

[15] Goldenberg, Edie N. (1975). "Making the Papers." Lexington, Massachusetts: D.C. Heath.

[16] *Ibid.*, p. 66.

[17] Fishman, Mark. (1980). "Manufacturing the News," p. 76. Austin, Texas: University of Texas Press.

[18] Goldenberg, Edie N. Page 145 in footnote 15, 1975.

[19] Gans, Herbert J. (1979). "Deciding What's News," p. 121. New York: Pantheon Books.

[20] Gitlin, Todd. (1980). "The Whole World is Watching." Berkeley, California: The University of California Press.

[21] *Ibid.*, p. 284.

[22] Paletz, David L., and Entman, Robert M. (1981). "Media Power Politics," pp. 138–146. New York: The Free Press.

[23] Ornstein, Norman J., and Elder, Shirley. (1978). "Interest Groups, Lobbying and Policy Making," p. 47. Washington, D.C.: Congressional Quarterly Press.

[24] U. S. Congress, House. Subcommittee on Commerce, Consumer and Monetary Affairs. Committee on Government Operations. (1978). "I.R.S. administration of tax laws related to lobbying,"

p. 2, 95th Congress, 2nd Session, May. Washington, D.C.: U.S. Government Printing Office.

25 Mayer, Caroline E. (1981). Nader, imitating fat cats, to hold big fund raiser. *Washington Post* (September 1), A1 ff; and Mayer, Caroline E. (1981). Nader of the lost bark. *The Washington Post* (September 13), F1 ff.

26 Internal Revenue Service. (1980). Department of the Treasury. Notice of proposed rule making: treatment for tax purposes, of expenditures for attempts to influence legislation (LR-190-77). *Federal Register 45* (No. 229) (Tuesday, November 25), 78167–78172.

27 U.S. Congress. Footnote 24, 1978.

28 *Ibid.*, p. 458.

29 *Ibid.*, p. 436.

30 Internal Revenue Service. Footnote 26, 1980.

31 *Ibid.*, p. 78168.

32 Public reference file folders 1–7, Internal Revenue Service (LR-190-77).

33 U.S. Congress. Page 346 in footnote 24, 1980.

34 Mobil Corporation. (1980). Notice of annual meeting (March 22), in Securities and Exchange Commission public file.

35 *Ibid.*, pp. 27–28.

36 Fulton, Bill. (1980). Should regulators pay the public to take part in their proceedings? *National Journal* (May 10), 776–778.

37 A late but decent burial. (1981). *Broadcasting* (October 5), 82.

38 Seligman, Daniel. (1979). The politics and economics of "public interest" lobbying. *Fortune* (November 5), 75, quoting Douglas Costle, administrator of the Environmental Protection Agency.

39 Fulton, Bill. Page 778 in footnote 36, 1980.

40 Bowie, Nolan. (1981). Emerging telecommunications technologies, public telecommunications and people of color. *In* H. Myrick and C. Keegan (Eds.), "In Search of Diversity," p. 142. Washington, D.C.: The Corporation for Public Broadcasting.

41 Parker, Edwin. (1973). "Information and Society," p. 19. Washington, D.C.: National Commission on Libraries and Information Science.

42 *Ibid.*

43 Baer, Walter. (1978). "Telecommunications technology in the 1980s." *In* G.O. Robinson (Ed.), "Communications for Tomorrow," p. 80. New York: Praeger Publishers.

44 *Ibid.*, pp. 90–91.

45 Pelton, Joseph N. (1981). The future of telecommunications: a Delphi survey. *Journal of Communication 31* (No. 1) (Winter), 181.

46 Jones, Mary. (1979). The new telecommunication technologies—an answer to consumer needs. *In* "Teletext and Viewdata in the U.S. a Workshop on Emerging Issues," p. 11. Menlo Park, California: Institute for the Future.

47 Sullivan, Walter. (1981). Data services map the way in labyrinths of information. *The New York Times* (August 23), E9.

48 Downie, Leonard, Jr. (1981). D.C. publisher plans to start a global intelligence service. *The Washington Post* (November 18), D1 ff.

49 *Ibid.*, p. D1.

50 Pelton, Joseph N. Pages 187–188 in footnote 45, 1981.

51 Smith, Anthony. (1980). "Goodbye Gutenberg," p. 153. New York: Oxford University Press.

52 Bagdikian, Ben H. (1971). "The Information Machines," p. 259. New York: Harper-Colophon Books.

53 LPTV reality seen as 18 months away. (1981). *Broadcasting* (November 16), 64.

54 The top 50 MSO's: as they are and will be. (1981). *Broadcasting* (November 30), 37.

55 House hearings examine how small business can get into the big business of cable. (1981). *Broadcasting* (September 28), 39–40.

[56] 2001 technology. (1981). *Broadcasting* (October 12), 252.

[57] Gitlin, Todd. (1981). New video technology: pluralism or banality. *Democracy 1* (No. 4)(October), 60–76.

[58] Thompson, Gordon B. (1979). ''Memo from Mercury: information technology *is* different,'' pp. 30–33. Montreal: Institute for Research on Public Policy.

[59] Smith, Anthony. Pages 193–201 in footnote 51, 1980.

[60] Carey, James W. (1981). McLuhan and Mumford: the roots of modern media analysis. *Journal of Communication 31* (No. 3) (Summer), 177–178.

10

Information Subsidies and Public Policy

The process begins with uncertainty and ends with action, but the uncertainty still remains. Public policy always involves a "second-best" solution because of the ever-present unknowns that threaten even the most complicated planning models. But it is not the random error in the system that has concerned us here. Instead, we have focused on the regular, patterned, and skillful manipulation of the information environment to ensure that shared perceptions of past, present, and future lead utlimately to the selection of a preferred option or plan. We have suggested that these patterns are reflections of some very simple economic rules guiding rational human behavior.

Information is seen to have both an objective market price and a personal, subjective utility. Information is valued in terms of its ability to reduce personal uncertainty, and guide personal decisions. It is also valued for its ability to generate uncertainty in others, or to influence individual and collective behaviors through the selective reduction of uncertainty. Because of the price of information, and the inequitable distribution of personal and economic resources, uncertainty is also maldistributed in society.

Influence or power over the decisions of others is a function of one's ability to manage their intake of information. Just as one may increase the demand for beef by lowering its price, the demand for information is sensitive to variations in its price. An information subsidy increases the demand for certain information by lowering its price to the consumer. Just as with other goods, the quality of information is also a factor in its use. Just as brand names provide consumers with some basis for evaluating the quality of a product with which they have no experience, the credibility of the information source carries some indication of the quality of the information in relation to its price.

Where a source's credibility is low, because of an obvious interest in the outcome of a decision, that source has an incentive to present the information through a more credible, disinterested source. Journalists, garbed in a cloak of objectivity, are valued as channels through which to deliver an information subsidy without having to pay a credibility tax. The use of journalists and media systems involves a two-stage subsidy. The journalist's costs of producing news are reduced through a variety of techniques utilized by sources to manage the information market. Some techniques are more successful than others in ensuring that the preferred message is faithfully reproduced in the media channel. Because of traditional relations between journalists and bureaucratically organized sources, departures from the daily routines of newswork raise the costs of "making the papers." The second stage of the subsidy is complete when the target of the subsidy, an actor in the policy process, gains access to the information at a near-zero cost, from a credible source, in a convenient, accessible form. Without the subsidy, the cost of gathering the information may have been excessively high, or the perceived utility too low for the policy actor (PA) to engage in a search.

The productivity of an information subsidy varies with the amount of competing information available to other participants in the policy process. Information from experience is cheap, and readily available from a highly credible source. Thus we have come to recognize that it is difficult to compete with such information in the production of influence. We have also come to recognize that some information is less productive than it might be because it is in conflict with widely held beliefs. Where information is in conflict with the prevailing ideology, there is a greater need for credibility, and reduced costs of access and use. It is similar to the kinds of barriers faced by the entrepreneur with a new product in a market with several heavily promoted competitors that have been around so long that their names are generics, like *Xerox* and *Scotch* tape. The size of the investment necessary to overcome the market advantage of these firms narrows the field of new entrants quite substantially.

Technical means for delivering information subsidies may also discriminate against the resource poor. The efficiency of many mass media systems may not reach acceptable limits until the scale of operation exceeds available resources, or expected benefits, or both. Because of these economies and diseconomies of scale, certain sources may be restricted to a very limited number of ways to deliver an information subsidy.

Corporate, political, and bureaucratic sources have greater resources and greater incentives to utilize information subsidies in the production of influence over public-policy decisions. Citizen consumers are greatly disadvantaged, and changes in the technology of communication promise to exacerbate the problems. That in a nutshell is what I have argued in these pages. After noting that the provision of information subsidies is not limited to the news media, but includes a variety of direct and indirect means, I described example after example of attempts by politicians, bureaucrats, citizens, and the corporate community to influence policy in education, health, energy, defense, and communications as well. Each example raises another question about the nature of power and its adaptation to the changing economic and social realities. It is to those questions that I would like to turn.

THE RESEARCH AGENDA

In Chapter Three (Figure 3.2), I described the flow of subsidized information and the impact of cultural norms and objective social conditions on that flow. And, although our knowledge about the effects of mass communication is far from complete, I have suggested that future research needs to go beyond agenda setting to consider the source of the agenda, and its impact on the quality of life. A great variety of approaches may be appropriate to the study of personal, institutional, and environmental influences that determine the use and effectiveness of information subsidies. It is not my intention, however, to suggest that we pursue the infinite regress of individual-differences psychology.

Clearly, at some level of analysis, each of us has a special, personal, or idiosyncratic reason or motivation that governs our efforts to communicate, and through that communication to influence others. If we desired, we could return to the methods of the phenomenologists and observe the differences in our own behavior from day to day, minute by minute, and produce volumes of detailed notes. But, at the end of that time, we would know very little about the nature of power, its production, and its use in the preservation of class relations. We need to struggle mightily with the problems of the individual as the unit of analysis. The traditionally atomistic focus of mass communications research is only disguised somewhat by a move to aggregate statistics.

Throughout this book I talked about sources as individuals or as aggregative types—Mobil Oil and the defense industry. My treatment of these sources is not unlike the conceptualization of audiences or information seekers. Just as audiences are classified according to race, sex, education, and income, we might begin to classify institutional sources into categories that would aid in the anticipation and interpretation of their communication behaviors.

The *size* of the corporation is bound to be an important conceptual unit. By size, I would hope to describe some measure of the resources available to the firm, as well as its relative importance in the national or world economy. A variety of measures might be appropriate, although as we see with the Fortune 500, the relative rankings of firms vary with the index chosen. Annual sales in dollars would perhaps be most appropriate as a standard for comparison.

Related to size is a measure of the relative market power of the firm. Industries are described in terms of the degree of *concentration*. Although interpretations vary, most comparisons between industries are concerned with the proportion of sales captured by the top 4, 8, and 20 firms in an industrial sector.[1] Just as the nature of price and quality varies between industries as a function of the degree of concentration or monopolization, it is quite likely that the production and utilitization of information subsidies will vary between firms, and across industries as a function of concentration.

Advertising is an information subsidy that has been shown to confer measurable economic advantage on those firms that use it. Other hidden or undercover subsidies should produce similar kinds of advantage, and we should expect to find that success reinforces the practice in corporations in the same way it does for individuals. I have noted, however, that subjective estimations of utility are important determinants of decisions to invest in an information subsidy. A rational actor would not spend more on an informational effort than he expected to receive in return. A small grocer would not invest in a television commercial, because it is unlikely that viewers from all over the state will come to her store in response to that ad. It would make more sense for her to place an ad in a local, community newspaper, where the probability is much higher that she would capture more of the benefits of the demand she would stimulate with her ad. For the same reason, it is unlikely that local or regional companies would invest in a national issue advertising campaign unless they could expect that they would capture sufficient benefits from the resultant policy to cover their costs. Thus, some measure of the *geographic distribution* of the firm's products or services might provide some insights into the nature and frequency of information subsidies they are likely to provide.

A related characteristic might differentiate between firms on the basis of the variety in their product line, or the degree to which it is linked to other products in the domestic or international market. A single-product firm, which produces tops that it makes from local wood, has less concern about the national energy policy than a dealer in automotive parts. A change in the price of oil may have only a limited impact on the cost of wooden tops, or the demand for them by children during the holiday season. But a rise in the price of oil has repercussions throughout the automotive industry.

Input-Output analysis uses matrix algebra to estimate the impact on an industrial sector that would be caused by a change in the output or demand of firms in another sector. Industries like the automotive industry, which are so highly linked to other industrial sectors, are much more sensitive to changes in the prices for intermediate inputs. Following the work of Leontief, Marc Porat[2] reconstructed the 1967 input-output matrix for the U.S. economy to see what the impact on the information sector might be if there were a 20% cut in defense spending. The model was able to identify who the biggest winners and losers would be if such a policy were adopted. The potential losers would in all likelihood have the greatest incentive for attempting to influence policy discussions on matters of defense. For our purposes, it might be useful to describe industries in terms of their *degree of integration* into the U.S. or the world economy. The greater the firms' sensitivity to a great number of policies, the greater the probability that those firms will engage in information subsidies.

Another measure of integration, and one that has been used quite frequently in the analysis of power and social-class domination,[3] may be seen in the degree to which firms in the industry share directors. Although competing firms are not supposed to have interlocking directorates, major institutional directors, like banks and financial institutions, may have officers who serve as directors on competing firms. Major New York banks hold substantial voting stock and directorial influence over supposed competitors in the communications industry. Such directors would have an incentive to influence policy that impacts on the *industry as a whole,* instead of limiting their concern to single firms. Industries characterized by such interlocking control would probably be characterized by more subsidies of a general nature—"defend our First Amendment rights."

It might also be possible and useful to characterize firms and industrial sectors in ideological terms—perhaps along a continuum from liberal to conservative. To the extent that the information policies of the firms reflect the political stance of their top-level management, some industries are clearly more liberal than others. The notion of a "liberal eastern establishment press" has taken on the quality of a cultural fact, but there is also considerable empirical verification to support such a view. Carol Weiss' examination of the reading habits and ideological beliefs of the nation's leaders finds media leaders in agreement with more liberal policies, and regular subscribers to liberal/intellectual periodicals.[4] She also found that corporate executives and the very wealthy also varied in their media use and ideological positions. Those who read the more liberal/intellectual periodicals were also more likely to hold liberal views. Of course, such an analysis does not suggest that holding liberal views predicts the frequency with which those views are expressed. We might speculate, however, that an industry that is fairly cohesive in its ideological perspective and its perception of common interest is more likely to speak out than one that has more diverse and often conflicting views. The U.S. Chamber of Commerce is seen to be limited in the number of issues on which it may take a position because of the varying perspectives and interests within its membership. Trade associations as representatives of such common *industrial* interests may find conflict among its members on the basis of ideological perspectives. How one might measure *ideological diversity* will be discussed later as we consider methodological issues.

Differences in corporate structure, integration in markets, and susceptibility to changes in public policy should be reflected in differences in the number and kind of information subsidies they provide. Firms that are not in the consumer goods markets have less of an incentive to engage in advertising in general audience media. Institutional advertising for the sake of "public image" would be limited to markets where the firm is more visible—as an employer, or perhaps as a source of environmental pollution. Firms in the defense industry might limit such self-promotion to trade publications and those newspapers read most faithfully by elite decision makers (DMs).

The following scheme might be useful in categorizing the various forms of information subsidy used by corporate or other bureaucratically organized PAs.

Direct Subsidies

Visits or personal contact with a PA; reports, letters, analyses or the like mailed or otherwise delivered directly to PAs; testimony in hearings, investigations, etc.; advertisements placed in media to which PAs are known to attend; contact with PAs by acknowledged representatives or agents.

Indirect Subsidies

a) where the identity of the source is purposely hidden: anonymous leaks, off-the-record statements, messages delivered through surrogates seen as acting independently, including reports by "independent research organizations," and "unsolicited testimonials";

b) where the identity of the source may be known, but the subsidy is delivered in such a way as to disguise the self interest: press conferences, news releases, and pseudo-events designed to win media attention as being legitimately newsworthy; open appeals to others to communicate with PAs.

It might be useful to classify the subsidies in terms of the strategies they use in the production of influence. In Chapter Two, I described a number of different approaches a source might take in an attempt to influence some PAs' perception of the relevant environment or their subjective evaluation of the risks and benefits associated with known options. Some subsidy efforts might attempt to suggest what decision rules a DM should follow, and then provide the information that increases the probability of the desired option's being selected. We might discover that a certain type of corporate or institutional source may favor a particular information strategy in general, or may vary those strategies as the nature of the threat changes. It is quite likely that strategies aimed at politicians will differ from those directed at bureaucrats and citizens. Because an information channel like *The Washington Post* will be used by all three, the nature of the strategies may vary with the medium selected for its delivery. The same source may be responsible for several journal articles and detailed reports that recommend the selection of policy options from a narrowly prescribed range and support that recommendation with sophisticated econometric analysis (with purposely omitted discussion of the assumptions underlying the specification of variables and parameters). This technical/rational appeal would be contrasted with a human interest story in a family magazine that illustrates in great detail the extent of human suffering that occurs (would occur) when the wrong option is selected. This emotional appeal might be contrasted with the political appeal made to congresspersons in their office, or through an avalanche of constituent mail stimulated by yet another emotional appeal. All these techniques may be used by a single institutional source, or one may be favored more than others.

The personal visits to legislative offices by the high-level corporate executive members of the Business Roundtable are thought to carry considerable weight—certainly more than a visit from a lobbyist with 40 clients. There may be definite patterns in the kind of firms, and the types of issues that result in personal visits.

It would be useful to determine the extent to which there is coordination within the corporate sector. Certainly the Business Roundtable plays a key role in organizing the corporate response. Trade associations play a similar role. It is not clear, however, how those associations come into play on an issue-by-issue basis, nor is it clear how much independence associations have from their invidividual members. I have noted several examples where existing organizations were seen to be incapable of responding to a particular policy issue, and a corporate task force was set up to coordinate the assault on something like a Consumer Protection Agency, or the call by Third World nations for a New International Information Order.[5]

The nature of corporate and bureaucratic decision making with regard to purposive communication has rarely been studied. There are numerous books telling readers *how* to communicate with the public, and *how* to improve the corporate image. There is very little research that tell us *when* a corporation is likely to engage in such efforts. In order to take us beyond agenda setting, researchers will have to begin to characterize corporate communication patterns at different points in time, under different competitive conditions, at times of technological and political change. Some have suggested that the present activism on the part of U.S. corporations is in response to a decade or more of consumer activism, and a response to lift the public image of business from the cellar it has been in for the last decade.

Politicians are thought to respond to public opinion. Do corporations respond, or do they attempt to anticipate or lead public opinion? If the cross-lagged correlations provide evidence that the media *lead* the public in assigning importance to issues and events, and if corporate information subsidies help to set the media agenda, then corporate communicators lead public opinion. We might ask if the change in the nature of corporate communication is a reflection of a change in corporate leadership, just as the change in political communication reflects a change in political leadership.

Elisabeth Noelle-Neumann's concept of a spiral of silence[6] with regard to public opinion may be seen to apply to corporate opinion as well. When individuals, corporate or private, perceive their ideas and perspectives to be poorly represented in the mainstream information channels, they are hesitant to express their own opinions. As conflicting opinions draw further and further into the background, the spiral of silence grows. But, when people find that their views either dominate, or are on the increase in the public channels of communication and no longer considered deviant, more and more people are willing to express similar views. This may be the case with the increased expression of racist beliefs, as well as with the willingness of corporate spokespersons to come out of their ideological closets.

We would expect to find that the ebb and flow of corporate communications with a particular ideological slant would operate independently of any single campaign, issue, or threat, but would be part of a cyclical pattern identifiable over the years. We might see occasional disturbances in the pattern around particularly contentious periods like the Vietnam war, but the pattern might be quite stable. That pattern might also reflect a changing of the guard within the ruling classes. Liberal ideas are replaced by more conservative notions as the liberal elites move into the background, but never out of power.

Bureaucratic communications might be seen to have an even more regular pattern. If bureaucratic uncertainty is the greatest around budget time, we should expect to see these subsidies provided in greater abundance around the time of congressional hearings for authorizations and allocations of agency budgets. Strategies used by these agencies will vary with the degree to which their clients

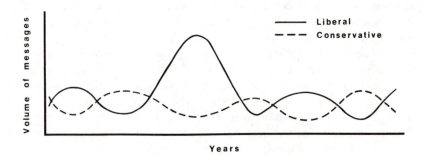

10.1 Volume of Policy Relevant Corporate Communication Over Time

are part of the general public. Indirect subsidies involving "spontaneous" expressions of gratitude or concern for the continued availability of one public service or the other are commonly orchestrated by social welfare agencies. These agencies are also important to the professionals who deliver those services, so teachers, social workers, and development specialists join in to provide useful human interest stories demonstrating the success of the program, and bureaucracy that administers it.

Yet the output of executive agencies is not limited to budgetary periods. There is considerable public information that is not aimed at a policy target, but may in fact be part of the day-to-day work of the agency required by a previous legislative mandate. It is in the departures from that *routine* that we will come to understand the nature of bureaucratic subsidy efforts.

There are differences between administrative agencies in the amount of information they release to the press each day. They differ as well in the degree to which they are successful in gaining media exposure. Those agencies that are not traditionally seen as being as newsworthy as the Department of State must engage in somewhat unusual efforts to overcome media inertia. Our knowledge of bureaucratic communications would be improved by a classification of these approaches that includes information about the resources required as well as their relative effectiveness.

Because tours and speaking engagements are more direct than press releases and reports for general distribution, a comparison of agencies on the basis of such appearances by higher-level bureaucrats provides a fairly reliable impression of the client/constituent network. Thus, we are likely to find that FCC commissioners rarely include conventions of performers and technicians in their yearly calendars, whereas broadcasters, program managers, and cable system operators are frequently given the opportunity to hear and question the regulatory DMs. Bureaucrats in the educational sector will speak before a meeting of publishers before they come before a meeting of parents.

Despite the prominence of electoral politics in the literature of political communication, there is very little that seeks to describe politicians as communicators. A few studies discuss the relative success politicians enjoy in gaining media coverage[7] and numerous analyses of presidential speeches, and the relation between presidential communications and presidential popularity.[8] Most of that work, however, is pursued from the perspective of journalists, and their response to presidential initiatives.

We need to be able to differentiate between information subsidies directed toward the voter as constituent, the financial contributer, the political opposition, the colleague as potential member of a coalition, the bureaucrat as an instrument for rewarding constitutents in a future election. Past studies have differentiated between politicians in terms of their region, the size of their home state, the wealth of their district, the security of their seat, their seniority, the importance of their committees, and the number of chairs they hold. It would be important to add information about the amount and source of the contributions they receive. As with the bureaucrats, the nature of their speaking engagements provides some identification of the breadth of their constituency. Of course, it would be instructive if one could compare acceptances with the volume of invitations received by politicians. While considerations of time and money may play some role in the choice between requests, it is reasonable to assume that choices are also reflections of the importance of the occasion as an opportunity to produce influence.

Several authors have noted the role of legislators in leading witnesses through their testimony in congressional hearings. These are clearly efforts to manage the construction of the official record. Committee chairs have the greatest power in building this record in establishing the number of witnesses and their order of presentation. Witnesses whose inclusion is prefunctory may be scheduled late in the day after the reporters have gone to file their stories. The importance of witnesses can be seen in the attendance of committee members at the sessions. Quite frequently the chair of the committee is the only member present to receive the testimony of an unimportant witness. The schedules are not random. There may be some value in examining the relationship between the institutional base of the witness, the topic of the investigation, and the attendance of committee members at a hearing. We may find consistent patterns in the number of questions, supporting comments, or expressions of agreement, and length of testimony from committee to committee, issue to issue, with regard to corporate, bureaucratic, and professional and public-interest representative testimony.

The *Congressional Record,* much maligned as an accurate record of what actually transpires in the Congress, is also a productive source of information about political subsidy efforts. In addition to personal statements by elected officials, published comments, reports, editorials, and other bits of information are introduced into the public record. I have noted that some of those insertions are made in partial payment to a constituent or a supporter who provided the material specifically for that purpose, that is, an indirect information subsidy. Other material is introduced because it reinforces a point a legislator wants to make, or makes it more eloquently than he could do on his own.

An analysis of such submissions would provide yet another index of information subsidization by politicians. In this analysis, we would be interested in the relationship between the perspective taken in the material introduced, and any objective indicators of constituent or contributor interest. Such a comparison might provide further insight into the relative importance of constituents and contributors to the actions of politicians.

METHODOLOGICAL CONSIDERATIONS

We have seen something of a change in recent years in the traditional approach to media decision making. Contemporary gatekeeping studies give greater importance to the ideological, professional, and organizational constraints that determine the content of mass media channels. A number of these studies[9] have given recognition to the significant role of the source, and some have even taken notice of the essentially economic relationship between source and journalist. I am suggesting that we must pursue this relationship further.

Measuring the behavior of sources seems always to be more difficult than measuring that of the receivers. At least there has always been more money available for research on audiences. But money is not the only problem. The methods developed for social research depend so heavily on subject compliance that it is more difficult to use those methods with sources who perceive their time to be too valuable to waste it filling out questionnaires. As a result, those of us who have been interested in studying the behavior of the powerful have concentrated our efforts on the evidence they leave behind as they go about their normal routines. Unfortunately, that evidence is usually several steps removed from its actual producer. That is, we may make inferences about the management or ownership of *The Washington Post* on the basis of regularities we observe in the content of the front page over time. But, as in the case of the *Post's* coverage of the Hanafi Muslim siege, there were more than 100 individuals carrying out their professional responsibilities in that space between the publisher and the morning edition. Occasionally, researchers may get as close as the program files in the standards and practices office or a television network, but that is still a long way down the hall from the chair of the board. We don't come anywhere near that close to the boardrooms of most Fortune 500 firms.

In the absence of more direct access to the locus of power, we try to characterize corporate sources on the basis of the messages they produce for our consumption. There are lessons to be learned from patterns of emphasis and structural forms that may vary over time, or more importantly, may vary with conditions in the environment. We learn more about a communicator from the messages they produce under stress than we do from those produced under careful, conscious control. We may learn things about our corporate sources as they communicate with different audiences. There may be an invariant underlying theme, but important and unexpected differences may emerge when we compare the tone, background, or seemingly incidental aspects of a message that appear only with certain audiences.

We learn some important things when we compare the messages produced by similar communicators that differ on some important dimension. Far too few studies have been published that compare the content of newspapers with independent or group ownership structures. I can think of no study that has attempted to compare the institutional ads of firms in competitive industries with those of firms in more highly concentrated markets.

Perhaps because of the difficulties we face in interpreting the relationships that emerge, we pay very little attention to the internal structure of messages—the kinds of things that frequently occur together, or the kinds of things that rarely appear together in texts produced by a single source.

It should be possible to characterize the responses of different industrial sectors to a variety of perceived threats to the industry, or to capitalist enterprise as a whole. For some issues, such as those raised by proposed regulations announced by an administrative agency in the *Federal Register,* the bulk of the responses come from the law offices of the corporation's Washington representative. In all probability, it was that representative who notified the executive of the proposed regulation several weeks before it actually appeared, and had long since been instructed to prepare a response. On other issues, responses may be forthcoming from trade associations, on still others, from local Chambers of Commerce. On just a few, such as the proposed change in the IRS regulations concerning efforts to stimulate grass-roots opposition or support for legislative action, a great number of firms, large and small, sent letters to the IRS. As public files, these direct subsidy efforts represent a rare opportunity to examine corporate communications.

While they still remain a requirement as a condition of licensure, the public files of broadcast stations may also provide some insight into both corporate and private attempts to influence media content. Many of the letters will be in response to a particular program or series, and as such, the letters could be seen to fit well within an investigational paradigm—differential responses to a common stimulus.

What corporate leaders have to say to their investors may also be seen as reflections of their political perceptions at a particular point of time. Comments by chief executive officers in the annual reports seek to build the confidence of shareholders at the same time they attempt to convince them that their financial well-being is dependent upon a favorable resolution of government policy issues. What executives have to say to the investment community is often more informative. *Wall Street Abstracts* frequently prints the text of speeches given by corporate executives at a variety of local and regional investors' and stock analysts' meetings. Quite frequently the presentation focuses on the present condition and prsopects of a particular firm, but those presentations are usually made in the context of the domestic and international economic and political environment.

This research cannot be limited to descriptions of texts. There is some value in a typology of corporate political ads as they appear in elite newspapers,[10] but there is much more value to be had when the research links examples of these types with the sources, the media channels, and the conditions of the economic and political environment at the time of their introduction into the public information stream. It matters *when* the National Maritime Council's "Don't Give Up the Ships" campaign came into being—whether it was before or after congressional deliberations about allocations for the Maritime Administration. The importance of timing was clearing in the minds of the PR firm eventually hired to do the job:

The ideal time to set sail on a public education and media relations program is before the sea of public opinion is tossed up with waves. It is our hope that the National Maritime Council and *Rafshoon Communications* will set out on this voyage together.[11]

It also matters when the American Gas Association, the National Association of Electric Companies, or the American Petroleum Institute began their separate, and then their coordinated, campaigns. We might expect to see a significant change in the amount and thrust of communications from these energy groups around the time of the TMI accident, and around the time of congressional discussion of deregulation and windfall profits taxes.

Attempts must be made to correlate regularities in texts with regularities and disturbances in the social, cultural, and political environment. The concern here is not necessarily with establishing causality. The effectiveness of subsidies is only of marginal theoretical interest. What is of primary importance is the discovery of conditions under which subsidies of a certain type will be introduced into a particular information stream, by a source with certain characteristics, where it meets with some degree of resistance on its way to its intended destination.

If it were possible, it would be useful to know the size of the budgets available to corporate, political, and bureaucratic sources for the provision of information subsidies. It is unlikely, however, that scholars will be given access to such detailed economic records. Even the IRS supposedly with the authority to require accurate reporting of expenditures, in a way that differentiates between deductible and nondeductible expenses, has not been able to get full compliance. Similarly, Congress has not solved the riddle of how much money the U.S. government spends trying to convince the people of the U.S. and the world that we are on the chosen path. We might work backward, of course, and estimate expenditures on the basis of what we know of the cost of full-page ads in the *Times,* and 30-second spots on local and network broadcasts. This might provide a rough estimate of the budgets for paid media messages, but as I have suggested, it is the *unpaid* coverage that matters the most in the policy game.

Although the Freedom of Information Act appears destined to self-destruct in a very short while, it might still be possible to describe the number and type of messages produced by different agencies of the government and delivered through their public-information offices. It might be a more manageable task if the analysis were limited to some subset of that output, such as the daily press releases. The output of agencies might be compared across time, events, administrations, and fluctuations in public opinion. The degree of conflict between agency and administration, agency and client, and agency and dependent supplier may be reflected in these releases, although it is also true that leaks and other forms of subsidy may play a more important role in times of conflict.

Where Leon Sigal's research[12] focused on the content as it appeared in the press, this approach would produce a more accurate picture of what the agency *wanted* to appear. A comparison of what was sent with what actually appears might provide some additional insight into the impact of professional, organizational, and competitive influences on the news production process, but that is not our primary concern.

A QUESTION OF IDEOLOGY

Radical, Marxist, and critical scholars have struggled with the role of ideology, and the hegemonic process that sets the boundaries of reasonableness within which needs and claims on resources are seen to be legitimate, and private and public responses are labeled as appropriate.[13] The dominant or ruling classes are seen to maintain their position through their control over the ideological sphere. In the cultural industries, this control is largely indirect, as the ruling ideology is translated into the professional norms guiding the work of journalists, writers, and producers. But, in a capitalist system where culture has taken on a commodity form, and to a large extent obeys the rules of the marketplace, the audience must play a role in its own domination. Because of this, the ideological content within the mass media channels must be acceptable to the masses of people. And it will be so, as long as it does not depart too radically from what they perceive as their own objective conditions.

Graham Murdock and Peter Golding have suggested a number of problems within this overall view of capitalist communications that could be addressed through empirical methods. The relationship between the ruling ideology and its realization in the decisions of media workers cannot be determined solely within the media.

> The first task is to spell out the nature of the ruling ideology, and to specify the propositions and assumptions of which it is composed. Secondly, the appearance and entrenchment of such propositions and assumptions in media output need to be clearly demonstrated.[14]

It is at that point that the "norms of production" may be related to the norms and assumptions of the ruling ideology. To focus solely on the content of the media is to *assume* complete hegemonic control, and it is to ignore the fact that ideology changes in response to objective historical conditions. Deliberations about matters of economic and political policy are in all probability the most likely source for evidence of both forces.

If, as has been argued, corporate, political, and bureaucratic leaders are the most closely aligned with the interests of the ruling classes, then their messages should bear the closest resemblance to the ruling ideology. If that ideology matures and takes shape in response to changing material conditions, and if the capitalist state exists to guarantee that ruling class interests are served, then public policy should be the reflection of the ruling response to changing material conditions. It is through study of the public policy process that we may come to answer some of the continuing questions about the role of mass media in society, and that is what I have proposed.

The impact of media on the social perceptions of the mass audience is an important question, and one that will increase in importance as less of our knowledge of reality is derived from personal experience. But that is not the primary question. The struggles between segments of the ruling class provide us with insight into the contradictions of capitalism, revealing the possibility for change, and that is where the work must begin.

CHAPTER TEN FOOTNOTES

[1] Scherer, F. M. (1973). "Industrial Market Structure and Economic Performance," pp. 50–57. Chicago, Illinois: Rand McNally.

[2] Porat, Marc. (1977). "The Information Economy: Definition and Measurement," pp. 72–103. Washington, D.C.: U.S. Department of Commerce.

[3] Domhoff, G. William. (1979). "The Powers That Be." New York: Vintage Books.

[4] Weiss, Carol H. (1974). What America's leaders read. *Public Opinion Quarterly 38* (Spring), 1–22.

[5] U. S. Congress. Senate. Committee on Foreign Relations. Hearings. (1977). "International communications and information." Washington, D.C.: U.S. Government Printing Office.

[6] Noelle-Neumann, Elisabeth. (1980). Mass media and social change in developed societies. *In* G. Wilhoit and H. de Bock (Eds.), "Mass Communications Review Yearbook," Vol. 1, pp. 657–659. Beverly Hills, California: Sage Publications.

[7] Weaver, David H., and Wilhoit, G. Cleveland. (1980). News media coverage of U. S. Senators in four congresses, 1953–1974. *Journalism Monographs* (No. 67) (April).

[8] Rivers, William L., Miller, Susan, and Gandy, Oscar. (1975). Government and the media. *In* S. Chaffee (Ed.), "Political Communication," pp. 217–236. Beverly Hills, California: Sage Publications.

[9] Gans, Herbert J. (1979). "Deciding What's News." New York: Pantheon Books; Fishman, Mark. (1980). "Manufacturing the News." Austin, Texas: University of Texas Press; Goldenberg, Edie. (1975). "Making the Papers." Lexington, Massachusetts: D.C. Heath; and Sigal, Leon V. (1973). "Reporters and Officials." Lexington, Massachusetts: D.C. Heath.

[10] Meadow, Robert G. (1981). The political dimensions of nonproduct advertising. *Journal of Communication 31* (No. 3) (Summer), 69–82.

[11] U.S. Congress. House. Subcommittee on Commerce, Consumer and Monetary Affairs of the Committee on Government Operations. Hearings. (1978). "IRS Administration of tax laws related to lobbying," p. 415. Washington, D.C.: U.S. Government Printing Office.

[12] Sigal, Leon. In footnote 9, 1973.

[13] A. Mattelart, and S. Sieglaub (Eds.). (1979). "Communication and Class Struggle," Vol. I. New York: International General.

[14] Murdock, Graham, and Golding, Peter. (1977). Capitalism, communication and class relations. *In* J. Curran, M. Gurevitch, and J. Woolacott (Eds.), "Mass Communications and Society," p. 35. Beverly Hills, California: Sage Publications.

Bibliography

ARTICLES IN JOURNALS AND OTHER PERIODICALS

Abelson, Philip H. (1979). Power in Washington. *Science 203* (No. 4376) (January), 129.

Adams, William, and Albin, Suzanne. (1980). Public information on social change: TV coverage of women in the workforce. *Policy Studies Journal 8* (No.5) (Spring), 726–729

Altman, Lawrence K. (1977). Manufacturer says a study shows X-ray scanner can reduce costs. *The New York Times* (July 26), 27.

———. (1979). Tough case for CAT scanner. *The Wall Street Journal* (October 30), C1 ff.

Ambrose, John. (1975). A brief review of the EMI scanner. *British Journal of Radiology 48*, 605–606.

Andrén, Gunnar. (1980). The rhetoric of advertising. *Journal of Communication 30* (No. 4) (Autumn), 74–80.

Armstrong, Scott. (1981). State reviewing Lefevre controversy on formula sales. *The Washington Post* (May 22), A1 ff.

Associated Press. (1981). Stockman vows allegiance to Reagan program. *The Washington Post* (December 9), A4.

Atkinson, Caroline. (1981). Supply side: is the bubble bursting? *The Washington Post* (November 9), A1 ff.

Atkinson, Caroline, and Kaiser, Robert G. (1981). Administration deeply split over further cuts in budget. *The Washington Post* (December 12), A1 ff.

Babcock, Charles R. (1981). Grand Jury probing for phony results on TMI safety tests. *The Washington Post* (October 16), A9.

Baldwin, Deborah. (1977). Ad Council prescription: public service pabulum. *The Washington Journalism Review* (October), 36–39.

Ball-Rokeach, Sandra, and DeFleur, Melvin. (1976). A dependency model of mass media effects. *Communication Research 3* (No.1) (January), 3–21.

Bander, Martin S. (1975). The physician and the press. *New England Journal of Medicine 293* (No. 3) (August), 402–403.

Barringer, Felicity. (1981). Nader to Stockman :U.S. rules saved economy $5.7 billion. *The Washington Post* (August 11), A13.

Beck, Mindy. (1975). Public interest groups tap into entertainment TV. *Access* (No. 18) (September), 8–11.

Behr, Peter. (1981). If there's a new rule, Jim Tozzi has read it. *The Washington Post* (July 10), A21.

Bennett, Harrison. (1972). Education and unemployment in the urban ghetto. *American Economic Review* (December), 796–812.

Bennett, Ivan L. (1977). Technology as a shaping force. *Daedalus 106* (No.1) (Winter), 125–133.

Benton, Marc, and Frazier, P. Jean. (1976). The agenda-setting function of the mass media at three levels of "information holding." *Communication Research 3* (No.3) (July), 261–274.

Berry, John M. (1981). '82 deficit jumps to $109 billion in Reagan estimates. *The Washington Post* (December 8), A1 ff.

Bethell, Tom. (1979). The gas price fixers. *Harpers* (June), 37 ff.

Bishop, Jerry. (1977). Maker of computerized X-ray scanners says they sharply cut diagnostic costs. *The Wall Street Journal* (July 26), 26. (a)

———. (1977). New X-ray device gives clear picture of beating heart. *The Wall Street Journal,* (March 11), 20. (b)

Bishop, Robert L. (1974). Anxiety and readership of health information. *Journalism Quarterly 51* (Spring), 40–46.

Blaiberg, Philip. (1968). To the last beat. *Readers Digest* (October), 274–306.

Blank, Joseph P. (1962). The man who wasn't allowed to die. *Readers Digest* (August), 101–105.

Blumler, Jay. (1978). Purposes of mass communications research: a transatlantic perspective. *Journalism Quarterly 55,* (No.3) (Summer), 219–230.

Bonafede, Dominick. (1981). Reporters' breakfast and lunch groups—good reporting or "socialized journalism?" *National Journal* (March 21), 487–491.

Bowers, Thomas A. (1973). Newspaper political advertising and the agenda-setting function. *Journalism Quarterly 50* (Autumn), 552–556.

Bowes, John E. (1976). Media technology: detour or panacea for resolving urban needs? *Journal of Broadcasting 20* (No. 3) (Summer), 333–343.

Branscomb, Lewis M. (1979). Information: the ultimate frontier. *Science 203* (January 12), 143–147.

———. (1981). The electronic library. *Journal of Communication 31* (No. 1) (Winter), 143–150.

Broder, Davis S. (1981). President is not soft on deficits, aides say. *The Washington Post* (December 10), A9.

Brody, Eugene B. (1975). The right to know. *Journal of Nervous and Mental Disease 161* (No. 2) (August), 73–81.

Brody, Jane. (1975). Three dimensional X-ray is tested for new view of body. *The New York Times* (October 22), 89.

———. (1976). Popular new X-ray unit could raise cost of care. *The New York Times* (May 8), 1 ff.

Bronson, Gail. (1980). As once bright market for CAT scanners dims, smaller makers of the X-ray devices fade out. *The Wall Street Journal* (May 6), 48.

Brown, Merrill. (1981). DOD faulted for use of AT&T data. *The Washington Post* (August 21), D8 ff. (a)

———. (1981). U.S. phone lines called vulnerable. *The Washington Post* (May 6), B1 ff. (b)

Brown, Warren. (1981). Donovan to reorganize the Department of Labor. *The Washington Post* (July 10), A3.

Chaffee, Steven, Ward, L. Scott, and Tipton, Leonard P. (1970). Mass communication and political socialization. *Journalism Quarterly 47* (Winter), 647–659.

Chaze, W. L. (1979). America's oil lobby—the way it works. *U.S. News and World Report* (May 7), 59–61.

Clark, Peter, and Fredin, Eric. (1978). Newspapers, television and political reasoning. *Public Opinion Quarterly 42* (No. 2) (Summer), 143–160.

Cloe, Lee. (1976). Health planners for computed tomography: perspectives and problems. *American Journal of Roentgenology 127* (July), 187–190.

Clymer, Adam. (1981). Conservative political committee evokes both fear and admiration. *The New York Times* (May 31), 1 ff.

Cohn, Victor. (1981). Reagan must decide what to prescribe for soaring hospital costs. *The Washington Post* (February 13), A1 ff. (a)

———. (1981). TV's Quincy tells Hill about rare diseases. *The Washington Post* (March 10), A4. (b)

Cohn, Victor, and Milius, Peter. (1979). A full house wins. *The Washington Post* (January 10), A1 ff. (a)

———. (1979). Behind Edward Cousins' $26,000 heart overhaul. *The Washington Post* (January 10), A6. (b)

———. (1979). Pay, practices of doctors on examining table. *The Washington Post* (January 11), A1 ff. (c)

———. (1979). The suppliers: saving lives, making a profit. *The Washington Post* (January 9), A1 ff. (d)

———. (1979). They make good by making well. *The Washington Post* (January 7), A1 ff. (e)

Cole, Bruce J. (1975). Trends in science and conflict coverage in four metropolitan newspapers. *Journalism Quarterly 52* (No. 3) (Autumn), 465–471.

Cooney, John E. (1977). If TV script needs a medical checkup, a doctor is on call. *The Wall Street Journal* (November 8), 1 ff.

Culbertson, Hugh M. (1980). Leaks—a dilemma for editors as well as officials. *Journalism Quarterly 57* (No. 3) (Autumn), 402–408.

Deficits: a challenge to GOP orthodoxy. (1981). *The Washington Post* (December 13), C6.

Demkovich, Linda E. (1980). Health report. *National Journal* (February 16), 276–280.

Denton, Herbert H. (1981). Only pieces of Reagan block grants plan remain in budget bills. *The Washington Post* (July 13), A2.

Deutch, Ronald, and Deutch, Patricia. (1966). These hearts need not die. *Readers Digest* (June), 181–184.

Dewar, Helen. (1981). Stockman leans on Senate to accept House budget. *The Washington Post* (July 10), A7.

Donohue, George A., Tichenor, Phillip, and Olien, Clarice. (1973). Mass media functions, knowledge and social control. *Journalism Quarterly 50* (No. 4) (Winter), 652–659.

———. (1975). Mass media and the knowledge gap. A hypothesis revisited. *Communication Research 2* (No. 1) (January), 3–23.

Downie, Leonard. (1981). D.C. publisher plans to start a global intelligence service. *The Washington Post* (November 18), D1 ff.

Dukert, Joseph M. (1980). Protecting America's energy future. *Exxon USA 29* (No. 3), 27–31.

Dunwoody, Sharon. (1980). The science writing inner club: a a communication link between science and the lay public. *Science, Technology and Human Values 5* (No. 30), 14–22.

Edelson, Alfred. (1981). Advocacy advertising. *Advertising Age* (March 30), 47 ff.

Elia, Charles J. (1975). Wall Street is zeroing in on latest advances in computerized X-ray scanning techniques. *The Wall Street Journal* (November 21), 47.

End of the H-bomb case. (1980). *The Progressive* (November), 8.

Evans, Ronald G., and Jost, R. Gilbert. (1976). Economic analysis of computed tomography units. *American Journal of Roentgenology 127* (July), 191–198.

Evans, Rowland, and Novak, Robert. (1981). The presidents' taxphobia. *The Washington Post* (December 21), A21.

Executive notes (1981). *The Washington Post* (August 6), A27.

Falcone, David, and Jaeger, B. Jon. (1976). The policy effectiveness of health services research: a reconsideration. *Journal of Community Health 2* (No. 1) (Fall), 36–51.

Farnsworth, Clyde H. (1980). Washington: the people who work for the Japanese. *The New York Times* (June 29), F3.

Ferraro, Eugene. (1967). Project ARISTOTLE. *Defense Industry Bulletin* (March).

Florence, B. Thomas. (1975). An empirical test of the relationship of evidence to belief systems and attitude change. *Human Communication Research 1* (No. 2) (Winter), 145–158.

Fowler out to slay big brother. (1981). *Broadcasting 101* (No. 13) (September 28), 19–20.

Fox, Renee C. (1977). The medicalization and demedicalization of American society. *Daedalus 106* (No. 1) (Winter), 9–22.

Frazier, P. Jean, and Gaziano, Cecile. (1979). Robert Ezra Parks' Theory of news, public opinion and social control. *Journalism Monographs* (No. 64) (November).

Friedman, Robert S. (1978). Representation in regulatory decision making: scientific, industrial and consumer inputs. *Public Administration Review* (May/June), 205 ff.

Friedman, Sharon M. (1981). Blueprint for breakdown: Three Mile Island and the media before the accident. *Journal of Communication 31* (No. 2) (Spring), 116–128.

Fugitive Scanners. (1979). *The Wall Street Journal* (August 29), 12.

Funkhouser, G. Raymond. (1973). The issues of the sixties: an exploratory study in the dynamics of public opinion. *Public Opinion Quarterly 37* (Spring), 62–75.

Gandy, Jr., Oscar H. (1979). On the use of qualifiers in medical headlines. *The Encoder 6* (No. 2) (Winter), 19–24.

———. (1980). Information in health: subsidized news. *Media Culture and Society 2* (No. 2) (April), 103–115.

Garvey, William, and Griffith, Belver. (1967). Scientific communication as a social system. *Science 157* (September 1), 1011–1016.

Genova, B. K. L., and Greenberg, Bradley. (1979). Interest in news and the knowledge gap. *Public opinion Quarterly 43* (No.1) (Spring), 79–91.

Gerbner, George, Gross, Larry, Morgan, Michael, and Signorielli, Nancy. (1980). The mainstreaming of America: violence profile No. 11. *Journal of Communication 30* (Summer), 10–29.

Gerbner, George, and Tannenbaum, Percy. (1961). Regulation of mental illness content in motion pictures and television. *Gazette 6*, 365–385.

Getler, Michael, (1981). Pentagon paints awesome portrait of Soviet arms. *The Washington Post* (September 30), A1 ff.

Ginzberg, Eli. (1977). Power centers and decision making mechanisms. *Daedalus 106* (No. 1) (Winter), 203–214.

Gitlin, Todd. (1981). New video technology: pluralism or banality. *Democracy 1* (No. 4), 60–76.

Glazer, Nathan. (1981). Democratic difficulties. *The New York Times Book Review* (June 14), 1 ff.

Gordon, Michael. (1980). The image makers in Washington—PR firms have found a natural home. *National Journal* (May 31), 884–890.

Gordon, Richard. (1981). Tugging away at Uncle Sam's ear. *Industrial Marketing* (March), 74–78.

Gottshalk, Earl C. (1979). TV's movies: looking at life in seven acts. *The Wall Street Journal* (September 14), 17.

Greenberg, Daniel S., and Randal, Judith E. (1977). Waging the wrong war on cancer. *The Washington Post* (May 1), C1 ff.

Grunig, James E. (1976). Organization and public relations: testing a communication theory. *Journalism Monographs* (No. 46) (November).

Greider, William. (1981). The education of David Stockman. *Atlantic Monthly* (December), 27–54. (a)

———. (1981). What David Stockman said. *The Washington Post* (November 22), C1 ff. (b)

Hagar, Barry. (1978). Executive lobbying. *Congressional Quarterly Weekly Report* (March 4), 579–586.

Haines, Pamela, and Moyer, William. (1981). No nukes is not enough. *The Progressive* (March), 34–42.

Halperin, Samuel. (1970). ESEA: Five years later. *Congressional Record, 116* (Part 23), 30916–30919.

Harper, Timothy. (1981). Poll backs separation of church, politics. *The Washington Post* (August 21), B14.

Henry, Nicholas. (1975). Bureaucracy, technology and knowledge management. *Public Administration Review* (November/December), 572–578.

Hilts, Philip J. (1981). Gene splicers' fear recedes, awe remains. *The Washington Post* (November 4), A1 ff. (a)

———. (1981). Sweeping reductions proposed in government support for science. *The Washington Post* (February 11), A2. (b)

———. (1981). The gold rush of companies into biotechnology is waning. *The Washington Post* (November 3), A1 ff. (c)

———. (1981). White House uses social sciences, but cuts funding for research. *The Washington Post* (June 29), A1 ff. (d)

Hirshleifer, John. (1973). Where are we in the theory of information? *American Economic Review 63* (May), 31–39.

Hughes, John. (1981). Memo outlining "Project Truth" campaign. *The Washington Post* (November 10), A11.

Ingrazzia, Lawrence, and Stevens, Charles W. (1980). New Mayo Clinic X-ray scanner promises to add to medical knowledge—and costs. *The Wall Street Journal* (March 6), 20.

Jackson-Beeck, Marilyn, and Meadow, Robert G. (1979). The triple agendas of presidential debates. *Public Opinion Quarterly* (Summer), 173–180.

Jacoby, Jacob, Chestnut, R., and Silberman, W. (1977). Consumer use of nutritional information. *Journal of Consumer Research 4* (September), 119–128.

Jensen, Michael C. (1977). Huge lobbying and legal drive being pressed for the Concorde. *The New York Times* (May 10), 1 ff.

Johnson, Haynes. (1981). The believe it or not show. *The Washington Post* (December 8), A1 ff.

Jones, William H. (1981). Stockman: clash of old and new. *The Washington Post* (May 7), B1.

Kaiser, Robert G. (1981). High visibility and higher stakes. *The Washington Post* (February 5), A1. (a)

———. (1981). Probably good politics, but budget problems remain unresolved. *The Washington Post,* (November 24), A6. (b)

———. (1981). Those embarrassing words have a familiar ring. *The Washington Post* (November 13), A1 ff. (c)

Kaplan, Morris B. (1975). The case of the artificial heart panel. *The Hastings Center Report 5* (No. 5), 41–48.

Kay, Peg. (1978). Policy issues in interactive cable television. *Journal of Communications 28* (No. 2) (Spring), 202–208.

Kearns, Doris. (1969). The growth and development of Title III, ESEA. *Educational Technology 9* (No. 5) (May), 7–14.

Keppling, Hans, and Roth, Herbert. (1979). Creating a crisis: German mass media and oil supply in 1973–74. *Public Opinion Quarterly 43* (Fall), 285.

Kilstrom, Richard. (1974). A general theory of demand for information about product quality. *Journal of Economic Theory 8,* 413–439.

Knaus, William A., Schrouder, Steven, and Davis, David. (1977). Impact of new technology: the CT scanner. *Medical Care 15* (No. 7) (July), 533–542.

Knight, Terry. (1981). Mythical "study" of market. NCPAC lobbying used in fight to keep tax straddle legal. *The Washington Post* (July 5), E1 ff.

Kovenock, David. (1973). Influence in the U.S. House of Representatives: a statistical analysis of communications. *American Politics Quarterly 1* (No. 4), 407–464.

Kraus, Sidney. (1973). Mass communication and political socialization: a reassessment of two decades of research. *Quarterly Journal of Speech 59* (December), 390–400.

Kriegbaum, Hillier. (1979). Three Mile Island: a crash course for readers. *Mass Comm Review 6* (No. 2) (Spring), 2–10.

Kristof, Nicholas D. (1981). Public, backing science, worries about change. *The Washington Post* (August 21), A3.

Lamberton, D. M. (1976). National policy for economic information. *International Social Science Journal 28* (No. 3), 449–465.

Lambeth, Edmund. (1978). Perceived influence of the press on energy policy making. *Journalism Quarterly 55* (No. 1) (Spring), 11.

Lancaster, Hal. (1980). CAT scanners put on wheels to cut costs. *The Wall Street Journal* (July 1), 25.

Langewiesche, Wolfgang. (1964). ICU–newest thing in nursing. *Readers Digest* (November), 208–214.

Lanouette, William J. (1980). Under scrutiny by a divided government, the nuclear industry tries to unite. *National Journal* (January 12), 44–48.

LaPorte, Todd, and Metlay, Daniel. (1975). Technology observed: attitudes of a wary public. *Science 188* (No. 4184) (April 11), 121–127.

Lardner, George. (1981). Assault on terrorism: internal security or witch hunt? *The Washington Post* (April 20), A1. (a)

———. (1981). CIA Doublespeak cloaks proposal for "Homespy" and "Datahide." *The Washington Post* (November 13), A19. (b)

———. (1981). New groups denounce bid to curb FOIA. *The Washington Post* (November Post (November 13), A5.

Larsen, James F. (1979). International affairs coverage on U.S. network television. *Journal of Communication 29* (No.2) (Spring), 136–147.

Latham, Aaron. (1979). Hollywood vs. Harrisburg. *Esquire* (May 22), 77–86.

Lembo, Diana, and Bruce, Carol. (1972). The growth and development of the Department of Audiovisual Instruction: 1923–1968. *Audiovisual Instruction* (March, April, May).

Lescaze, Lee. (1981). Reagan rejects Stockman offer to quit. *The Washington Post* (November 13), A1. (a)

———. (1981). Reagan silent on admission by Stockman. *The Washington Post* (November 12), A2. (b)

Loehwing, David A. (1966). The learning industry. *Barrons* (October 3), 10.

Lublin, Joan S. (1976). CAT scanner seen effective at detecting cancer of pancreas and other organs. *The Wall Street Journal* (November 17), 20.

———. (1979). Hospitals turning to bold marketing to lure patients and stay in business. *The Wall Street Journal* (September 11), 33.

Lucas, William, and Adams, William. (1978). Talking, television and voter indecision. *Journal of Communication 28* (No.4) (Autumn), 120–131.

Luxenberg, Stanley. (1979). Image agencies thrive on crises. *The New York Times* (July 29), 3, 9.

MacPherson, Myra. (1981). Notes from the real life drama. *The Washington Post* (November 17), B1 ff.

Madison, Christopher. (1980). Energy consultants—what do they do and why should they be doing it? *National Journal* (August 30), 1442–1446. (a)

———. (1980). Synfuels go Hollywood. *National Journal* (September 13), 1528. (b)

Maisel, Albert Q. (1969). The shortage of transplant hearts. *Readers Digest* (August), 69–73.

Marder, Murray. (1981). Propaganda role urged for Voice of America. *The Washington Post* (November 13), A1 ff. (a)

————. (1981). U.S. sharpening information policy overseas. *The Washington Post* (November 10), A1 ff. (b)

Margolis, Richard J. (1977). National Health Insurance—the dream whose time has come? *The New York Times Magazine*. (January 9), 12 ff.

Marquis, Donald, and Allen, Thomas. (1966). Communication patterns in applied technology. *The American Psychologist 21*, 1052–1062.

Mazur, Allan. (1981). Media coverage and public opinion on scientific controversies. *Journal of Communication 31* (No. 2) (Spring), 106–115.

McCombs, Maxwell E., and Shaw, Donald L. (1972). The agenda-setting function of the mass media. *Public Opinion Quarterly 36* (Summer), 176–187.

McEwan, William J. (1978). Bridging the information gap. *Journal of Consumer Research 4* (March), 247.

McGuire, William J. (1976). Some internal psychological factors influencing consumer choice. *Journal of Consumer Research 2* (March), 302–319.

McHale, John. (1965). Business enlists for the war on poverty. *Trans-action 2* (No. 4) (May/June), 3–9.

Mead, Lawrence M. (1977). Health policy: the need for governance. *The Annals of the American Academy of Political and Social Sciece 434* (November), 39–57.

Meadow, Robert G. (1981). The political dimensions of non-product advertising. *Journal of Communication 31* (No. 3) (Summer), 69–82.

Mendelsohn, Harold. (1979). Delusions of technology. *Journal of Communication 29* (No. 3) (Summer), 141–143.

Meuller, Dennis L. (1976). Public choice: a survey. *Journal of Economic Literature 14* (No. 2) (June), 395–424.

Meyer, Lawrence. (1977). New machines send costs soaring. *The Washington Post* (May 8), A1 ff.

Miller, Arthur H. (1981). What mandate? What realignment? *The Washington Post* (June 28), D1 ff.

Miller, Susan H. (1978). Reporters and Congressman: living in symbiosis. *Journalism Monographs* (No. 53) (January).

Miller, S. Michael. (1976). The coming of the pseudo-technocratic society. *Sociological Inquiry 46* (Nos. 3–4), 219–221.

Molotch, Harvey, and Lester, Marilyn. (1974). News as purposive behavior: on the strategic use of routine events, accidents and scandals. *American Sociological Review 39* (February), 101–112.

Montgomery, Katheryn. (1981). Gay activists and the networks. *Journal of Communication 31* (No. 3) (Summer), 49–57.

More to FCC proposals than meets the eye. (1981). *Broadcasting 101* (No. 13) (September 28), 41–44.

Morgan, Daniel. (1981). Conservatives: a well-financed network. *The Washington Post* (January 4), A1 ff.

Nadel, Mark V. (1975). The hidden dimension of public policy: private governments and the policy making process. *Journal of Politics 37* (No. 1) (February), 2–34.

Nelkin, Dorothy. (1979). Scientific knowledge, public policy, and democracy: a review essay. *Knowledge 1* (No. 1) (September), 106–122.

Neuman, Geoffrey. (1976). An institutional perspective on information. *International Social Science Journal 28* (No. 3), 466–492.

Neumann, Jonathan, and Gup, Ted. (1980). Billion dollar U.S. deals with industry unchecked. *The Washington Post* (June 22), A1 ff.

New X-ray device is said to detect brain tumors better. (1974). *The Wall Street Journal* (December 4), 22.

Noll, Roger. (1976). Information, decision-making procedures and energy policy. *American Behavioral Scientist 19* (No. 3) (January), 267–285.

Obler, Jeffry. (1979). The odd compartmentalization: public opinion, aggregate data and policy analysis. *Policy Studies Journal 7* (No. 3) (Spring), 524–539.

O'Connor, John J. (1981). When "based on" loses touch with reality. *The New York Times* (June 7), D29.

Operating rooms in the round. (1963). *Time* (September 13), 84–85.

Orr, Richard, and Crouse, Eleanor. (1962). Secondary publication in cardiovascular, endocrine and psychopharmacologic research. *American Documentation 13* (April), 197–203.

Page, Irving H. (1970). Science writers, physicians, and the public—ménage à trois. *Annals of Internal Medicine 73,* 641–647.

Palmgreen, Philip, and Clarke, Peter. (1977). Agenda setting with local and national issues. *Communication Research 4* (No. 4) (October), 435–452.

Paskowski, Marianne, and Donath, Robert. (1981). Telling the Corporate story. *Industrial Marketing* (March), 543–548.

Peacock, Howard. (1980). Oildom's most independent people. *Exxon USA 29* (No. 4), 16–21.

Pelton, Joseph N. (1981). The future of telecommunications: a Delphi survey. *Journal of Communication 31* (No. 1) (Winter), 177–189.

Perry, James M. (1981). Washington PR staffs dream up ways to get agencies' stories out. *The Wall Street Journal.* (May 23), 1.

Pfund, Nancy, and Hofstadter, Laura. (1981). Biomedical innovation and the press. *Journal of Communication 31* (No. 2) (Spring), 138–154.

Prize for the CAT. (1979). *The Wall Street Journal* (October 17), 26.

Reid, T. R. (1981). Affirmative action is under a new gun. *The Washington Post* (March 27), A8.

Rich, Spencer. (1981). Medical costs up 15.2% in '80: hit $247 billion. *The Washington Post* (October 30), A1. (a)

———. (1981). Plight of Social Security is being exaggerated, Democrats charge. *The Washington Post* (July 8), A3. (b)

Robinson, Michael J., and Appel, Kevin R. (1979). Network news coverage of Congress. *Political Science Quarterly 64* (No. 3), 407–418.

Rosnow, Ralph L. (1977). Gossip and marketplace psychology. *Journal of Communication 27* (No. 1) (Winter), 158–163.

Rotzoll, Kim B., and Christians, Clifford G. (1980). Advertising Agency practitioners' perceptions of ethical decisions. *Journalism Quarterly 57* (No. 3) (Autumn), 425–431.

Rowen, Hobart. (1981). Deficits prove supply-side theory false. *The Washington Post* (December 20), F1. (a)

———. (1981). Reaganomics and the recession. *The Washington Post* (November 22), F1. (b)

Rubin, David M., and Hendy, Val. (1977). Swine influenza and the news media. *Annals of Internal Medicine 87* (No. 6), 769–774.

Russell, Louise B. (1976). The diffusion of new hospital technologies in the United States. *International Journal of Health Sciences 6* (No. 4), 557–580.

———. (1977). The diffusion of hospital technologies: some econometric evidence. *Journal of Human Resources 12* (No. 4), 482–501.

Sandman, Peter M. (1976). Medicine and mass communications: an agenda for physicians. *Annals of Internal Medicine 85* (No. 3), 378–383.

Schanche, Donald A. (1972). One day in the life of a heart surgeon. *Readers Digest* (July), 54–61.

———. (1973). For failing hearts—atomic power. *Readers Digest* (May), 39–48.

Schiller, Daniel. (1979). An historical approach to objectivity and professionalism in American news reporting. *Journal of Communication 29* (No. 4), 46–57.

Schmeck, Harry M. (1973). New cross-section X-rays insure high precision. *The New York Times* (October 10), 8.

———. (1977). Experts urge controls on device that takes cross-section X-ray. *The New York Times* (May 3), 28.

Schram, Martin. (1981). A safe performance. *The Washington Post* (October 3), A1. (a)

———. (1981). President reportedly to downplay Stockman as budget spokesman. *The Washington Post* (November 15), A20. (b)

———. (1981). Reagan the tax lobbyist: an artist at work. *The Washington Post* (August 13), A 3. (c)

Schwartz, George. (1979). The successful fight against a Federal Consumer Protection Agency. *Michigan State University Business Topics* (Summer), 45–57.

Schwartz, Harry. (1977). The government puts a damper on the scanner bonanza. *The New York Times* (December 18), F3.

———. (1979). Cost cuts never get a Nobel. *The New York Times* (October 12), A31.

Selinger, Susan. (1977). Newsletters: the fourth and a half estate. *Washington Journalism Review* (October), 26 ff.

Shabecoff, Philip. (1979). Big business is on the offensive. *The New York Times Magazine* (December 9), 134 ff.

Shaheen, Jack G. (1979). Do television programs stereotype the Arabs? *The Wall Street Journal* (October 12), 23.

Shales, Thomas. (1978). Violence at home. *The Washington Post* (September 26), C1 ff.

———. (1981). A gun in the house: taking cheap shots with a low-caliber thriller. *The Washington Post* (February 11), C3.

———. (1981). TV's look at the town's fight over "free speech." *The Washington Post* (November 17), B1 ff.

Shapiro, Stuart, and Wyman, Stanley. (1976). CAT fever. *The New England Journal of Medicine 294* (April 22), 954–956.

Silver, George A. (1977). Lessons of the Swine Flu debacle. *The Nation* (February 12), 166–169.

Singer, S. Fred. (1981). OPEC has no oil weapon. *The Washington Post* (July 10), A23.

Social research on broadcasting: a colloquy on the Katz Report for the BBC and the issues it raises. (1978). *Journal of Communication 28* (No. 2) (Spring), 89–141.

Sorenson, J. S., and Sorenson, D. D. (1973). A comparison of science content in magazines in 1964–65 and 1969–70. *Journalism Quarterly 50* (Spring), 97–101.

Spivak, Jonathan. (1975). A glamour machine is hailed by doctors as a boon to diagnosis. *The Wall Street Journal* (December 10), 1 ff.

Stauffer, John, Frost, Richard, and Rybolt, William. (1978). Literacy, illiteracy and learning from television news. *Communication Research 5* (No. 2) (April), 221–232.

Stephens, Mitchell, and Edison, Nadyne. (1980). Coverage of events at Three Mile Island. *Mass Comm Review 7* (No. 3) (Fall), 3–9.

Stone, Peter H. (1981). Conservative brain trust. *The New York Times Magazine* (May 3), 18 ff.

Struck, Myron. (1981). Publications come down to final word. *The Washington Post* (November 9), A13.

Sullivan, Walter. (1981). Data services map the way in labyrinths of information. *The New York Times* (August 23), E9.

Suominen, Elina. (1976). Who needs information and why. The *Journal of Communication 26* (No. 4) (Autumn), 115–119.

Surgery. The best hope of all. (1963). *Time* (May 3), 44–60.

Technicare, EMI unit announce new models of CT scanner systems. (1977). *The Wall Street Journal* (November 22), 40.

Ter-Pogossian, Michael M. (1976). The challenge of computed tomography. *American Journal of Roentgenology 127* (July), 1–2.

The riddle of the Nobel scanner. (1979). *The New York Times* (October 15), A18.

Thomas, Lewis. (1977). On the science and technology of medicine. *Daedalus 106* (No. 1) (Winter), 35–46.

Tichenor, Philip, Donohue, George, and Olien, Clarice. (1973). Mass communication research: evolution of a structural model. *Journalism Quarterly 50* (Autumn), 419–423.

Torgerson, Ellen. (1977). Violence takes a beating. *TV Guide* (June 4), 5 ff.

Tuchman, Gaye. (1980). Who cares who says what to whom? *Studies in Communication 1*, 143–158.

Tuchman, Mitch. (1977). Who's turning what into movies? *Esquire* (April), 72–74.

Turow, Joseph. (1978). Casting for TV parts: the anatomy of serial typing. *Journal of Communication 28* (No. 4), (Autumn), 18–24.

United Press International. (1981). Memo urges PR drive for nuclear power. *The Washington Post* (October 12), A11. (a)

————. (1981). OSHA official has cotton dust booklets destroyed. *The Washington Post* (March 27), A8. (b)

Use less, pay more. (1979). *Time* (April 16), 66–68.

Walton, Eugene. (1975). Self-interest, credibility, and message selection in organizational communication: a research note. *Human Communication Research 1* (No. 2) (Winter), 180–181.

Walum, Laurel Richardson. (1975). Sociology and the mass media: some major problems and modest proposals. *The American Sociologist 10* (February), 28–32.

Weaver, David H., and Wilhoit, Cleveland. (1980). News media coverage of U.S. Senators in four congresses, 1953–1974. *Journalism Monographs* (No. 67) (April).

Weaver, Warren. (1981). House panel may create a separate institute for arthritis. *The New York Times* (June 14), 40.

Weisman, John. (1981). Why big oil loves public TV. *TV Guide* (June 20), 4 ff.

Weiss, Carol. (1974). What America's leaders read. *Public Opinion Quarterly 38* (Spring), 1–22.

————. (1980). Knowledge creep and decision accretion. *Knowledge 1* (No. 3) (March), 381–404.

White, Robert A. (1980). Bias in the news. *Communication Research Trends 1* (No. 4) (Winter), 1 ff.

Wildavsky, Aaron. (1977). Doing better and feeling worse: the political pathology of health policy. *Daedalus 106* (No. 1) (Winter), 105–124.

Williams, Sherman, and Wysong, Jere. (1975). The use of research in national health policy: an assessment and agenda. *Medical Care 13* (No. 3) (March), 256–267.

Wilson, George. (1980). With Vietnam defused, weapon-makers ballyhoo their firepower. *The Washington Post* (November 25), A2.

Wilson, James Q. (1981). Does Reagan have a mandate? *The New York Times Book Review* (June 7), 3 ff.

Wilson, Ronald, Feldman, Jacob, and Kovar, Mary. (1978). Continuing trends in health and health care. *The Annals of the American Academy of Political and Social Science 435* (January), 140–156.

Wolin, Sheldon. (1981). The new public philosophy. *Democracy 1* (No. 4) (October), 23–36.

Wright, W. Russell. (1975). Mass media as sources of medical information. *Journal of Communication* (Summer), 171–173.

Xhignesse, Louis, and Osgood, Charles. (1967). Bibliographic citation characteristics and the psychological journal network in 1950 and 1960. *The American Psychologist 22*, 778–791.

Zevin, Robert B. (1981). The new economic faith. *The Atlantic Monthly* (April), 25–36.

BOOKS

Aaron, Henry. (1978). "Politics and the Professors: The Great Society in Perspective." Washington, D.C.: The Brookings Institution.

Altheide, David L., and Johnson, John M. (1980). "Bureaucratic Propaganda." Boston, Massachusetts: Allyn and Bacon.

Annett, John. (1972). "Feedback and Human Behavior." New York: Penguin Books.
Arlen, Michael J. (1977). "The View From Highway One." New York: Ballentine Books.
Asbell, Bernard. (1978). "The Senate Nobody Knows." Garden City, New York: Doubleday, Inc.
Bagdikian, Benjamin H. (1971). "The Information Machines." New York: Harper Colophon Books.
Barnouw, Eric. (1978). "The Sponsor." New York: Oxford University Press.
Bartlett, Randall. (1973). "Economic Foundations of Political Power." New York: The Free Press.
Beard, Edmund, and Horn, Stephen. (1975). "Congressional Ethics. The View From the House." Washington, D.C.: The Brookings Institution.
Becker, Gary. (1964). "Human Capital." New York: Columbia University Press.
Bethell, Tom. (1980). "Television Evening News Covers Inflation: 1978–79." Washington, D.C.: The Media Institute.
Boffey, Phillip M. (1975). "The Brain Bank of America." New York: McGraw Hill.
Brembeck, Winston L., and Howell, William S. (1976). "Persuasion: A Means of Social Influence." Englewood Cliffs, New Jersey: Prentice Hall.
Brown, Lester. (1971). "Television. The Business Behind the Box." New York: Harcourt, Brace, Jovanovich.
Bukoski, William, and Lorotkin, Arthur. (1978). "Computing Activities in Secondary Education." Washington, D.C.: The American Institutes for Research.
Comanor, William S., and Wilson, Thomas A. (1974). "Advertising and Market Power." Cambridge, Massachusetts: Harvard University Press.
Commoner, Barry. (1979). "The Politics of Energy." New York: Alfred A. Knopf.
Dahl, Robert A. (1961). "Who Governs?" New Haven, Connecticut: Yale University Press.
———. (1963). "Modern Political Analysis." Englewood Cliffs, New Jersey: Prentice-Hall.
Daubert, Harold. (1974). "Industrial Publicity." New York: John Wiley and Sons.
Davis, Karen. (1975). "National Health Insurance." Washington, D.C.: The Brookings Institution.
Deakin, James. (1966). "The Lobbyists." Washington, D.C.: Public Affairs Press.
Domhoff, G. William. (1978). "The Powers That Be." New York: Vintage Press.
Downs, Anthony. (1957). "An Economic Theory of Democracy." New York: Harper and Row.
Ebbin, Steven, and Kasper, Raphael. (1974). "Citizen Groups and The Nuclear Power Controversey: Uses of Scientific and Technical Information." Cambridge, Massachusetts: The Massachusetts Institute of Technology Press.
Ehrenreich, Barbara, and Ehrenreich, John. (1971). "The American Health Empire." New York: Vintage Books.
Ellul, Jacques. (1964). "The Technological Society." New York: Alfred A. Knopf.
Erikson, Robert, and Guttberg, Norman. (1973). "American Public Opinion: Its Origins, Content and Import." New York: John Wiley and Sons.
Finn, Chester E. (1977). "Education and the Presidency." Lexington, Massachusetts: D.C. Heath.
Fishman, Mark. (1980). "Manufacturing the News." Austin, Texas: University of Texas Press.
Franklin, Marc A. (1968). "The Dynamics of American Law." Mineola, New York: The Foundation Press.
Freeman, S. David. (1974). "Exploring Energy Choices." New York: The Ford Foundation.
Fuchs, Victor R. (1974). "Who Shall Live?" New York: Basic Books.
Gans, Herbert J. (1979). "Deciding What's News." New York: Pantheon Books.
Gitlin, Todd. (1980). "The Whole World is Watching." Berkeley, California: The University of California Press.
Goldenberg, Edie N. (1975). "Making the Papers." Lexington, Massachusetts: D.C. Heath.
Goodell, Rae. (1975). "The Visible Scientists." Boston, Massachusetts: Little, Brown & Company.
Graber, Doris A. (1980). "Mass Media and American Politics." Washington, D.C.: Congressional Quarterly, Inc.
Greenberg, Daniel S. (1967). "The Politics of Pure Science." New York: New American Library.
Gunther, Jonathan. (1978). "The United States and the Debate On The World 'Information Order.' " Washington, D.C.: Academy for Educational Development.

Gurley, John G. (1976). "Challengers to Capitalism." San Francisco, California: San Francisco Book Company.

Hennesey, Bernard. (1981). "Public Opinion," 4th ed. Monterey, California: Brooks/Cole Publishing Company.

Hess, Stephen. (1981). "The Washington Reporters." Washington, D.C.: The Brookings Institution.

Hiltz, Starr R., and Turoff, Murray. (1978). "The Network Nation." Reading, Massachusetts: Addison-Wesley.

Hoban, Charles. (1946). "Movies that Teach." New York: Dryden Press.

Homans, George Caspar. (1961). "Social Behavior. Its Elementary Forms." New York: Harcourt, Brace & World, Inc.

Ilitskaya, Lenina (Trans.). (1976). "ABC of Dialectical and Historical Materialism." Moscow: Progress Publishers.

Illich, Ivan. (1977). "Medical Nemisis: The Expropriation of Health." Toronto, Ontario: Bantam Books.

Jencks, Christopher, Smith, Marshall, Acland, Henry, Bane, Mary Jo, Cohen, David, Gintis, Herbert, Haynes, Barbara, and Michelson, Stephen. (1972). "Inequality." New York: Harper and Row.

Key, Jr., V. O. (1958). "Politics, Parties, and Pressure Groups," 4th ed. New York: Thomas Y. Crowell Company.

Kingdon, John W. (1973). "Congressmen's Voting Decisions." New York: Harper and Row.

Kirschenmann, Peter. (1970). "Information and Reflection." Holland: D. Reidel Publishing.

Kriegbaum, Hillier. (1967). "Science and the Mass Media." New York: New York University Press.

Krippendorff, Klaus. (1980). "Content Analysis." Beverly Hills, California: Sage Publications.

Machlup, Fitz. (1962). "The Production and Distribution of Knowledge in the United States." Princeton, New Jersey: Princeton University Press.

Mankiewicz, Frank, and Swerdlow, Joel. (1978). "Remote Control." New York: Ballentine Books.

Mansfield, Edwin. (1970). "Microeconomics." New York: W.W. Norton & Company.

Martin, James S. (1977). "Future Developments in Telecommunications," 2nd ed. Englewood Cliffs, New Jersey: Prentice-Hall.

Marx, Karl. (1975). "Value, Price and Profit." New York: International Publishers.

McKeown, Thomas. (1976). "The Role of Medicine." London: The Nuffield Provincial Hospitals Trust.

Melman, Seymour. (1970). "Pentagon Capitalism: The Political Economy of War." New York: McGraw-Hill.

Menges, Günter. (1973). "Economic Decision Making." New York: Longmans Press.

Miller, David W., and Starr, Martin K. (1967). "The Structure of Human Decisions." Englewood Cliffs, New Jersey: Prentice-Hall.

Nimmo, Daniel. (1978). "Political Communication and Public Opinion in America." Santa Monica, California: Goodyear Publishing.

Niskanen, William A. (1971). "Bureaucracy and Representative Government." Chicago, Illinois: Aldine-Atherton.

Okun, Arthur M. (1975). "Equality and Efficiency. The Big Tradeoff." Washington, D.C.: The Brookings Institution.

Oleszek, Walter J. (1978). "Congressional Procedures and the Policy Process." Washington, D.C.: Congressional Quarterly Press.

Ornstein, Norman J., and Elder, Shirley. (1978). "Interest Groups, Lobbying and Policymaking." Washington, D.C.: Congressional Quarterly Press.

Paletz, David L., and Entman, Robert. (1981). "Media Power Politics." New York: The Free Press.

Raskin, Marcus G. (1978). "The Federal Budget and Social Reconstruction." Washington, D.C.: The Institute for Policy Studies.

Rettig, Richard. (1977). "Cancer Crusade." Princeton, New Jersey: Princeton University Press.

Rivers, William L. (1970). "The Adversaries. Politics and the Press." Boston, Massachusetts: Beacon Press.

Rodgers, William. (1970). "Think. A Biography of the Watsons and IBM." New York: The New American Library.

Saettler, Paul. (1968). "A History of Instructional Technology." New York: McGraw-Hill.

Schiller, Herbert I. (1973). "The Mind Managers." Boston, Massachusetts: Beacon Press.

Schultz, Charles. (1972). "Setting National Priorities. The 1973 Budget." Washington, D.C.: The Brookings Institution.

Sigal, Leon V. (1973). "Reporters and Officials." Lexington, Massachusetts: D.C. Heath.

Silverman, Milton, and Lee, Philip R. (1974). "Pills, Profits and Politics." Berkeley, California: University of California Press.

Simon, Herbert A. (1965). "Administrative Behavior," 2nd ed. New York: Free Press.

Smith, Anthony. (1980). "Goodbye Gutenberg." New York: Oxford University Press.

Sproul, Lee, Weiner, Stephen, and Wolf, David. (1978). "Organizing an Anarchy." Chicago, Illinois: University of Chicago Press.

Steinberg, Charles. (1980). "The Information Establishment." New York: Hastings House.

Stevens, Rosemary. (1971). American Medicine and the Public Interest." New Haven, Connecticut: Yale University Press.

Summerfield, Harry L. (1974). "Power and Process." Berkeley, California: McCutcheon Publishing Corporation.

Sweezy, Paul M. (1972). "Modern Capitalism and Other Essays." New York: Monthly Review Press.

Thomas, Norman. (1975). "Education in National Politics." New York: David McKay.

Tuchman, Gave. (1978). "Making News: A Study in the Construction of Reality." New York: The Free Press.

Udall, Stewart, Conconi, Charles, and Osterhout, David. (1974). "The Energy Balloon." New York: McGraw-Hill.

Wellford, Harrison. (1972). "Sowing the Wind." New York: Grossman Publishers.

Wildavsky, Aaron. (1964). "The Politics of the Budgetary Process." Boston, Massachusetts: Little, Brown & Company.

EDITED VOLUMES

Anderson, James E. (1970). "Politics and Economic Policy-making." Reading, Massachusetts: Addison-Wesley.

Archer, Clive, and Maxwell, Stephen. (1980). "The Nordic Model: Studies in Public Policy Innovation." Westmend, England: Gower Publishing Company.

Blanchard, Robert O. (1974). "Congress and the News Media." New York: Hastings House.

Blumler, Jay, and Katz, Elihu. (1974). "The Uses of Mass Communications: Current Perspectives on Gratifications Research." Beverly Hills, California: Sage Publications.

Chaffee, Steven. (1975). "Political Communication: Issues and Strategies for Research." Beverly Hills, California: Sage Publications.

Clarke, Peter. (1973). "New Models for Communication Research." Beverly Hills, California: Sage Publications.

Cloward, Richard A., and Piven, Frances Fox. (1975). "The Politics of Turmoil." New York: Vintage Books.

Curran, James, Gurevitch, Michael, and Woolacott, Janet. (1977). "Mass Communication and Society." Beverly Hills, California: Sage Publications.

David, S. M., and Peterson, Paul. (1973). "Urban Politics & Public Policy." New York: Praeger Publishers.

Dexter, Lewis A., and White, David M. (1964). "People, Society and Mass Communications." New York: The Free Press.

Egdahl, Richard, and Gertman, Paul. (1978). "Technology and the Quality of Health Care." Germantown, Maryland: Aspen Systems, Inc.

Greenstein, Fred, and Polsby, Nelson. (1975). "Micropolitical Theory: Handbook of Political Science," Vol. 2. Reading, Massachusetts: Addison-Wesley.

Gove, Samuel, and Wirt, Frederick. (1976). "Political Science and School Politics." Lexington, Massachusetts: D.C. Heath.

Harris, C. Lowell. (1973). "Government Spending and Land Values." Madison, Wisconsin: University of Wisconsin Press.

Hirsch, Paul, Miller, Peter, and Kline, F. Gerald. (1977). "Strategies for Communication Research." Beverly Hills, California: Sage Publications.

Kline, F. Gerald, and Tichenor, Philip J. (1972). Current Perspectives in Mass Communication Research." Beverly Hills. California: Sage Publications.

Lerner, Daniel, and Nelson, Lyle. (1977). "Communication Research—A Half-Century Appraisal." Honolulu, Hawaii: East-West Center.

Lévy-Garboua, Louis. (1979). "Sociological Economics." Beverly Hills, California: Sage Publications.

Mattelart, Armand, and Siegelaub, Seth. (1979). "Communication and Class Struggle," Vol. 1. New York: International General.

McAnany, Emile, Schnitman, Jorge, and Janus, Noreene. (1981). "Communication and Social Structure." New York: Praeger Publishers.

Moore, John. (1979). "The Washington Lobby," 3rd ed. Washington, D.C.: Congressional Quarterly Press.

Myrick, Howard, and Keegan, Carol. (1981). "In Search of Diversity." Washington, D.C.: Corporation for Public Broadcasting.

Nagi, S., and Corwin, R. (1972). "The Social Contexts of Research." New York: Wiley Interscience.

Oatman, Eric F. (1980). "Prospects for Energy in America." New York: H. W. Wilson.

Ray, Michael, and Ward, Scott. (1976). "Communicating with Consumers." Beverly Hills, California: Sage Publications.

Robinson, Glen O. (1978). "Communications for Tomorrow." New York: Praeger Publishers.

Rosen, Sumner M. (1975). "Economic Power Failure: The Current American Crisis." New York: McGraw-Hill.

Schramm, Wilbur, and Roberts, Donald F. (1972). "Process and Effects of Mass Communication." Urbana, Illinois: University of Illinois Press.

Shaw, Donald, and McCombs, Maxwell. (1977). "The Emergence of American Political Issues: The Agenda-setting Function of the Press." St. Paul, Minnesota: West Publishing.

Theberge, Leonard J. (1981). "Crooks, Conmen and Clowns." Washington, D.C.: The Media Institute.

Tickton, Sidney. (1971). "To improve Learning," Vol II. New York: R.R. Bowker.

Tuchman, Gaye. (1974). "The TV Establishment, for Power and Profit." Englewood Cliffs, New Jersey: Prentice-Hall.

Warner, Raleigh, and Silk, Leonard. (1979). "Ideals in Collision. The Relationship Between Business and the News Media." New York: Carnegie Mellon University Press.

Weaver, James H. (1973). "Modern Political Economy." Boston, Massachusetts: Allyn and Bacon.

Wendt, Dirk, and Vlek, Charles. (1975). "Utility, Probability and Human Decision Making." Boston, Massachusetts: D. Reidel Publishing, Company.

Wilhoit, G. Cleveland, and deBock, Harold. (1980). "Mass Communication Review Yearbook," Vol. 1. Beverly Hills, California: Sage Publications.

———. (1981). "Mass Communication Review Yearbook," Vol. 2. Beverly Hills, California: Sage Publications.

Wirt, Frederick M. (1975). "The Polity of the School." Lexington, Massachusetts: D.C. Heath.
Withey, Stephen B., and Abeles, Ronald P. (1980). "Television and Social Behavior: Beyond Violence and Children." Hillsdale, New Jersey: Lawrence Erlbaum Associates.

PAPERS, GOVERNMENT DOCUMENTS, AND OTHER SPECIAL PUBLICATIONS

Abbott Laboratories. (1980). *1980 Annual Report.*

Bell and Howell, Inc. (1961–1973). *Annual Reports.*

Bergstrom, Rosemary, and Olson, Paul. (1975). "A Time Half-Dead at the Top." Lincoln, Nebraska: Study Commission on Undergraduate Education and the Education of Teachers.

Council of Economic Advisors. (1978). "Annual Report, with Economic Report of the President." Washington, D.C.: U.S. Government Printing Office.

Dervin, Brenda. (1977). "Communicating with, not to the Urban Poor." New York: ERIC Clearinghouse on Urban Education.

Electronic Industries Association. (1974). "Electronic Market Data Book." Washington, D.C.: Electronic Industries Association.

Finn, James, and Perrin, Donald G. (1962). "Teaching Machines and Programmed Learning. A Survey of the Industry, 1962." Washington, D.C.: U.S. Department of Health, Education and Welfare.

Ford Foundation and the Fund for the Advancement of Education. (1959). "Teaching by Television." New York: Ford Foundation and the Fund for the Advancement of Education.

Fry, Donald. (1979). "The Knowledge Gap Hypothesis and Media Dependence: An Initial Study. (Conference paper, Association for Education in Journalism, Houston, Texas (August)).

Gandy, Jr., Oscar H. (1974). "The Economics and Structure of Bias in Mass Media Research." (Conference paper, International Association for Mass Communication Research, Leipzig, German Democratic Republic.)

———. (1976). "Instructional Technology: The Reselling of The Pentagon (An examination of a subsidy for the capitalization of education)." PhD. dissertation, Stanford University.

———. (1980). "Beyond Agenda Setting: Information Subsidies and The Capitalist State." (Conference paper, International Association for Mass Communication Research, Caracas, Venezuela (August).)

Garcia, Rogelio, and Laurencall. (1978). "An analysis of responses to a questionnaire by the Commerce, Consumer and Monetary Affairs Subcommittee of the House Government Operation Committee concerning representational activities of large American corporations and companies." Washington, D.C.: Congressional Reference Service (May).

Gerbner, George, Morgan, Michael, and Signorielli, Nancy. (1981). Programming health portrayals: what viewers see, say and do. Paper prepared for "Television and Behavior: Ten Years of Scientific Progress and Implications for The 1980s" to be published by the National Institute of Mental Health. Philadelphia, Pennsylvania: The Annenberg School of Communication (January).

Gerbner, George, Gross, Larry, Eleey, Michael, Jackson-Beeck, Marilyn, Jeffries-Fox, Susanne, and Signorielli, Nancy. (1977). "Violence Profile No. 8." Philadelphia, Pennsylvania: Annenberg School of Communications (March).

Getty Oil Company. (1980). *Annual Report.*

Goodfield, June. (1977). Communicating science: the special problems of reporting scientific enquiry in the media. (Conference paper, International Institute of Communication (September).)

Gulf Oil Corporation. (1980). *Annual Report.*

Guthrie, James. (1968). "The 1965 ESEA: The National Politics of Educational Reform." PhD. Dissertation, Stanford University.

Hope Reports, Inc., Rochester, New York. (1975). "Av-USA, 1973–74. Current Hope Reports."

Institute for the Future, Menlo Park, California. (1979). "Teletext and Viewdata in the U.S.: A Workshop on Emerging Issues" (June).

McLaughlin, James Michael. (1975). "Characters and Symbolic Functions of Fictional Televised Medical Professionals and their Effect on Children." Masters thesis, University of Pennsylvania, Annenberg School of Communication.

National Analysts, Inc. (1972). "A Study of Health Practices and Opinions." Philadelphia, Pennsylvania.

National Security Industrial Association. (1970). "Proceedings of a conference on the Application of Computers to Training." Washington, D.C.

The Network Project. (1971). "The Fourth Network." New York.

Parker, Edwin B. (1973). Information and society: A report to the National Commission on Libraries and Information Science. Washington, D.C.: U.S. Office of Education (March).

Pietilä, Viekko. (1977). "On the scientific status and position of communication research." Paper No. 35. Institute of Journalism and Mass Communication, University of Tampere, Finland.

Porat, Marc Uri. (1977). "The Information Economy: Definition and Measurement." Washington, D.C.: U.S. Government Printing Office.

President's Commission on the Accident at Three Mile Island. (1979). "Report of the Public's Right to Information Task Force." Washington, D.C.: U.S. Government Printing Office.

Raytheon Company. (1966). *Annual Report.*

RCA Corporation. (1969–1974). *Annual Reports.*

Rockwell, M. (1969). "A Summary of Coronary Care Unit Literature," RM-5944-RR. Santa Monica, California: Rand Corporation.

Scott, Geraldine. (1975). "Statistics of the State School Systems, 1971–72." Washington, D.C.: U.S. Government Printing Office.

Shaw, Eugene F. (1977). Agenda setting and mass communication theory. (Conference paper, Popular Culture Association (October).)

Siebert, Ivan. (1975). "Educational Technology. A Handbook of Standard Terminology and a Guide for Recording and Reporting Information about Educational Technology." Washington, D.C.: U.S. Government Printing Office.

Thompson, Gordon B. (1979). "Memo from Mercury: Information Technology *is* Different." Montreal, Quebec: Institute for Research on Public Policy.

Time, Inc. (1971). *Annual Report.*

U.S. Congress. House. Committee on Instructional Technology. (1970). "To Improve Learning. A Report to the President and the Congress." Washington, D.C.: U.S. Government Printing Office.

U.S. Congress. House. Subcommittee on Commerce and Monetary Affairs. Committee on Government Operations. (1978). "Hearings. IRS Administration of Tax Laws Related to Lobbying. Parts I and II." Washington, D.C.: U.S. Government Printing Office.

U.S. Congress. House. Subcommittee on Education. Education and Labor Committee. (1967). "Study of the United States Office of Education." Washington, D.C.: U.S. Government Printing Office.

U.S. Congress. House. Subcommittee on Science, Research and Technology. (1978). "Scientific and Technical Information Activities: Issues and Opportunities." Washington, D.C. U.S. Government Printing Office.

U.S. Congress. Joint Committee on Atomic Energy. Subcommittee on Research and Development. (1956). "Shortage of Scientific and Engineering Manpower." Washington, D.C.: U.S. Government Printing Office.

U.S. Congress. Senate. Committee on Energy and National Resources. (1978). "Hearings. The Relationship Between the Department of Energy and Energy Industries." Washington, D.C.: U.S. Government Printing Office.

U.S. Congress. Senate. Committee on Governmental Affairs. (1979). "Lack of Accountability in Government Public Information and Publishing Programs." Washington, D.C.: U.S. Government Printing Office.

U.S. Congress. Senate. Select Committee to Study Governmental Operations with Respect to Intelligence Activities. (1975). "Hearings. Intelligence Activities." Washington, D.C.: U.S. Government Printing Office.

U.S. Congress. Senate. Subcommittee on Civil Services and General Services. (1979). "Hearings. Federal Government's Use of Consultant Services." (October).

U.S. Department of Commerce. Office of the Secretary. (1977). U.S. Technology Policy. Draft Study. *Federal Register 42* (No. 65) (April 5), 18121–18124.

U.S. Department of Health, Education and Welfare. (1966). "Proceedings of the Conference on the impact of a coronary care unit on hospital, medical practice and community." Arlington, Virginia.

U.S. Department of Health, Education and Welfare. Social Security Administration. (1975). "Medical Care Expenditures, Prices, and Costs. Background Book." Washington, D.C.: U.S. Government Printing Office (September).

U.S. Office of Management and Budget. (1976). Special analyses. "Budget of the United States Government for fiscal years 1974–76." Washington, D.C.: U.S. Government Printing Office.

Varis, Tapio, and Salinas, Raquel. (1977). "International News and the New Information Order." Tampere, Finland: University of Tampere.

Westinghouse Electric Company. (1969–1974). *Annual Reports.*

Williams, Erik D. (1975). "Report of Progress for the Field Test of the TICCIT system of CAI." Washington, D.C.: The National Science Foundation. (a)

———. (1975). "Report of Progress for the Field Test of the University of Illinois PLATO System of CAI." Washington, D.C.: National Science Foundation. (b)

Index

*Page numbers in *italic* indicate where a complete reference can be found, n indicates footnote,
and t indicates table.